MW01070492

COMMON LAW AND NATURAL LAW IN AMERICA

Speaking to today's flourishing conversations on both law, morality, and religion, and the religious foundations of law, politics, and society, *Common Law and Natural Law in America* is an ambitious four-hundred-year narrative and fresh reassessment of the varied American interactions of "common law," the stuff of courtrooms, and "natural law," a law built on human reason, nature, and the mind or will of God. It offers a counter-narrative to the dominant story of common law and natural law by drawing widely from theological and philosophical accounts of natural law, as well as primary and secondary work in legal and intellectual history. With consequences for today's natural-law proponents and critics alike, it explores the thought of the Puritans, Revolutionary Americans, and seminal legal figures including William Blackstone, Joseph Story, Christopher Columbus Langdell, Oliver Wendell Holmes, and the legal realists.

Andrew Forsyth is Lecturer in the Department of Religious Studies, and Assistant Secretary in the Office of the Secretary and Vice President for Student Life, at Yale University. A Cambridge law graduate, he studied theology and religious studies at Glasgow, Harvard, and Yale. He has recently published articles in the *Yale Journal of Law & the Humanities, Soundings: An Interdisciplinary Journal*, and *Scottish Journal of Theology*.

LAW AND CHRISTIANITY

Series Editor
John Witte, Jr., Emory University

The Law and Christianity series publishes cutting-edge work on Catholic, Protestant, and Orthodox Christian contributions to public, private, penal, and procedural law and legal theory. The series aims to promote deep Christian reflection by leading scholars on the fundamentals of law and politics, to build further ecumenical legal understanding across Christian denominations, and to link and amplify the diverse and sometimes isolated Christian legal voices and visions at work in the academy. Works collected by the series include groundbreaking monographs, historical and thematic anthologies, and translations by leading scholars around the globe.

Books in the series

Under Caesar's Sword: How Christians Respond to Persecution
edited by Daniel Philpott and Timothy Samuel Shah

God and the Illegal Alien
Robert W. Heimburger

Christianity and Family Law
John Witte, Jr. and Gary S. Hauk

Christianity and Natural Law
Norman Doe

Agape, Justice, and Law
Robert F. Cochran, Jr. and Zachary R. Calo

Great Christian Jurists in English History
Mark Hill, QC and R. H. Helmholz

Great Christian Jurists in Spanish History
Rafael Domingo and Javier Martinez-Torron

Calvin's Political Theology and the Public Engagement of the Church
Matthew J. Tuininga

God and the Secular Legal System
Rafael Domingo

How Marriage Became One of the Sacraments
Philip Reynolds

Christianity and Freedom (Volume I: Historical Perspectives, Volume II: Contemporary Perspectives)
edited by Timothy Samuel Shah and Allen D. Hertzke

The Distinctiveness of Religion in American Law
Kathleen A. Brady

Pope Benedict XVI's Legal Thought
Marta Cartabia and Andrea Simoncini

The Western Case for Monogamy over Polygamy
John Witte, Jr.

Church Law in Modernity: Toward a Theory of Canon Law Between Nature and Culture
Judith Hahn

Care for the World: Laudato Si' and Catholic Social Thought in an Era of Climate Crisis
Frank Pasquale

Common Law and Natural Law in America: From the Puritans to the Legal Realists
Andrew Forsyth

Common Law and Natural Law in America

FROM THE PURITANS TO THE LEGAL REALISTS

ANDREW FORSYTH

Yale University

CAMBRIDGE
UNIVERSITY PRESS

CAMBRIDGE
UNIVERSITY PRESS

University Printing House, Cambridge CB2 8BS, United Kingdom

One Liberty Plaza, 20th Floor, New York, NY 10006, USA

477 Williamstown Road, Port Melbourne, VIC 3207, Australia

314–321, 3rd Floor, Plot 3, Splendor Forum, Jasola District Centre, New Delhi – 110025, India

79 Anson Road, #06–04/06, Singapore 079906

Cambridge University Press is part of the University of Cambridge.

It furthers the University's mission by disseminating knowledge in the pursuit of education, learning, and research at the highest international levels of excellence.

www.cambridge.org
Information on this title: www.cambridge.org/9781108476973
DOI: 10.1017/9781108576772

© Andrew Forsyth 2019

First published 2019

Printed and bound in Great Britain by Clays Ltd, Elcograf S.p.A.

A catalogue record for this publication is available from the British Library.

ISBN 978-1-108-47697-3 Hardback

FOR J.R.G.

Contents

Preface   *page* xi

Acknowledgments   xv

1   Puritan Natural Law: Early New England and the
     Colonial Colleges   1

2   Modern Natural Law: Revolutionaries and Republicans   24

3   Organizing Common Law: William Blackstone in America   46

4   Subsuming Natural Law into Common Law: Joseph Story   70

5   Law as Science: Christopher Columbus Langdell   105

6   Breaking with Natural Law: Oliver Wendell Holmes and
     the Legal Realists   125

     Epilogue   146

Index   149

Preface

Invocations of natural law in contemporary legal circles are almost guaranteed to generate more heat than light. Proponents frame natural law as essential to the defense of civilization and its critics as perversely denying universally accessible truths; critics regard natural-law discourse as a Trojan horse for the imposition of a minority's conservative religious convictions on an increasingly pluralistic nation. The idea that common law – the stuff of quotidian courtrooms in America – might be in fundamental harmony with natural law, or even structured and justified by it, is accordingly fantastical or nightmarish.

This was not always so. Despite today's prevailing wisdom that common law and natural law are separate and distinct ideas, in reality, a centuries-long stream of American legal thought presupposed – sometimes tacitly, sometimes explicitly – that natural law and common law are intertwined. Natural law, in short, undergirded the development of American jurisprudence. Contemporary debates on law, morality, and religion lack this historical memory and suffer accordingly.

What the concepts of "natural law" and "common law" meant to those who invoked them, however, requires careful delineation. We cannot generalize. The Puritans' "natural law," we shall see, was not the Revolutionaries'. Nor was the "common law" of Joseph Story, the fabled nineteenth-century jurist, altogether that of William Blackstone, its chief eighteenth-century organizer.

Still, we must start somewhere, and initial definitions will be helpful.

By "common law," I mean the system of laws in England and the United States in which laws – whatever their seeming source in a constitution, statutes, orders, or cases – are made explicit through interpretation by judges; judicial decisions in individual cases expound and develop the law.[1] To speak

---

[1] "Common law" also has narrower meanings. For instance, it can refer to the body of law distinct from "equity," or those areas of the law – contract, torts, and property, etc. – which

of common law is to invoke, too, the institutions, procedures, and conventions that allow for the functioning of a system of case law. For instance, common-law jurisdictions typically have adversarial court proceedings in which lawyers prosecute or defend, a judge impartially determines the law, and a jury decides the facts in a case. These institutions, procedures, and conventions set England and the United States apart from continental Europe's various civilian systems, in which court proceedings are inquisitorial rather than adversarial, with judges playing an active role in the collection of evidence and interrogation of witnesses.

This definition of common law is uncontroversial today. But its easy famil-iarity – at least to lawyers – is more obscuring than illumining of certain historical aspects of the common-law tradition. Far from the creation of judges, in our seventeenth- through early twentieth-century story, American common law was understood as deeper rooted: the custom of the people perhaps, or even nothing less than common reason. The common law was to be interpreted by judges, yes, but as *found*, not created, in interpretation.[2] Indeed, it was wholly orthodox, we shall see, for judges and jurists – sharing the same intellectual worlds as philosophers and theologians – to treat natural law as a source or justification for common law.

What, then, is natural law? For its proponents, "natural law" is law that proceeds from or is grounded in – variously – the mind or will of God, nature, or human reason. In the broadly shared Western tradition of moral reflection found in the centuries we will explore, "natural law" is the understanding that there is a *universal morality naturally accessible to all rational people*. Among contemporary common-law legal practitioners and Anglophone legal philo-sophers, "natural law" often simply refers to any approach that treats law as necessarily having a connection to morality. This meaning is essentially the converse of "legal positivism," which is often defined, minimally, as the contention that law has no necessary connection with morality.[3]

How the details of natural law are further specified matters acutely for its relationship to common law. What is natural law's source and content? How is it perceived and enacted? These details are spelled out differently by the Puritans, Revolutionary Americans, and the seminal legal figures we will

having no initial legislative source are instead formed, most proximately, by the reasoned judgments of courts.

[2] See Gerald Postema, "Philosophy of the Common Law," in *The Oxford Handbook of Jurisprudence and Philosophy of Law*, ed. Jules Coleman and Scott Shapiro (Oxford: Oxford University Press, 2004), 588–623.

[3] H. L. A. Hart, "Positivism and the Separation of Law and Morals," in *Essays in Jurisprudence and Philosophy* (Oxford: Clarendon, 1983), 54.

encounter, whether Blackstone, Story, or Christopher Columbus Langdell, the creator of the modern law school.

Ultimately, our story ends with the rejection of natural law by Oliver Wendell Holmes and the "legal realists," a loose group of early twentieth-century jurists and practitioners skeptical about whether legal rules are rational or even coherent. But the narrative of the following pages is not simply a story of the concretion of natural law within common-law thought, followed by the erosion of its significance, even its outright rejection.[4] It is also a story of the history of natural-law reflection not as a linear novel, but as overlapping essays of differing quality and durability, written by common lawyers who – consciously or otherwise – recognized or ignored or fudged the differences between natural law's varied expressions.

* * *

A word on my choices may be helpful. My focus is a connected set of American conceptions of natural law and common law that form a specific tradition of moral and legal inquiry, from the seventeenth-century Puritans to the early twentieth-century legal realists. I do not replicate available studies – for example, on Revolutionary era discussions of natural law and natural rights (its sometime cousin) – but dust off lesser known discourses and debates.[5] I do so not for antiquarian reasons, but because contemporary proponents and critics of natural law alike miss the potent materials at hand by too readily accepting the distinctions between natural law and common law drawn by the legal realists. Otherwise vibrant twentieth-century visions of natural law – whether the rise of universal human rights discourse, Martin Luther King, Jr.'s appeals to natural law, or the "new natural law" of John Finnis and others – spend little if any time on the sweep of American legal reflection before the realists. Those who care about the relationship of law, morality, and religion in contemporary America will benefit from knowing how natural law and common law were connected and parsed over four hundred years of

[4] Earlier critiques of this narrative include Charles Grove Haines, *The Revival of Natural Law Concepts: A Study of the Establishment and of the Interpretation of Limits on Legislatures with Special Reference to the Development of Certain Phases of American Constitutional Law* (Cambridge, MA: Harvard University Press, 1930).

[5] For studies of natural law and natural rights in the thought of the founding fathers, see, e.g., Carl Becker, *The Declaration of Independence: A Study in the History of Political Ideas* (New York: Harcourt, Brace, 1922); Susan Ford Wiltshire, *Greece, Rome, and the Bill of Rights* (Norman: University of Oklahoma Press, 1992); Michael Zucker, *The Natural Rights Republic: Studies in the Foundation of the American Political Tradition* (Princeton, NJ: Princeton University Press, 1996); Mark David Hall, *The Political and Legal Philosophy of James Wilson, 1742–1792* (Columbia: University of Missouri Press, 1997).

American history, as, too, will those who study the history of moral philosophy or who seek to advance or critique religious arguments for natural law.

I do not argue, to be clear, that readers adopt a natural-law interpretation of American law, of whatever variety. This is not a political tract or religious pamphlet. Instead, I show how and why Americans appealed to natural law. Some appeals may convince you. Others will not. Needless to say, natural law has its detractors and opponents across disciplines and topics. Many philosophers reject wholesale the idea that the goodness of actions relates to claims about human nature and flourishing. Many lawyers see no need to talk of law beyond the social fact of its existence. Many theologians dismiss natural law for a perceived lack of emphasis on the authority of God's will and commands. The chapters that follow are not shaped to convince them – or you – otherwise.

Nor will I convince many contemporary advocates of natural law – including in the legal academy – that what we find in American common law's recourse to natural law is necessarily worth their attention. This is a consequence of refusing to appeal to or incorporate a predetermined standard for "natural law." I do not take for granted, for instance, that the natural law of Thomas Aquinas is normative and then judge all other expressions against it. Instead, by giving proper attention to the changing connections between American law both common and natural, I show the pitfalls and trade-offs of embracing any particular historical appeal to natural law. The Puritans' natural law, for instance, was chastened by their belief that human reason is necessarily corrupted by sin. Blackstone's influential rooting of common law in natural law shared this basic assumption, at least to some degree. This is missed by many contemporary champions of Blackstone, who assume he shares the more epistemologically ambitious natural law of Hugo Grotius and Samuel Pufendorf that was influential at the time of the Revolution.

And so, even as we recognize that American understandings of common law, natural law, and their relationship have changed, whether for good or ill, we can see that for much of American history it was assumed that common law – far from wholly detached from moral considerations – was, indeed, not just in fundamental harmony with natural law, but structured and justified by way of reference to it. Or put another way: When we consider law, morality, and religion in America today, we can freshly pull upon or push against the long-standing if variegated tradition of lawyers and legal thinkers who said that to know or interpret our laws is first to determine how things ought to be.

Acknowledgments

It is a pleasure to record my thanks to the Louisville Institute for fellowships in 2016–17 and 2013–15, and to recognize its funder, the Lilly Endowment, Inc.

Jennifer Herdt has read well-nigh everything I have written, at least since 2011. Her comments have improved papers and presentations and this book a good deal. She is both generous and precise, a model to emulate. I thank her.

I am grateful, too, for careful readings of earlier versions of this text, not least from Jerry McKenny, Olivia Stewart Lester, Kathy Tanner, and, particularly, Cathy Kaveny, whose comments helped frame and focus the project. Judicious advice was received from Marie Griffith and other participants in the 2017 Louisville Institute winter seminar. Chapter One was honed in conversation with members of a 2015–16 Yale law and humanities working group.

My thanks to John Berger and Cambridge University Press for shepherding this project to print. I am pleased to be counted in the Law and Christianity series edited by John Witte.

In New Haven, Rona Gordon was a sterling editor. Josh Goodbaum's edits have been essential and his patience remarkable. He likely knows this project too well by now. I have accepted *nearly all* his counsel. The book, however, is dedicated to him and not to Mungo, the dog.

Acknowledgments

1

Puritan Natural Law

Early New England and the Colonial Colleges

Animated by promise and anxiety, the Puritan colonists of the Massachusetts Bay Company founded a college in 1636.[1] They desired to "advance learning and perpetuate it to posterity," dreading to leave "an illiterate ministry to the churches, when our present ministers shall lie in the dust."[2] A conduit of European natural-law thinking, the college became a seedbed for Puritan natural law and a nursery for natural law's engagement with common law. Through collegiate education the Puritans' truth was to be specified, evinced, and systematically transmitted to the generations who would follow.

Prominent among the colonists were men educated at Cambridge University, many in its puritan-leaning institutions, such as Emmanuel College. Following his death in 1638, and bequest of money and books, the new college in Cambridge, Massachusetts, was named for Emmanuel graduate the Reverend John Harvard (b. 1607). In their teaching and preaching, the puritans of both these Cambridges, we shall see, took for granted a connection

---

[1] Following current scholarly conventions, the use of "Puritans" with a capital "P" refers to the particular group of settlers in New England, while use of "puritans" with a lower-case "p" refers to the sometimes amorphous set of individuals and protestant groups who shared a reforming spirit within the English Church. The use of a capital "P" emphasizes that the New England Puritans were a distinct group (despite scholarly disagreement as to whether this group was a haggard collection of refugees – their identity forged in their shared expulsion from the Old World – or a self-consciously utopian band). See John Coffey and Paul Chang-Ha Lim, ed., *The Cambridge Companion to Puritanism* (Cambridge: Cambridge University Press, 2008); and Stephen Foster, *The Long Argument: English Puritanism and the Shaping of New England Culture, 1570–1700* (Chapel Hill: University of North Carolina Press, 1991).

[2] The quotations are from "New Englands First Fruits," in *The Eliot Tracts: With Letters from John Eliot to Thomas Thorowgood and Richard Baxter*, ed. Michael Clark (Westport, CT: Praeger, 2003), 55–78. Published in London, and edited – and probably composed – by Thomas Weld and Hugh Peter, *New Englands First Fruits* informs its readers about the climate, products, and religion of New England, and offers a description of Harvard College. It likely served as publicity or fundraising material.

1

between rationality and morality: The human ability to form valid judgments by use of intellectual powers, they thought, is intimately tied to how to live rightly and well. How the world truly *is* relates profoundly to how it *ought* to be.

This connection between is and ought has grounded most expressions of natural law – a universal morality accessible to all rational persons – that proved a broad mainstream of Western moral thought until modernity.[3] Whatever their disagreements with the Church of England, in their views of the connection of reason and morals, the New World Puritans did not deviate far from the thinking of the Europe they fled.

A PURITAN NATURAL LAW?

The Puritans shared the common sense of their time. They operated with their age's organized body of considered knowledge.[4] This seemingly obvious truth is repeatedly hidden from the record: The most influential theological and historical framings of the Puritans have obscured the natural-law worldview they shared with Europe. Systematic and classificatory work in theology has often placed the Puritans among those Protestants who can be recognized as distinct from Roman Catholics precisely on account of their presumed suspicion of natural law. (If Thomas Aquinas's thought is the *sine qua non* of natural law, the Puritans are not natural lawyers.) Likewise, when natural law is treated as an "extra-biblical" body of morality, the Puritans are excluded from its bounds, for they are known for their commitment to the authority of the preached biblical text and not the traditions of the Church.

The Puritans are excluded too from many American historians' narratives of natural law. Prominent historians of the American Revolution, for instance, readily equate "natural law" with "modern natural law" – the thought of John Locke is their usual example – which they understand as providing the founding fathers with a secular grounding for human equality and rights. As such, one convenient result is that "natural law" – as they conceive it – indicates, and even accounts for, the intellectual breaking point between America's colonial period and its seemingly Enlightenment-inspired

---

[3]   Some contemporary expressions of "natural law" seek to avoid a connection between *is* and *ought*. The "New Natural Lawyers," for instance, speak of "basic goods" that are "self-evident" rather than deduced from facts about nature. See Germain Grisez, Joseph Boyle, and John Finnis, *Practical Principles, Moral Truth, and Ultimate Ends*, 32 Am. J. Legal Hist. 99 (1987).

[4]   See Clifford Geertz, "Common Sense as a Cultural System," *The Antioch Review* 33, no. 1 (1975): 5–26.

Revolution. Where natural law is equated solely with its modern form, "natural law" is the thought of broadly secular Revolutionaries, with the Puritans left as Biblicist theocrats for whom natural law can have no major force.[5]

These faulty theological and historical framings fail to place the Puritans in their intellectual world or account for the specific basis, lineage, and scope of natural law as they understood it. In assuming the normativity of a particular form of natural law – Roman Catholic scholastic or modern – they fail to recognize *Puritan* natural law. Natural law thus appears the child of philosophical and theological efforts, cultivated by medieval scholastics, whom the Puritans reject, or of Enlightenment philosophes, whom they precede.

The Puritans, however, understood natural law to have a biblical basis. Natural law survived the Puritans' scouring of the perceived accretions of Church tradition. While the Puritans did indeed self-consciously look to the early Church as normative – and not to traditions of interpretation as did, arguably, Roman Catholics – and correspondingly sought to model their civic affairs on the record of the Old and New Testaments, the Christianity they espoused was not separate from the Western Christian tradition of natural law. For they found in Scripture the idea that even those who have not heard God's law are obliged to follow this law and have the capacity to do so. In the language of the Geneva Bible:

> For when the Gentiles which have not the Law, do by nature the things *contained* in the Law, they having not the Law, are a Law unto themselves,
> Which show the effect of the Law written in their hearts, their conscience also bearing witness and their thoughts accusing one another, or excusing. (Romans 2:14–15.)[6]

This "law written in their hearts" found further biblical support in the Puritans' reading of the first chapter of the biblical book of Genesis, and, in particular, its account of human creation in the *image of God*.[7] In accord with a significant line of Western Christian interpretation, the Puritans understood

---

[5] For one vigorous recent version of this position, see Matthew Stewart, *Nature's God: The Heretical Origins of the American Republic* (New York: Norton, 2014).

[6] Generations of historians have treated the Geneva Bible as the Puritans' standard translation. Bruce Metzger provides a helpful brief introduction to the work: "The Geneva Bible of 1560," *Theology Today* 17, no. 3 (1960): 339–52. However, the Puritans also used the Authorized (that is, King James) version of the Bible. See Harry Stout, "Word and Order in Colonial New England," in *The Bible in America: Essays in Cultural History*, ed. Nathan Hatch and Mark Noll, 19–37 (New York: Oxford University Press, 1982).

[7] The Geneva Bible renders Genesis 1:27, for example: "Thus God created the man in his image: in the image of God created he him: he created them male and female." See also: Genesis 5:1 and 9:6, 1 Corinthians 11:7, 2 Corinthians 3:18–4:4, Hebrews 2, and James 3:9.

rationality as the content of the *imago Dei*: Human beings mirror God in their ability to think and form judgments. Rationality distinguishes human beings from the rest of creation, they thought, and accounts for the human ability to apprehend natural law. Indeed, with John Calvin, and others in the Reformed tradition of Protestantism to which they cleaved, the Puritans placed particular theological emphasis both on human creation in the image of God and on the corruption or deformation of this image in humanity's fall from original perfection.[8]

Not that the Puritans based their natural law solely on the biblical narrative. Puritan leaders received an education in Cambridge that, as throughout Europe, was built on the re-emergence of classical learning in the later Middle Ages and, with it, the recovery of the natural law of the Stoics and Roman law. Indeed, Renaissance humanism and its protestant appropriators strengthened a commitment to careful engagement with the texts and thought of Greece and Rome, alongside the biblical texts.[9] So, while there was no confusion as to the authority or pre-eminence of the biblical texts over the classical in puritan thought, the lineage of their own *Christian* thought was articulated through the philosophical and rhetorical categories of the classical world, received through the Christian centuries in the work of Augustine and others, and later recast in Christian wresting with the rediscovered corpus of Aristotle.[10] Most educated puritans, therefore, broadly expected the consonance of Christian truth and the best of classical literature. They read the

---

[8]   Important discussions of Calvin and natural law include: Susan Schreiner, *The Theater of His Glory: Nature and the Natural Order in the Thought of John Calvin* (Durham, NC: Labyrinth Press, 1991); Brian Gerrish, "The Mirror of God's Goodness: A Key Metaphor in Calvin's View of Man," in *The Old Protestantism and the New: Essays on the Reformation Heritage*, 150–59 (Edinburgh: T. & T. Clark, 1982); Günter Gloede, *Theologia Naturalis Bei Calvin* (Stuttgart: W. Kohlhammer, 1935); Jane Dempsey Douglass, "The Image of God in Humanity: A Comparison of Calvin's Teaching in 1536 and 1559," in *In Honor of John Calvin, 1509–64*, ed. E. J. Furcha, 175–203 (Montreal: Faculty of Religious Studies, McGill University, 1987); Luke Anderson, "The Imago Dei Theme in John Calvin and Bernard of Clairvaux," in *Calvinus Sacrae Scripturae Professor*, ed. Wilhelm Neuser, 178–98 (Grand Rapids, MI: Eerdmans, 1994).

[9]   For general discussions of the place of classical learning in the Renaissance, see Albert Rabil, Jr., ed., *Renaissance Humanism: Foundations, Forms, and Legacy* (Philadelphia: University of Pennsylvania Press, 1988); and Charles Nauert, Jr., *Humanism and the Culture of Renaissance Europe* (Cambridge: Cambridge University Press, 2006).

[10] For discussion of the reception of Aristotle, see Bernard Dod, "Aristoteles latinus," in *The Cambridge History of the Later Medieval Philosophy: From the Rediscovery of Aristotle to the Disintegration of Scholasticism, 1100–1600*, ed. Norman Kretzmann, Anthony Kenny, and Jan Pinborg, 45–79 (Cambridge: Cambridge University Press, 1988); and C. H. Lohr, "The Medieval Interpretation of Aristotle," in Kretzmann et al., *Later Medieval Philosophy*, 80–98.

Latin Stoic moralists in particular: Calvin wrote on Seneca, for instance, and the work of Cicero featured in every curriculum.[11] These "wise heathens" were understood as speaking from the remainder of the image of God within them, the law written on their hearts. John Cotton (1585–1652), the leading minister of the first generation of New England Puritans, was one of many who could say: "Heathen Law-givers, Philosophers, and Poets have expressed the effect of all the Commandments save the tenth."[12] Yet the influence ran in both directions. It was Christian beliefs that accounted, in the first place, for the very favoring of the Stoics over other ancient schools of philosophy. (For the Stoics, after all, were viewed as monotheistic, devoted to the will of God and God's service, cosmopolitan, and concerned with cultivating a disciplined life.)[13] Likewise, in American teaching of Greek, it was the New Testament and morally improving Hellenistic sources that found favor, rather than the seemingly amoral tales from the Greek classics.[14]

Puritan natural law – biblically warranted, classically interpreted – differed significantly from medieval scholastic accounts, however, in its scope. Natural law for the Puritans concerned not the economics of salvation, but – as for Calvin and others in the Reformed tradition – civil authority and human sociability. For the Puritans, nature or reason provided no saving knowledge of God as such. Instead, a primary purpose for natural law was the continuation of civilization precisely *apart* from knowledge of God's revealed will. Calvin

[11] See Ford Lewis Battles and André Malan Hugo, trans. and ed., *Calvin's Commentary on Seneca's De Clementia* (Leiden, The Netherlands: E. J. Brill, 1969).

[12] *A Practical Commentary, or, an Exposition with Observations, Reasons, and Verses upon the First Epistle Generall of John* (London: Printed by R. I. and E. C. for Thomas Parkhurst, 1656), 234.

[13] For discussion of the last point, *askesis* (spiritual exercises), see Pierre Hadot, Philosophy as a Way of Life: Spiritual Exercises from Socrates to Foucault, ed. Arnold I. Davidson, trans. Michael Chase (Oxford: Blackwell, 1995). More generally, see also Brad Inwood, *Reading Seneca: Stoic Philosophy at Rome* (New York: Oxford University Press, 2005), 224–48; Gerald Watson, "The Natural Law and Stoicism," in *Problems in Stoicism*, ed. A. A. Long, 217–36 (London: The Athlone Press, 1971). There is a vast literature on the reception of Cicero. For a recent example, see William Altman, ed., *Brill's Companion to the Reception of Cicero* (Leiden, The Netherlands: Brill, 2015).

[14] Benjamin Lord, a 1714 graduate of Yale, noted that "we recited the Greek Testament; knew not Homer, &c."; Franklin Bowditch Dexter, *Biographical Sketches of the Graduates of Yale College with Annals of the College History, October, 1701–May, 1745* (New York: Henry Holt, 1885), 115. Accordingly, when Caroline Winterer suggests that classicism was "irresistible" to eighteenth-century protestant ministers who "happily reconciled the ethics of the heathens with the morality of Christianity," this does not hold for the Puritans. In the Puritan world, the classics both came along with the Christian worldview – and not as a separate source – and *were selected for reading* as a result of their correspondence with fundamental Christian convictions. Caroline Winterer, *The Culture of Classicism: Ancient Greece and Rome in American Intellectual Life, 1780–1910* (Baltimore, MD: Johns Hopkins University Press, 2002), 14.

had spoken of natural law, for instance, as concerned with "terrestrial matters" (*res terrenae*), where natural law explains why adherence to the second table of the Law – duties to neighbors – is possible for all people.[15] In particular, he was concerned to show that there are God-given norms for the state (*politia*), household management (*oeconomia*), and the mechanical and liberal arts. With his humanist sensibilities and training, Calvin urged an appreciation of sculpture, painting, medicine, the mathematical sciences, Roman law, and so forth, and, regardless of their human source, insisted that these are to be understood as gifts given by God.[16]

Such a distinction between the salvific and the terrestrial, however, is far from neat, and the Puritans accordingly debated the boundaries of natural law. One long-running controversy was whether the Sabbath was mandated by natural law. Calvin thought not, and likewise Boston clergyman Samuel Willard (1640–1707) insisted that the details of the sacraments and ordinances of the Church "must come entirely from Christ; [for] the realm of the church is entirely separate from the realm of nature, and to decide upon its law Christ consulted only His own pleasure."[17] Yet even Willard suggested that the light of nature might suggest "a convincing reason of the equity and suitableness" of any sacrament or ordinance.[18] From nature, in other words, the Church might not deduce or demand Sabbath-keeping, but once known through revelation, a day of rest might appear reasonable and well suited to human life.[19]

---

[15] The second table of the Law refers to Commandments 4–10 of the Ten Commandments, which are seemingly concerned with human relationships rather than human relations with God. " Institutionis Christianae religionis [1559]," in *Joannis Calvini opera selecta*, ed. Petrus Barth (Monachii: C. Kaiser, 1926–59), 2.2.13. *The standard English translation of the 1559 edition is: Institutes of the Christian Religion: In Two Volumes*, ed. John McNeill and trans. Ford Lewis Battles (Philadelphia: Westminster Press, 1960).

[16] Calvin, *Institutes*, 1.2.14–15; 1.21.12. Irena Backus notes that, surprisingly, and unlike Thomas Aquinas, Calvin does not mention a human instinct to reproduce, rear children, or respond to violence. He does, however, consider at some length humanity's sociable nature and inclinations to preserve society, not least in civic order and honesty (2.2.13). " Calvin's Conception of Natural and Roman Law," *Calvin Theological Journal* 38 (2003): 7–26.

[17] Samuel Willard, *A Compleat Body of Divinity* (Boston: Printed by B. Green and S. Kneeland for B. Eliot and D. Henchman, 1726), 613.

[18] Ibid.

[19] The debate over whether the Sabbath could be known by nature was long-standing. In the generation before Willard, Thomas Shepard (1605–49) – the influential minister of the First Church of Cambridge – suggested that while humanity can know the natural law today, its knowable rules and principles are *not* those "most perfect impressions of the law of nature, in man's first creation and perfection." Shepard's position is an intensification of Willard's in its suggestion that, before the fall, human beings might well have grasped Sabbath-keeping *solely* through natural law. In the primordial past, at least, human beings could truly know God's will apart from revelation. *Theses Sabbaticae: Or, The doctrine of the Sabbath* (London: Printed by T. R. and E. M. for John Rothwell, 1649), thesis, 12, 4.

The Puritans, then, are best viewed within the broader intellectual and social climate of their age. They adhered to a broad natural-law common sense. Yet in seeking to assuage their particular anxieties, the Puritans emphasized the ways in which natural law can explain the decency in human life apart from God's direct revelation; made in God's image, so with God's law written on our hearts, all human beings can avoid disobeying the commandments against murder, adultery, theft, false witness, and covetousness, and live sociably with their neighbors.

PURITAN REASON

Debates over whether the Sabbath is commended by natural law are a reminder, however, that despite their natural-law worldview many Puritans retained a hearty suspicion of the operation of reason apart from revelation.[20] With Western Christians through the ages, the Puritans understood humanity to have fallen from a state of original righteousness and fellowship with God. With Reformed Protestants, they insisted that *all* of human nature is corrupted, including human reason and will.[21] As John Cotton's 1646 children's catechism *Milk for Babes* puts it: "My corrupt nature is empty of Grace, bent upon sinne, and onely unto sinne, and that continually."[22]

And yet, the Puritans continued to insist that if human beings are created in God's image then they image God's rationality, however much this rationality

---

[20] Perry Miller suggests that "the frequency with which the preachers insisted upon an inherent rationality of man is truly startling"; *The New England Mind: The Seventeenth Century* (Cambridge, MA: Belknap Press of Harvard University, 1984), 184. John Morgan, however, suggests that reason played a far more restricted role. *Godly Learning: Puritan Attitudes towards Reason, Learning, and Education, 1560–1640* (New York: Cambridge University Press, 1986).

[21] While this distinguishes the Puritans from Roman Catholic thought, the extent to which Puritans differed with other Protestants including those in the English Church is disputed. Distinctions are often exaggerated in retrospect. See Dewey Wallace, Jr., *Puritans and Predestination: Grace in English Protestant Theology, 1525–1695* (Chapel Hill: University of North Carolina Press, 1982). For the classic Roman Catholic position forged at the Council of Trent, see Giuseppe Alberigo, ed., *The Oecumenical Councils of the Roman Catholic Church from Trent to Vatican II (1545–1965)* (Turnhout, Belgium: Brepols, 2010). John O'Malley provides an excellent overview of the Council: *Trent: What Happened at the Council* (Cambridge, MA: Belknap Press of Harvard University, 2013).

[22] John Cotton (1585–1652), *Milk for Babes. Drawn Out of the Breasts of Both Testaments. Chiefly, for the Spirituall Nourishment of Boston Babes in Either England: But May Be of Like Use for Any Children* (London: Printed by J. Coe for Henry Overton, 1646), 2. This was reprinted many times on both sides of the Atlantic, and at least eight editions from the seventeenth century are known. Sometime between 1690 and 1701 it was first incorporated into *The New England Primer*, and it remained an essential component of that work and thereby an integral part of American religious education for the next 150 years.

is obscured or defaced by sin. Reason remains definitive of what it means to be human. For Thomas Hooker (1586–1647): "A man is a living creature indued with a reasonable soul: and every living creature indued with a reasonable soul, is a man."[23]

We find, therefore, that even when defending the primacy of revelation, Puritans turned to reason. In a 1785 election sermon to the Connecticut General Assembly, Samuel Wales (1748–94) commended "a divine and supernatural influence" as necessary for "true religion," but added that this view, "clearly taught in divine revelation," was also "perfectly consonant to the dictates of reason." "It has been taught," he said, "even by heathen philosophers, such as Socrates and Plato, Cicero and Seneca."[24] For Wales, true religion needs recognition of revelation apart from reason, and yet it is both from revelation and reason that this is known to be true.

If no Puritan denied that after the Fall human beings still possess a "remainder" of God's image, they nonetheless disputed what this inheritance entailed for postlapsarian human beings' ability to grasp the tenets of God's law.[25] The view of William Ames (1576–1633), an influential figure for the first and second generations of New England Puritans, is instructive.[26] In Ames's account – as too in Wales's view of "true religion" – reason and revelation are neither unrelated nor, ultimately, in conflict. They both point to the same body of principles: "the moral law of God revealed through Moses is completely the

---

[23] A *Survey of the Summe of Church-Discipline, Part I: Ecclesiastical Policie Defined* (London: Printed by A. M. for John Bellamy, 1648), 44. Such was John Cotton's confidence both in "an essential wisdome in us, namely, our Reason which is natural" and this reason's being the "same nature" as our very selves, that his chosen analogy for God's Trinitarian life was reason: Christ "who is the reason and wisdome of the Father … is of the same nature with him." A *Practical Commentary, or, an Exposition with Observations, Reasons, and Verses upon the First Epistle Generall of John* (London: Printed by R. I. and E. C. for Thomas Parkhurst, 1656), 8.

[24] Samuel Wales, *The dangers of our national prosperity; and the way to avoid them. A sermon, preached before the General Assembly of the state of Connecticut, at Hartford, May 12th, 1785* (Hartford, CT: Printed by Barlow & Babcock, M,DCC,LXXXV [1785]), 26. *Political Sermons of the American Founding Era, 1730–1805*, ed. Ellis Sandoz, 2nd ed. (Indianapolis, ID: Liberty Fund, 1998), 835–64.

[25] Christians today disagree as to whether the image of God is, indeed, possessed – an inherent capacity (such as reason) – or a bestowed worth (resulting from God's redemptive love). The latter view has gained traction as Christian thinkers argue that human beings with severe impairments – cognitive disabilities from birth, say, or obtained through injuries or Alzheimer's disease – possess human rights or dignity on account simply of their being human.

[26] Cotton Mather called Ames "that *profound*, that *sublime*, that *subtil*, that *irrefragable* – yea, that *angelic doctor*"; *Magnalia Christi Americana* (Hartford, CT: S. Andrus and Son, 1853), Book 3, 236. *Magnalia* was first published in 1702. And see Keith Sprunger, "William Ames and the Settlement of Massachusetts Bay," *New England Quarterly* 39, no. 1 (1966): 66–79.

same with that which is said to be inscribed in the hearts of men."[27] Human access to the moral law is possible through the conscience, where *synderesis* – habitual knowledge of basic moral principles – is the "light of nature" given to humanity by God in order to know God.[28] Synderesis guarantees knowledge of basic moral principles, even if human conscience errs in its interpretation of these principles or the application of moral principles to facts. We are assured, nonetheless, that all humans possess the building blocks of morality. In Ames's account, moreover, God's moral law – pre-eminently known in the Ten Commandments – is also rightly termed "natural law" because through humans' "*natural* conscience" its principles can be intuited.[29]

And yet Ames insists that this natural law is only partially grasped. The human mind, in his telling – whether regenerated by God's grace or in its "natural" state – does, indeed, possess conscience, and this provides human access to the moral law of God. But, after the Fall, human beings only have access to "some relics of the law" akin to "some dim aged picture," which only the "voice and power of God" can "renew[] as with a fresh pencil."[30]

In Ames's account it is only in the "written law of God," then, that one can find "true right practical reason [*recta ratio practica*], pure and complete in all its parts."[31] In this judgment, Ames and many puritans shared the broad consensus of the age. In his later writings John Locke too would simultaneously affirm the reasonableness of Christianity yet argue that human beings need a divine lawgiver, for "'tis too hard a task for unassisted Reason, to establish Morality in all its parts upon its foundations; with a clear and convincing light."[32] In Scripture, the puritans and Locke say alike: We see face-to-face what reason glimpses only through a glass, darkly.

---

[27] William Ames, *Philosophemata* (Cambridge: Printed by Roger Daniels, 1646), 108–9. The translation is Perry Miller's *New England Mind*, 196. James Gustafson sees this position as in continuity with Calvin: *Protestant and Roman Catholic Ethics: Prospects for Rapprochement* (Chicago: University of Chicago, 1978), 165n37.

[28] See Lee Gibbs, *The Puritan Natural Law Theory of William Ames*, Harvard Theological Review 64, no. 1 (1971): 37–57.

[29] Emphasis added. Ames's equation of the commandments and natural law illustrates what Perry Miller takes to be the Puritans' "perverse tendency to make revelation natural and redemption rational." *New England Mind*, 187.

[30] See Julia Ipgrave's discussion in her *Adam in Seventeenth-Century Political Writing in England and New England* (Abingdon, England: Routledge, 2017), 61.

[31] William Ames, *Conscience with the Power and Cases Thereof, Divided into Five Bookes* (London: Printed by E. G. for I. Rothwell, T. Slater, L. Blacklock, 1643), V.I.28, 108. See also J. B. Schneewind, *The Invention of Autonomy: A History of Modern Moral Philosophy* (New York: Cambridge University Press, 1998), 63–64n8.

[32] *The Reasonableness of Christianity: As Delivered in the Scriptures*, ed. John Higgins-Biddle (New York: Clarendon Press, 1999), chapter XIV, 148. In a reply of March 30, 1696 to William Molyneux's request that he write a treatise on morality, Locke wrote: "But the Gospel contains so

PURITAN CIVIL LAW

But how did the New England Puritans' understandings of natural law and reason fit with their understanding of the laws applicable to them as members of a particular political community, *civil* laws distinguishable – in part, at least – from laws applicable to them as Church members? In other words: How did their understanding of the law governing their lives as colonists and subjects relate to their understanding of the law to which they were bound as Christians? The distinctions of our time are not the Puritans'.

We understand better the Puritans' view of life together, life in society under civil law, when we understand that natural law was its assumed backdrop. Most often natural law was taken for granted by the Puritans. It undergirded their very understanding of reason. More explicit considerations of natural law's relationship to the civil law were most often scholarly concerns. In his treatise on conscience, for example, William Ames, when talking of law, declared: "This civil law [*jus hoc civile*] in as much as it is right [*rectum*] is derived from the law of nature [*jure naturale*]; for that is not law which is not just and right."[33]

But explicit consideration of natural law was not restricted to academic treatises. Natural law was the justification, too, for elements of the Puritans' civil legal system: both its overall jurisprudential rationale and laws governing daily living. The 1647 *Lawes and Libertyes of Massachusetts* – which functioned as something of a constitution for the colony – begins with a preamble, which, in part, offers justifications for the content of the various laws and liberties thereafter enumerated.[34] As with any (quasi-)constitutional document, the question of *authority* is central to *Lawes and Libertyes*: Who or what can rightly give orders and make decisions, and justifiably demand obedience?

---

perfect a body of Ethicks, that reason may be excused from that enquiry, since she may find man's duty clearer and easier in revelation than in herself." *Reasonableness*, ed. Higgins-Biddle, 148n3.

In his *Essay Concerning Human Understanding*, Locke suggests that "*Reason* is natural *Revelation*, whereby the eternal Father of Light, and Fountain of all Knowledge communicates to Mankind that portion of Truth, which he has laid within the reach of their natural Faculties: *Revelation* is natural *Reason* enlarged by a new set of Discoveries communicated by GOD immediately, which *Reason* vouches the Truth of, by the Testimony and Proofs it gives, that they come from GOD. So that he that takes away *Reason*, to make way for *Revelation*, puts out the Light of both, and does much the same, as if he would persuade a Man to put out his Eyes the better to receive the remote Light of an invisible Star by a Telescope." *An Essay Concerning Human Understanding*, ed. Peter H. Nidditch (Oxford: Clarendon Press, 1975), 4.19.4, 698.

[33] Ames, *Conscience*, V.I.22, 105; Gibbs, "Puritan Natural Law," 48–49.

[34] *Laws and Liberties of Massachusetts: Reprinted from the Copy of the 1648 Edition in the Henry E. Huntington Library* (Cambridge, MA: Harvard University Press, 1929).

The preamble identifies a difficulty in quickly answering the question of authority. What is the status of the colony's laws vis-à-vis the law of God known in the Scriptures? The Puritans worried about a particularly troublesome answer. (Whether this was a live issue of debate in the colony or the rehearsal of a perennial concern is not clear.) Distinguishing the "Lawes of God" from the "laws of men," the preamble suggests, can be a "snare to many" if so distinguishing the two suggests either that civil law does not possess authority or that the civil law's authority is different than God's. Neither anarchy nor a nondivine posited authority were reasonable answers for the Puritans. Attempting to avoid these twin threats, the preamble thereafter offers a clear if variegated account of "civil Authoritie."

In the first place, the preamble offers a bald *genealogical* account of authority. If the traceable *source* of a law possesses proper authority, then the law itself must possess authority. "[W]hen the Authoritie is of God and that in way of an Ordinance *Rom.* 13.1 . . . [a civil law] is mediately a law of God, and that in way of an Ordinance which all are to submit unto and that for conscience sake." The preamble suggests, in other words, that the Puritans' civil laws come from God, even if they are promulgated through the mediation of human actors. When traceable to the command of one with proper authority, a law itself has authority and must be followed.

The law is to be followed, however, not out of fear or self-interest. Laws are not merely commands backed up by credible threats.[35] Instead, in the Puritans' telling, if God is the source of law's authority, the law is properly followed out of conscience, the human capacity to know good and evil and apply moral principles to facts. In this light, the preamble's reference to the New Testament book of Romans offers a familiar proof text for civil power: "Let every soul be subject unto the higher powers: for there is no power but of God: and the powers that be, are ordained of God." As the marginal notes of the Geneva Bible explains:

> Now he [the Apostle Paul] showeth severally, what subjects owe to their Magistrates, to wit, obedience: From which he showeth that no man is free: and in such sort that it is not only due to the highest Magistrate himself, but also even to the basest, which hath any office under him.[36]

---

[35] This is the basic positivist account of laws offered by John Austin (1790–1859). See his 1832 *The Providence of Jurisprudence Determined*, ed. Wilfred E. Rumble (Cambridge: Cambridge University Press, 1995).

[36] For a contemporary treatment of civil authority in the Reformed tradition that attempts to pull away from the implications of acquiescence to established civil power, whatever its seeming merits, see Nicholas Wolterstorff, *The Mighty and the Almighty: An Essay in Political Theology* (New York: Cambridge University Press, 2012).

The preamble, however, also includes a more *substantive* account of legal authority, which, while interwoven with the genealogical account, stands in some tension to the idea that genealogy alone grants laws their authority. In the substantive account, a civil law is a law of God, and thus to be submitted to, where "the administration of it is according to deductions, and rules gathered from the word of God, and the clear light of nature in civil nations." The preamble, in effect, invites the reader to understand the laws that follow in *Lawes and Libertyes* as drawn from Scripture and the natural law. The laws of Massachusetts – given this basis – should, therefore, agree with the laws of other civilized nations. Laws might have authority because of their genealogy – their pedigree directly or mediately from God – but also because of their substantial resemblance to the moral authority of the Bible and natural law.

Finally, the preface suggests that "surely there is no humane law that tendeth to the common good . . . but the same is mediately a law of God, and in way of an Ordinance which all are to submit unto and that for conscience sake." This, we might think, is merely a pious attribution of all good things to God, or an ex post facto account of the verified goodness of certain laws. Yet this preamble idea is also a proclamation that the laws outlined in the *Lawes and Libertyes of Massachusetts* will readily be comprehended as civilized and communally effective. Laws will be humane and for the common good. When Increase Mather (1639–1723) condemned drunkenness, for example, he not only appealed to the written word of God, but also suggested that "the very Light of Nature condemns this practice. Drunkards sin . . . against that light and law which is written in their Consciences."[37] *Lawes and Libertyes* operates with the assumption that colonists should be able to readily comprehend both the utility and rationality of the laws to which they are subject.

We need not think that this emphasis on the correspondence of God's, nature's, and society's laws was something peculiar to New England Puritans. In the history of English common law, influential voices had long accounted for the authority of human laws in their correspondence with nature.[38] The Puritans' *explicit* treatment of natural law in their civil law, however, was distinctive. Reference to their civil law's relationship to natural law served, in part, as a reference point and justification for the community

---

[37] Increase Mather, *Wo to drunkards. Two Sermons Testifying against the Sin of Drunkenness: Wherein the Wofulness of That Evil, and the Mistery of All That Are Addicted to It, Is Discovered from the Word of God* (Cambridge, MA: Printed by Marmaduke Johnson, and sold by Edmund Ranger, bookbinder in Boston, 1673).

[38] See Richard Helmholz, *Natural Law and Human Rights in English Law: From Bracton to Blackstone,* 3 Ave Maria. L. Rev. 1 (2005): 1–22.

they were building. In responding to attacks, real and perceived, from inside and outside their nascent community, natural law was at hand to justify their practices.[39]

The newness of the New World's laws and procedures, moreover, compelled attention to the claimed natural-law basis of civil laws. In England, laws and procedures had already undergone centuries of accumulation and refinement.[40] Where there is precedent, laws need not continually revert to their sources. The Puritans' legal order was not simply new, however, but deliberately formed in reference to perceived English injustices. Dislike of lawyers is partly attributable to the legal persecutions of puritans in England, and, in time, lawyers' association with the increasingly unpopular royal government in the colonies.

Suspicion of legal practice, however, was not merely reactive. By design there was to be little need for lawyers in the New World. Indeed, there was only one lawyer resident in the Massachusetts Bay Colony in 1640: Thomas Lechford came to Boston from Lincoln's Inn in London in 1638, stayed three years, and then returned. Individuals ideally represented themselves before magistrates. Legal practice was a legerdemain the Puritans sought to exclude from their honest society.

Cumbersome forms of English procedure were likewise discarded.[41] In Plymouth, Massachusetts, deeds of land were merely acknowledged and recorded by a magistrate, not signed or sealed as true in Plymouth, England.[42] Puritan suspicion of legal practice, however, did not indicate that civil law

---

[39] When attacked, the Puritans pulled upon all resources to hand, natural law included. In his influential *Vindication of the Government of New-England Churches*, for instance, John Wise (1652–1725) offers arguments from *"Antiquity;* The *Light of Nature; Holy Scripture;* and from the *Noble* and *Excellent Nature* of the *Constitution* itself. And lastly from the *Providence of God* dignifying of it." John Wise, A *Vindication of the Government of New England Churches* (1717): *A Facsimile Reproduction with an introduction by Perry Miller* (Gainesville, FL: Scholars' Facsimiles & Reprints, 1958), 3. For more information, see Thomas Johnston, Jr., "John Wise: Early American Political Thinker," *Early American Literature Newsletter* 3, no. 1 (1968): 30–40.

[40] While Francis Bacon (1561–1626), to take a prominent counterpoint, expressed the view that English law must be in conformity with nature and reason, his attention was on middle axioms (rules generalized from specific cases), which provided, in his view, the premises by which new cases might properly be decided. The "maxims" Bacon identified, nonetheless, were simultaneously generalizations from cases *and* "general dictates of reason" or "conclusions of reason," and he expected, therefore, that "for the most part nearly the same rules [will be] found in the civil laws of different states; except perhaps that they may sometimes vary with reference to the forms of constitutions." See Paul Kocher, "Francis Bacon on the Science of Jurisprudence," *Journal of the History of Ideas* 18, no. 1 (1957): 3–26, 10.

[41] See, e.g., Scott Gerber, *Law and Religion in Colonial Connecticut*, 55 Am. J. Legal Hist. 142 (2015).

[42] See Angela Fernandez, *Record-Keeping and Other Troublemaking: Thomas Lechford and Law Reform in Colonial Massachusetts*, 23 Law & Hist. Rev. 235 (2005). For discussions of "puritan jurisprudence," see Gail Sussman Marcus, "'Due Executive of the Generall Rules of

lacked importance, but rather that law merited broad engagement by all of society. Law – and with it, governance – were to be the preserve not of a professional caste, but of all in a society committed to a disciplined way of living.

THE COLONIAL COLLEGES

Founded before the Revolution, the colonial colleges were small in number and scale.[43] As one of the few institutions in the British New World, however, they exercised considerable influence on their broader communities.[44] Training ministers of religion and other leaders in the colonies, the colleges not only contributed to the colonies' social and economic orders, but also transmitted the higher learning of the age and influenced the developing thought world of the new colonies.[45]

In the curriculums of these colonial colleges, and the lives, too, of their teachers and students, we find a particularly potent distillation of the Puritans' understanding of reason and both natural law and civil law. Indeed, if we do not presume that today's pedagogical practices exhaust all the possibilities for legal education, we can see that these fledgling colleges taught law.

This is not the usual depiction of the colonial colleges or the history of legal education in America. For the beginnings of legal education in America, legal scholars' have most often focused on the 1817 birth of university graduate law schools *separate* from colleges, and the continuities or discontinuities between these early law schools' practices and today's. The broad dominance of legal positivism in the imagination of twentieth-century legal scholarship,

---

Righteousnesse': Criminal Procedure in New Haven Town and Colony, 1638–1658," in *Saints and Revolutionaries: Essays on Early American History*, ed. David Hall, John Murrin, and Thad Tate, 99–137 (New York: Norton, 1984); *The Many Legalities of Early America*, ed. Christopher Tomlins and Bruce Mann (Chapel Hill: University of North Carolina Press, 2001); and George Haskins, *Law and Authority in Early Massachusetts: A Study in Tradition and Design* (New York: Macmillan, 1960).

[43] Surveys of the history of the American college include: Frederick Rudolph, *The American College and University, A History* (New York: Knopf, 1961); Laurence R. Veysey, *The Emergence of the American University* (Chicago: University of Chicago, 1965), and John R. Thelin, *A History of American Higher Education* (Baltimore: Johns Hopkins University Press, 2004).

[44] For a brief recent treatment, see Roger L. Geiger, *The History of American Higher Education: Learning and Culture from the Founding to World War II* (Princeton, NJ: Princeton University Press, 2016), 1–90.

[45] See J. David Hoeveler, *Creating the American Mind: Intellect and Politics in the Colonial Colleges* (Lanham, MD: Rowman & Littlefield, 2002).

moreover, has helped mask earlier approaches to law, including the Puritans', that do not begin with the assumption that law is separate from morality.

Historians of education, too, have helped render American collegiate study of law invisible. This obfuscation, in part, has been the result of their broadly shared understanding that antebellum American colleges "failed." Through much of the twentieth century, historians of education viewed the colonial college as an "obstacle" to the development of higher education in America. Early colleges were portrayed – often correctly – as small, parochial, sectarian, and fixed – even fixated – on a narrow curriculum involving rote learning of dead languages. The colonial college, accordingly, stood as the "virtual antithesis" of the twentieth-century secular, science-driven, research university they admired, and so merited only a particular kind of historical interest as the problem that was solved.[46]

Twentieth-century historians of education could simply point to demographics to make their case that nothing much of use happened in the colonial colleges. Students were younger than today, they noted, with the median age at Harvard from 1673 to 1707 hovering between fifteen and sixteen years old.[47] And the tone of student life was more "aristocratic . . . than popular," even as poorer, older students attended college to enter the professions.[48] The focus in the colonial colleges was not, then, as twentieth-century critics wished, the development of new knowledge, but what Cotton

---

[46] For example, R. Freeman Butts's *The College Charts Its Course* (New York: McGraw-Hill, 1939) is premised on the triumph of the elective system over a defined curriculum. For a historiography of twentieth-century treatment of the colleges, see Roger Geiger, "Introduction: New Themes in the History of Nineteenth-Century Colleges," in *The American College in the Nineteenth Century*, ed. Roger Geiger (Nashville: Vanderbilt University Press, 2000), 1–37.

[47] Iran Cassim Mohsenin, "Note on Age Structure of College Students," *History of Education Quarterly* 23, no. 4 (1983): 491–98. In the seventeenth century, students were admitted to college based not on age, as such, but on competency, not least in Latin, the language of instruction, knowledge of which was required and assumed, rather than taught. Their basic reading and writing skills were reliant on the books brought from England: psalter, "Testament," and Bible; a horn book, A. B. C., Primer, *Book of Civilitie*, and spelling book. Edwin Dexter, *A History of Education in the United States* (New York: Macmillan, 1904).

By 1685, books were printed in New England, with *The Protestant Teacher for Children* among the first. Sometime between 1687 and 1690 came the *New England Primer*, which was the most widely used book in America until sometime later than 1783, when Webster's *American Spelling Book* was published. See Gillian Avery, *Origins and English Predecessors of the New England Primer* (Worcester, MA: American Antiquarian Society, 2000); and Henry Perkinson, "The Role of Religion in American Education: An Historical Interpretation," *Paedagogica Historica* 5, no. 1 (1965): 109–21.

[48] Theodore Crane, *The Colleges and the Public, 1787–1862* (New York: Teachers College, Columbia University, 1963), 8. With the increased prominence of social history from the 1970s onward, the consensus of the scholarship today is that colleges reflected their surroundings.

Mather (1663–1728) called the "collegiate way of living."[49] Assuming the connection of reason and morals, the colleges were to inculcate, without undue separation, how to know and how to live. Ideally for Mather and his contemporaries, students would follow a disciplined life of study and chapel worship, and would live and eat together with peers and tutors. Formation was at its heart: the development of faith and character in young men, primarily to form an elite for leadership in the community.[50] The colleges sought to develop in students a "lively faith in Christ" and strong character, but they inculcated habits for social advancement too: the refinement of writing and speaking to the standards of the day, social graces, and the ability to get along (and ahead) in the world.[51]

The intellectual and social background that fostered this vision of a collegiate way of living had predecessors in the Old World, but the vision's enactment took a particularly American form. Whatever their intention, the earliest colonial leaders and teachers could not help but be innovators – they founded new institutions, wrote governance documents, and determined curriculums – yet they inhabited, and *wanted to inhabit*, the same thought world as European protestants. Scholarly debates continue as to the particular genealogies of the colonial colleges, but it is fairest to say that they built upon various models: The early presidents and tutors worked with what they knew, and with what was doable given the social and economic circumstances they inhabited. But also – and this is often overlooked – they sought for the colleges what they imagined to be true and best.

The British universities were the closest models for the colleges. Many of the founding personalities of Harvard were graduates of Emmanuel College, Cambridge, and other puritan colleges of that university.[52] Graduates of Oxford and the Scottish universities brought other influences. Following the Scottish model, the colonial colleges located in chief towns, little cared to distinguishing "college" and "university," found ways to include poor boys

---

[49] *Magnalia Christi Americana* (Hartford, CT: S. Andrus and Son, 1853), Book IV, §2, 10.

[50] To these fundamental policies of character formation, the colleges held steadfastly and without essential change for nearly 200 years. See John Brubacher and Willis Rudy, *Higher Education in Transition: A History of American Colleges and Universities, 1636–1968* (New York, Harper & Row, 1968), 23–24.

[51] Even a century later, a 1754 newspaper advertisement for King's College (later Columbia) announced that "The chief thing that is aimed at in this College is to teach and engage the Children to *know God in Jesus Christ*, and to love and serve him in all *Sobriety, Godliness*, and *Righteousness* of life, *with a perfect heart, and a willing mind.*" *New York Gazette*, June 3, 1752.

[52] Samuel Eliot Morison, *The Founding of Harvard College* (Cambridge, MA: Harvard University Press, 1935). Appendix D is a list of "English University Men who Emigrated to New England before 1646."

among their number, and – as in the English dissenters' colleges – taught divinity in the arts curriculum.[53]

British political subjects that they were – in law and mostly in mindset – Americans looked to Cambridge, Oxford, and the Scottish universities as their models well into the eighteenth century.[54] In preparing to lead Yale, Thomas Clap borrowed histories of the English universities, and sought information from Americans who held their degrees. Seeking a new charter for Yale in 1745, he first gave careful attention to the governance and administration of Oxford and Cambridge.[55]

What unified the colonial colleges with the puritan colleges of Oxford and Cambridge, and aligned them in part with the Scottish universities and English dissenters' academies, was their mission as New World "schools of the reformation."[56] The colonists brought traditions of classical learning, shared throughout Europe, but put these traditions into practice to defend the Reformed faith. Classical learning was sifted for its utility to form pious and useful subjects, and to forge a godly commonwealth.

The colonial colleges, then, had a vocational purpose.[57] In part this followed from the governance structure of the early American colleges, which – following

[53] Elbert Willis, *The Growth of American Higher Education: Liberal, Professional and Technical* (Philadelphia: Dorrance, 1936), 158. See also George Pryde, *The Scottish Universities and the Colleges of Colonial America* (Glasgow: Jackson, Son & Company, 1957).

[54] Whether and how Americans viewed themselves as British, and in relation to what other ideals, remains a topic of significant interest. For the often forgotten losing side in the Revolutionary era and the importance of local, over national, identity, see William Nelson, *The American Tory* (Oxford: Clarendon, 1961); Maya Jasanof, *Liberty's Exiles: American Loyalists in the Revolutionary World* (New York: Knopf, 2011); and Gregory Knouff, *The Soldiers' Revolution: Pennsylvanians in Arms and the Forging of Early American Identity* (University Park: Pennsylvania State University Press, 2004).

[55] Brubacher and Rudy, *Higher Education*, 3.

[56] The American colleges were ambiguously secular or ecclesiastical: They were concerned with ministerial education, but with their external boards, they were not self-governing *collegium scholasticum* made up of divines. Neither were they akin to municipal grammar schools or the *gymnasium illustre*, for their focus was on the whole of the colony. Jurgen Herbst, *From Crisis to Crisis: American College Government, 1639–1819* (Cambridge, MA: Harvard University Press, 1982), 5. See, also, in particular, 1–62. For the influence of the English dissenting academics, see David Humphrey, "Colonial Colleges and English Dissenting Academies: A Study in Transatlantic Culture," *History of Education Quarterly* 12, no. 2 (1972): 184–97. For the Protestant arts college model following the 1560 Scottish reformation, see Steven Reid, *Humanism and Calvinism: Andrew Melville and the Universities of Scotland, 1560–1625* (Burlington, VT: Ashgate, 2011).

[57] The ideal of the "liberal arts" college as an institution pursuing academic inquiry as an end in itself, or perhaps formative of students' general habits of inquiry – "mental discipline" – is anachronistic for the colonial period. The famous "Yale Report" of 1828, which rejected elective courses in favor of a core curriculum based on the classics for the purpose of forming

the Scottish universities over Oxford and Cambridge – placed the control of the college in the hands not of its teachers, but of an external board of prominent clergy and laymen: that is, men who generally favored education for public professions over "pure learning."[58] Foremost in their mission was the education of clergy. The 1643 pamphlet *New Englands First Fruits* recounts the founding of Harvard College as tied to the colonists' desire for educated ministers.[59] Likewise, the founding motivation for Yale and the College of New Jersey (now Princeton) was straightforwardly to train up literate clergy.[60] As late as 1753, the General Assembly of Connecticut resolved in respect to Yale that "one principal end proposed in erecting the college was to supply the churches in this Colony with a learned, pious and orthodox ministry."[61]

But from the start, the colleges' concern was also to produce educated orthodox laymen to lead the government and the churches (a necessity, given congregational polity). The College of New Jersey responded to the need for "a competent number of men of letters" for "the bench, the bar, and seats of legislation," fearing that the competencies required were "seldom the spontaneous growth of nature, unimproved by education."[62]

THE COLONIAL CURRICULUM

In the content of its teaching and learning, Harvard followed the puritan colleges of Cambridge, and thus brought to the New World a *scholastic*

---

well-rounded graduates with the capacities for further study on their own initiative was *neo-traditionalistic*. It was a conscious articulation of a desired framework created when the givenness of academic practices was challenged. It re-presented aspects of the "classical" curriculum, but without the eminently practical orientation of the earliest American colleges.

[58] Brubacher and Rudy, *Higher Education*, 4. The Charter of William and Mary suggests an institution akin to the Scottish "unicollege": a degree-granting college, with an external governing board. A. Bailey Cutts, "Educational Influence of Aberdeen in 17th Century Virginia," *William and Mary Quarterly* 15, no. 4 (1935): 229–49. Personality as much as policy played a role in particular links to Europe. John Blair at William and Mary, for example, was a graduate of the Marischal College in Aberdeen, and Edinburgh University. William Smith, who planned much of the curriculum at King's College and the College of Philadelphia, studied at the University of Aberdeen. John Witherspoon was an Edinburgh graduate.

[59] Clark, *Eliot Tracts*, 55–78. The historicity of the pamphlet is mixed. It was likely written as publicity material to encourage donations, and we might think, therefore, that its emphases were an attempt to find a sympathetic audience.

[60] As Samuel Blair put it: "Religious societies were annually formed, in various places; and had they long continued vacant, or been supplied with an ignorant illiterate clergy, Christianity itself, in a course of years, might have become extinct among them." *An Account of the College of New Jersey* (Woodbridge, NJ: James Parker, 1764), 5–7.

[61] Quoted in Benjamin Trumbull, *A Complete History of Connecticut, Civil and Ecclesiastical*, vol. 2. (New Haven, CT: Maltby, Goldsmith, and Samuel Wadsworth, 1815), 264.

[62] Blair, *Account of the College of New Jersey*, 5–7.

curriculum.[63] This was a "logical, systematic, and largely Aristotelian" enter-prise, taught by lecture, disputation, and declamation.[64] Henry Dunster (1609–59), a graduate of Magdalene College, Cambridge, introduced a curriculum at Harvard that essentially followed the Cambridge model: "Primus annus Rhetoricam docebit, secundus et teritus Dialecticam, quartus adiungat Philosophiam."[65] (The first year will teach rhetoric; the second and third, dialectic; the fourth will add philosophy.)[66]

In a 1779 letter to Yale's President Stiles, a graduate of 1714 recalled Yale's earliest curriculum:

> Books of the Languages and Sciences recited in my Day were Tully and Virgil, but without any Notes; Burgersdicius and Ramus's *Logick*, also Heerebord's *Set Logic*, &c.; Pierson's manuscript of Physicks, which I have no copy of. We recited the Greek Testament; knew not Homer, &c.; recited the Psalms in Hebrew . . . We recited Ames' *Medulla* on Saturdays, and also his *Cases of Conscience* sometimes; the two upper classes used to dispute syllogistically twice or thrice a week.[67]

Students focused on the arts. In the vocabulary of scholasticism and the colonial colleges, the *arts* were the branches of study concerned with action.[68] (The *sciences* were concerned with abstract knowledge.)[69] *Rhetoric*, then, was

---

[63] Morison, *Founding of Harvard College*. For a general history of the colonial curriculum, see Louis Franklin Snow, *The College Curriculum in the United States* (New York: Teachers College, Columbia University, 1907).

[64] William Costello, *The Scholastic Curriculum at Early Seventeenth-Century Cambridge* (Cambridge, MA: Harvard University Press, 1958). At Oxford and Cambridge, the arts courses began with grammar out of Priscian and Donatus, logic out of Aristotle and Boethius, rhetoric out of Aristotle, Cicero, and Boethius, geometry out of Euclid, astronomy out of Ptolemy, and the three philosophies (natural, moral, and mental) out of Aristotle.

[65] Snow, *The College Curriculum in the United States*, 23.

[66] In his history of the university, Josiah Quincy (1772–1864), president of Harvard from 1829 to 1845, suggests that the principles of education that Dunster established did not materially change through the seventeenth century. *History of Harvard University* (Cambridge, MA: Josiah Owen, 1840).

[67] Benjamin Lord's letter of May 28, 1779 in Dexter, *Biographical Sketches*, 115–16. In 1753, the Yale Corporation reaffirmed its commitment to ordering the College's doctrine, discipline, and mode of worship "according to the Assembly's Catechism, Dr. Ames's Medulla, and Cases of Conscience." "At a Meeting of the President and Fellows of Yale-College, November 21, 1753" in Thomas Clap, *The Annals or History of Yale-College, in New Haven, In the Colony of Connecticut, From the First Founding thereof, in the Year 1700, to the Year 1766* (New Haven, CT: Printed for John Hotchkiss and B. Mecom, M, DCC, LXVI [1766]).

[68] Costello, *Scholastic Curriculum*, 147.

[69] The sciences included: metaphysics (the study of "being" in general); physics ("being" as qualified); mathematics ("being" as quantified); and cosmology (the being of the geographical world).

the art of expression according to established principles of *eloquentia*. Students studied Greek and Latin orators, historians, and poets to gain precepts of *ars dicendi*, and wrote in imitation of their voices. The aim was to form a well-rounded Latin style, although English orations were studied too. What Dunster called "dialectic" is *logic*, which taught students the patterns of what was understood to constitute proper thinking.[70] This topic too had an active aim: Students studied to hone their abilities of apprehension, judgment, and the linking of judgments in a process of reasoning. The purpose was notably practical with students learning to sift arguments for fallacies. *Philosophy* was three-fold (natural, moral, and mental), and learned primarily through study of Aristotle's works. Moral philosophy taught students principles of moral behavior, primarily as those principles were understood to be discoverable by reason from the natural law.

From the beginnings of American college education, ethics, politics, and law were yoked together for a broad education in character and leadership. At Harvard, lectures on "Ethicks and Politicks" were delivered to second-year students.[71] President Dunster tried to obtain books in law – as well as medicine – so that the school might play a role in professional training.[72] Meanwhile at Yale, President Clap attempted to offer a broad program of preparation for law and other professions, even while emphasizing the priority of ministerial training. He taught a course on "the nature of civil government," "the various kinds of Courts," and "Statute, Common, Civil, Canon, Military and Maritime Laws."[73]

This combination of teaching was something new. The American ideal of a liberal arts education – so powerful until recently – wrongly dulls our surprise that seventeenth- and eighteenth-century colleges taught natural law

---

[70] Norman Kretzmann and Eleonore Stump, eds. *Logic and the Philosophy of Language*, vol. 1 of *The Cambridge Translations of Medieval Philosophical Texts* (Cambridge: Cambridge University Press, 1988); Alexander Broadie, *Introduction to Medieval Logic* (Oxford: Clarendon, 1993).

[71] "New Englands First Fruits," in Clark, *Eliot Tracts*. Similar content was thereafter taught throughout the colonies under the names of "Moral Philosophy" or "Natural Law." See Alfred Zantzinger Reed, *Training for the Public Profession of the Law: Historical Development and Principal Contemporary Problems of Legal Education in the United States* (New York: Carnegie Foundation for the Advancement of Teaching, 1921), 113; Mark Bailey, *Early Legal Education in the United States: Natural Law Theory and Law as a Moral Science*, 48 J. Legal Edu. 311 (1998).

[72] Robert Lovett, ed., *Publications of the Colonial Society of Massachusetts*, vol. XLIX, *Documents from the Harvard University Archives, 1638–1750* (Boston: Published for the Society, 1975); Books Printed At Cambridge [January 26, 1655/56]."

[73] Clifford K. Shipton, *Biographical Sketches of Those Who Attended Harvard College in the Classes, 1722–1725* (Boston: Massachusetts Historical Society, 1945), 34.

and principles of government. This was not the pattern of English education. The colonists had known Oxford and Cambridge universities to teach only Roman and canon law, with study of the common law and Chancery courts solely in the hands of practitioners.[74]

Not that teaching law meant teaching the necessary means to enter the legal profession. Until the twentieth century, entry to the legal profession came mostly through apprenticing with a senior practitioner and passing bar examinations; college, therefore, played little formal role in producing lawyers.[75] Most contemporary scholars have, therefore, seen little continuity between the traditions of American collegiate study of the law and the now-standard graduate teaching of lawyers.[76] Nonetheless, the early American colleges taught the body of rules, and corresponding institutions – "the law" – that their students recognized as binding on their actions as subjects of their political community.

True, from the standard viewpoint of contemporary legal scholars, a viewpoint formed within a general commitment to legal positivism – the separation of law and morality – the colonial colleges' teaching to cultivate citizens' virtue, where law is an admixture of moral philosophy or the study of

[74] London's Inns of Court were the sites of barristers' education, while solicitors and attorneys learned their craft as apprentices. For a brief introduction see chapter 10 "The Legal Profession," in J. H. Baker's *An Introduction to English Legal History* (London: Butterworths LexisNexis, 2002). See also Wilfrid Prest, *The Inns of Court under Elizabeth I and the Early Stuarts, 1590–1640* (Totowa, NJ: Rowman & Littlefield, 1972); C. W. Brooks, *Pettyfoggers and Vipers of the Commonwealth: The "Lower Branch" of the Legal Profession in Early Modern England* (Cambridge: Cambridge University Press, 1986). As we have seen, the principal university experience of the puritans of Cambridge, Massachusetts, was that of Cambridge, England, where Elizabethan statutes of 1561–71 governed the curriculum. Heavy traces of the medieval trivium (grammar, rhetoric, logic) and quadrivium (arithmetic, geometry, astronomy, music) marked a student's study, albeit alongside some treatment of the three philosophies (natural, moral, mental). See Costello, *Scholastic Curriculum*, 42–43; Joe Kraus, "The Development of a Curriculum in the Early American Colleges," *History of Education Quarterly* 1, no. 2 (1961): 64–76; Thelin, *History*, 19.

[75] Some bar organizations gave preferential treatment to college graduates. Certain counties reduced the length of college graduates' apprenticeships, for instance. And in 1771, Suffolk County in Massachusetts, at least, required would-be lawyers to have a college education in order to be admitted to the bar. Reed, 112–13. Robert Stevens suggests that the profession's support for college education partly accounts for American collegiate study of the law. *Law School: Legal Education in America from the 1850s to the 1980s* (Chapel Hill: University of North Carolina Press, 1983), 4.

[76] John Thelin comments "[a] college might have had a professor who delivered lectures on law, but the subject was combined with such topics as 'police,' a field that was most likely a forerunner to what is known today as political science and public administration." *History*, 31. Or as Alfred Reed notes: Study of the law "resembled what we should now term government and jurisprudence rather than law, and were still only partially differentiated from ethics and philosophy." *Training*, 135.

good governance, is not properly legal study. But this prematurely assumes agreement as to law's nature. In some distinction to this now-standard positivist view, significant traditions of American collegiate study of law represented and perpetuated two ideas about law that positivism does not: first, that discussion of law cannot be avoided when political morality is considered; and, second, that the study of the law, far from exhausted by study for its practice, should begin with philosophical reflection, broadly conducted within the terms of the natural-law tradition. This model of collegiate study of the law made sense as part of an education intended to inculcate piety and character, and commitment to the common weal.

* * *

What directed and chastened the colonial colleges' broadly scholastic curriculum – which emphasized, too, classical and "oriental" languages – was a particular understanding of learning, and its relationship to maintaining protestant orthodoxy. In his work on the New England Puritans, Perry Miller popularized the idea of the Puritans' debt to Petrus Ramus (1515–72) and the Ramian belief in *technologia* – the systematic connection between the arts – or *encyclopedia*, the circle of the arts, whereby all fields of learning are held together by their correspondence to a divine order, accessible through proper method.[77] Many scholars now doubt any direct links between Puritan teachings and Ramus. Yet Ramus and the Puritans shared a common protestant humanist vision: Truth had a unity, which the pursuit of the arts could profitably track; and learning was a means to pursue true happiness grounded in love of God.[78] Ethics, law, and politics – including Yale President Clap's treatment of various courts and forms of law – formed part of this curriculum, and was embedded in a culture where reason and morality, and natural and civil law, cohered.

The colleges founded before the American Revolution taught ethics, law, and government to form pious and energetic men for leadership in the colonies. As schools of the Protestant reformation they inculcated a collegiate way of life aimed at forming ministers of religion and civil leaders for the colonies. That they did so within a particular natural-law framework

---

[77] For work on Ramus, see Mordechai Feingold, Joseph Freedman, and Wolfgang Rother, eds., *The Influence of Peter Ramus: Studies in Sixteenth and Seventeenth Century Philosophy and Sciences* (Basel, Switzerland: Schwabe, 2001); Peter Sharratt, "The Present State of Studies on Ramus," *Studi francesi* 47–48 (1972): 201–13; Peter Sharratt, "Recent Work on Peter Ramus (1970–1986)," *Rhetorica* 5 (1987): 7–58; Peter Sharratt, "Ramus 2000," *Rhetorica* 18 (2000): 399–455.

[78] Margo Todd, *Christian Humanism and the Puritan Social Order* (New York: Cambridge University Press, 1987).

resulted from the refracting of their Old World intellectual heritage through their self-understanding of a New World mission. They sought a better understanding of the world, and thought that such reflection cultivated proper personal piety and morality. Indeed, in the Puritan mind, seeking knowledge and cultivating character were frequently one and the same pursuit. What might seem to us arcane disputes on the boundaries of natural law and human reason – whether the Sabbath-keeping is known apart from scriptural commands – were debates, too, on how to live with God and neighbor.

Not that the Puritans, or other colonists, necessarily took active steps to inculcate a natural-law vision of the society. Such a vision simply formed the background assumptions of the age: rationality and morality go together, they thought, and human laws accordingly derive their authority from their correspondence with the moral order. And yet, the particular rigors and anxieties of the New England Puritans – and their outsized impact on American education – did foster a *particular* vision of natural law in the colleges. In the colonial curriculum, natural law accorded with Scripture and the best of antiquity, and was focused on civil affairs. Natural law offered an account of the authority of the civil law, and, increasingly in time, arguments for the veracity of Christian revelation.

When we attend to the history of the colonial colleges, therefore, and particularly as sources of natural-law thinking and sites for natural law's engagement with common law, we find distinctive ways of talking about law. The natural-law traditions of the Puritans ensured that teaching on law was not restricted to teaching skills for its practice. College instruction, indeed, seemingly inextricably encompassed ethics, law, and government: To ask "what we know" and "how we should live well" was to seek the just ordering of society and its institutions; questions of law were explicitly tied to broader questions of theology, morality, and politics, and were rightly the concern not of a professional caste but all who would lead church and colony.

The Puritans' understanding of natural law, we have seen, differs significantly from today's leading theological and legal accounts. It is neither the natural law of Roman Catholic scholasticism – it does not speak to eternal law, as such, or the economy of salvation – nor the natural law of the "new natural lawyers," for it treats "nature" both descriptively and normatively. (Nature is both how things are and how they ought to be.) What the Puritans offer, instead, is a particularly "protestant" form of natural law, focused on Scripture and committed to an understanding of human moral incapacity apart from God's grace. This is a distinctive combination. The Revolutionaries who followed placed far greater confidence in human instincts as potentially generative of moral and legal norms.

2

Modern Natural Law

Revolutionaries and Republicans

The colonial colleges had sought to form students' whole character in proper love of God and neighbor. By the Revolutionary War, however, the colleges' focus was instead the aptitudes and virtues that tend toward good citizenship. Proper knowledge of God and neighbor requires revelation, said the Puritans; the basic standard for life in society – the natural law knowable by all – is only fully understandable through the biblical motifs of humanity's creation in God's image and possession of a law written on the heart. By the outbreak of the Revolution, however, it increasingly seemed that the aptitudes and virtues for civic life could be known as much from self-evident principles in nature as from reflection on the Puritan's God. From schools of the reformation, the colonial colleges were becoming schools of the Republic.

MODERN NATURAL LAW

Amid the various intellectual changes of the later eighteenth century, the curriculum of American colleges came to embrace an increasingly dominant strain of natural-law reflection, variously known as "secular," "modern," or "protestant" natural law.[1] Modern natural law was to be based on claims universally accessible, on sense perception or rational moral principles, and not on the theological or metaphysical grounds championed in the colonial colleges.

While scholars trace the methods of modern natural law to the early sixteenth-century School of Salamanca, and even identify its roots in antique

---

[1] Michael Seidler's entry "Pufendorf's Moral and Political Philosophy" in the *Stanford Encyclopedia of Philosophy* provides a good introduction to the historiography of modern natural law; last modified November 3, 2015, https://plato.stanford.edu/entries/pufendorf-moral.

Stoicism and Roman law, eighteenth-century Americans' most immediate sources were the writings of Hugo Grotius (1583–1645), Samuel Pufendorf (1632–94), and other authors formed in the wake of the European wars of religion. In the work of Grotius, Pufendorf, and their peers, Americans found a scientific system for natural law. Deeply conscious of the destructiveness of European religious disputes, the modern natural lawyers placed *reason* as the bedrock of humanity, a bulwark amid clashing dogmatisms.[2]

To embrace modern natural law, however, was not to indiscriminately reject the natural-law inheritance found and forged in the earliest American colleges nor the colonial reverence for the classical models of Greece and Rome.[3] Earlier Puritan debates about reason's relative corruption, or otherwise, prepared the ground. What distinguished modern natural law from its Puritan predecessor was the purported sufficiency of rationally based moral principles without reliance upon a theological anthropology. This confidence in reason shifted attention procedurally, if not ultimately in American minds, from God to humanity. For most of its proponents, this was not an antireligious move: The emphasis on human reason was a particular form of religious

---

[2]   Recent scholarship, however, has revised enduring assumptions about the religious origins of seventeenth-century European conflicts. See Ronald Asch, *The Thirty Years War: The Holy Roman Empire and Europe, 1618–1648* (Basingstoke, UK: Macmillan, 1997); Johannes Burkhardt, *Der Dreißigjährige Krieg* (Frankfurt: Suhrkamp Verlag, 1992); Johannes Arndt, *Der Dreißigjährige Krieg 1618–1648* (Stuttgart: Reclam, 2009); and Peter Wilson, *The Thirty Years War: Europe's Tragedy* (Cambridge, MA: Belknap Press of Harvard University, 2009). Wilson also surveys the historiography in his "New Perspectives on the Thirty Years War," *German History* 23 (2005): 237–61. For an argument that a "myth of religious violence" is used to justify the nation-state, see William Cavanaugh, *The Myth of Religious Violence: Secular Ideology and the Roots of Modern Conflict* (Oxford: Oxford University Press, 2009).

[3]   The role of the orator as public conscience gained prominence through the time of the American Revolution. Cicero was the prime example of this form of statesmanship forged through political and moral science, a training in history, politics, and law. David Robson, *Educating Republicans: The College in the Era of the American Revolution, 1750–1800* (Westport, CT: Greenwood Press), 61. Latin language acquisition was tied to character formation. The *Distichs of Cato*, a collection of proverbial wisdom and morality, was the common Latin teaching aid, as it had been in Europe. Benjamin Franklin published James Logan's translation in 1735. By their fourth year of instruction, boys would read Ovid's *De Tristibus* and *Metamorphoses* and Cicero's epistles. Later they would turn to Cicero's *Orations* and Hesiod. See, e.g., Robert Middlekauff, *Ancients and Axioms: Secondary Education in Eighteenth-Century New England* (New Haven, CT: Yale University Press, 1963); Kenneth Murdock, "The Teaching of Latin and Greek at the Boston Latin School in 1712," *Publications of the Colonial Society of Massachusetts* 27 (March 1927): 21–29; Meyer Reinhold, ed., *Classick Pages: Classical Reading of Eighteenth-Century Americans* (University Park, PA: American Philological Association, 1975); C. K. Shipton "Secondary Education in the Puritan Colonies," *New England Quarterly* 7 (1934): 646–61; and The System of Public Education Adopted by the Town of Boston, 15th October, 1789.

humanism, a celebration, of sorts, of humanity placed at the pinnacle of created order.

The shift from the colonial curriculum to its republican successor, more-over, was tied to theological shifts; God's will, once known in history, was now understood in nature and its laws.[4] What might seem like ambivalence, double consciousness, and contradiction in Puritan understandings of the relationship between revelation and reason – human beings, they said, were totally corrupt in their capacities yet could know the law of nature – could be reconciled in a more optimistic view of human abilities. God's grace, which to earlier Puritans seemed an alien in-breaking into human affairs – Damascene experience – was later the perfector of existing human actions or traits: God's grace was understood no longer as beyond and without humanity but as the reinvigorator of *natural* human capacities.[5]

Not that these changes were simple, linear, or uncontested. Even as the early Puritans believed in a God who acts decisively in history, and understood their lives in New England as directed and bound by God's special provi-dence, they were suspicious of the "miraculous."[6] Most Puritans subscribed to the idea that miracles – events not ascribable to human action or natural forces – had served a particular purpose in securing the early Church and its scriptural canon, but had, accordingly, ceased with the apostles.[7]

Likewise, most proponents of the republican curriculum thought that their scholarship was complementary to Christian faith: In their telling, morality was discoverable through the reason that originated with the author of nature. And, as taught in the American colleges, at least, this rational morality *would not contradict* revelation.[8] Reason could reinforce a divinely sanctioned ethics.

---

4   Catherine Albanese, *Sons of the Fathers: The Civil Religion of the American Revolution* (Philadelphia: Temple University Press, 1976), 34.

5   Perry Miller, *The New England Mind: The Seventeenth Century* (Cambridge, MA: Belknap Press of Harvard University, 1984), 200.

6   Thus the "miraculous," instead, suggested the demonic. See Cotton Mather's account of the Salem Witch Trials in *The Wonders of the Invisible World. Observations as Well Historical as Theological, upon the Nature, the Number, and the Operations of the Devils* (Boston: Printed by Benj. Harris for Sam. Phillips, 1693).

7   Garnet Howard Milne, *The Westminster Confession of Faith and the Cessation of Special Revelation: The Majority Puritan Viewpoint on whether Extra-biblical Prophecy is still possible* (Waynesboro, GA: Paternoster, 2007). Jonathan Edwards recognized spiritual gifts in the apostolic era, but thought that "the ordinary influences of the Spirit of God working grace in the heart is a far greater privilege than any of them; a greater privilege than the spirit of prophecy, or the gift of tongues, or working miracles even to the moving of mountains." *The Works of Jonathan Edwards*, vol. 8, *Ethical Writings*, ed. Paul Ramsey (New Haven, CT: Yale University Press, 1989), 157.

8   George Marsden, *The Soul of the American University: From Protestant Establishment to Established Nonbelief* (New York: Oxford University Press, 1994), 50.

Indeed, reason offered, in effect, one further argument for the veracity of God's laws.

The vocabularies of Puritan and Revolutionary cultures and their treatments of natural law vied and overlapped. In his May 1775 election sermon to the provincial congress meeting at Watertown, Harvard President Samuel Langdon (1723–97) employed the traditional language of the jeremiad, for instance, to indict sin around him and British corruption.[9] But he praised God too for humanity's "natural rights independent of all human laws" and "the law of nature" that allows for the beginning and continuing of human society.[10] Most famously, the Declaration of Independence also harmonized the varied sentiments of the age.[11] It strikes a tone of modern natural law in its invocation of "Nature's God" who sets up the laws of nature.[12] But the Declaration speaks too with a traditional vocabulary where God is creator and supreme judge of the world, and where Congress is to commit itself to divine providence. The document offers no doctrinal specifics.

A certain vagueness in the Declaration was surely no accident. It helped secure broad agreement. But for some, at least, lack of specificity was also an imprimatur of universality. John Adams spoke of Christianity, for example, as the means to bring the multitudes to "the great Principle of the Law of Nature and Nations, Love your Neighbour as yourself, and do to others as you would that others should do to you."[13] For others, this abstraction and emphasis on rationally accessible natural law seemed to render Christianity instrumental, even superfluous. Yale's Thomas Clap worried. He introduced modern

---

[9]   See Cathleen Kaveny, *Prophecy without Contempt* (Cambridge, MA: Harvard University Press, 2016). Kaveny treats the genre of the "election sermon" at 156–59.

[10] *Government corrupted by vice, and recovered by righteousness. A sermon preached before the honorable Congress of the colony of the Massachusetts-Bay in New England, assembled at Watertown, on Wednesday the 31st day of May, 1775. Being the anniversary fixed by charter for the election of counsellors* (Watertown, MA: Printed and sold by Benjamin Edes, MDCCLXXV [1775]), 23.

[11] Matthew Harris and Thomas Kidd, *The Founding Fathers and the Debate over Religion in Revolutionary America: A History in Documents* (New York: Oxford University Press, 2012), 11.

[12] Indeed, it strikes something of a Deist note: the acknowledgment of God based on reason, and the rejection of revealed religion. There is a vast collection of work on the role of religion in the Declaration, the Constitution, and the lives of the founding fathers. See, e.g., Vincent Muñoz, *God and the Founders: Madison, Washington and Jefferson* (New York: Cambridge University Press, 2009); and Edwin Gaustad, *Faith of Our Fathers: Religion and the New Nation* (San Francisco: Harper & Row, 1987). On questions of church and state, see John Witte, Jr., and Joel A. Nichols, *Religion and the American Constitutional Experiment*, 3rd ed. (Boulder, CO: Westview, 2011); and Frank Lambert, *The Founding Fathers and the Place of Religion in America* (Princeton, NJ: Princeton University Press, 2003).

[13] John Adams's diary entry for August 14, 1796; *The Works of John Adams*, ed. Charles Frances Adams (Boston: Little, Brown, 1850), III:423.

science into his college's curriculum yet strove to maintain Puritan policies, and resist liberalization of doctrine and morals.[14] Jonathan Edwards, likewise, while conversant with the ideas of Lord Shaftesbury and Francis Hutcheson, disputed human ability to access true virtue apart from revelation. Adherents of modern natural law, in his mind, were just too optimistic about human nature. God's grace was needed to sanctify the reasoning process.[15]

THE UNITY OF TRUTH

Despite differing views of the sufficiency, or otherwise, of human reason, the colonial and Revolutionary curriculums operated with a shared understanding of truth. Both understood truth to be singular and unified. In their telling: The truth of experimental science, art, literature, and religion all speak to the same reality. Temperature is true. Beauty is true. God is true.

This assumption of the unity of truth is confusing to contemporary commentators and critics, and is one reason why colonial and Revolutionary discussions of "nature" are found intellectually suspect. The concept of nature used by the colonists and Revolutionaries seems slippery to many: imprecisely bound to the proper regime of science, say, or the separate regime of morals.

Two sorts of complaint are frequently made. First, when critics look at colonial and Revolutionary proponents of natural law, they find that nature is sometimes that which is primitive and original, simple and uncorrupted. Nature, in this depiction, is universal. It is found in all people, irrespective of custom, culture, education, or the like. Yet sometimes when critics look at colonial and Revolutionary treatments of natural law they find nature to mean that which does not exist everywhere, but which ought to exist. Nature, in this depiction, is a norm to be sought.[16]

At least for the Puritans, however, this double depiction was not contradictory. The scriptural narrative explained both. All of nature, in their view, was created good: "And God saw all that he had made, and lo, it was very good."[17] And yet, after the Fall, human beings are estranged from their good created nature, even as they are called to its restoration through God's grace. Detached from this narrative of Fall and restoration, however, there are

[14]   Louis Tucker, *Puritan Protagonist: President Thomas Clap of Yale College* (Chapel Hill: University of North Carolina Press, 1962).

[15]   See, e.g., *The Works of Jonathan Edwards*, vol. 18, The Miscellanies, 501–832, ed. Ava Chamberlain (New Haven, CT: Yale University Press, 2000), 155.

[16]   See Edwin Gaustad, *Neither King nor Prelate: Religion and the New Nation, 1776–1826* (Grand Rapids, MI: Eerdmans, 1993), 87.

[17]   Genesis 1:31a, Geneva Bible.

tensions between the depictions, even despite the popularity of secular "fall from grace" narratives and naturalistic calls to "being who you truly are."

The second complaint about talk of nature, which divides the working assumptions of today from both the Puritan and the Revolutionary eras, is a taken-for-granted understanding that the physical and the moral are commensurate. The laws of nature – physical forces – were not divorced from natural law understood as moral philosophy. The educated, working view of science from the time of the Revolution through to the middle of the nineteenth century was an equation of Newtonian and Baconian theories of induction. Knowledge was grown through linking together the natural laws derivable from clear-eyed observation of facts in the world.[18] The purpose of investigating nature around us was to discover its laws. And the laws of the physical universe and moral law were both equally God's law.[19] Colonials and Republicans alike possessed a strong sense of the compatibility of science and morals, of natural and revealed religion.[20]

This idea that God is known in "two books" – by revelation and by nature or reason – was far from new. But it received new impetus with the rise of experimental science, and the corresponding emphasis on induction. Whereas the Puritans often deduced natural law from Scripture and doctrine, by the Revolutionary era Americans had turned to careful observation of particular phenomena. The commands of God, in effect, could be known through principles discoverable in nature.

Physical and moral science alike were understood as built up from individual facts. Science was the conglomerate of pieces of knowledge. This vision generated confidence in the veracity of science: Common sense and experimental methods could surely prove small pieces of evidence, and bigger discoveries, in this telling, simply consisted of adding together smaller pieces.[21] This level of epistemic confidence stood in some distinction to the views of the Puritans. The early Puritans held, after all, that man has "knock't his head in the fall, and craz'd his understanding." After the Fall, humanity is

---

[18] For instance, in Isaac Newton's *Regulae philosophandi*. See Julie Reuben, *The Making of the Modern University: Intellectual Transformation and the Marginalization of Morality* (Chicago: University of Chicago, 1996), 36.

[19] See, e.g., Robert Boyle, *Some Considerations Touching the Usefulness of Experimental Natural Philosophy* (Oxford: Printed by Henry Hall for Richard Davis, 1663).

[20] Barbara Shapiro, *Probability and Certainty in Seventeenth-Century England: A Study of the Relationships between Natural Science, Religion, History, Law, and Literature* (Princeton, NJ: Princeton University Press, 1983).

[21] See Larry Laudan, "Thomas Reid and the Newtonian Turn of British Methodological Thought," in *Science and Hypothesis: Historical Essays on Scientific Methodology* (Dordrecht, The Netherlands: Reidel, 1981), 86–110.

left, they said, with only "some broken fragments, & moth-eaten registers, old rusty outworn monuments" so indistinct that there "are but very few of them, that he can spell out what they mean, and in others he is mistaken."[22] And yet, as Perry Miller notes, despite Puritan distrust of human understanding, their writings came to

> expound upon the coincidence of natural law or the law of reason with the law promulgated at Sinai, until there are times when the reader wonders whether Puritans had not come to regard Biblical dispensation as a corroboration to the conclusions of reason rather than the one true and perfect revelation.[23]

If Miller captures the Puritans' increasing embrace of reason, he overstates the shift in epistemic priority. While there were continuities between the colonial and Revolutionary mindsets – particularly if compared to the views of today – the Puritans, nonetheless, began with the revealed law as they understood it, whereas the Revolutionaries began with nature. The Puritans found in nature corroboration for revelation; the Revolutionaries found nature sufficient.

REPUBLICAN COLLEGES

The colonial college sought to form ministers and virtuous laymen for leadership. Following the Revolution, in the new Republic, colleges increasingly emphasized the formation of learned magistrates and informed citizens. A 1779 bill to reform the College of William and Mary, for example, explains how, by character formation and good laws, those "whom nature hath endowed with genius and virtue, should be rendered by liberal education worthy to receive, and able to guard the sacred deposit of the rights and liberties of their fellow citizens."[24] The principles articulated in the University of Virginia's later founding are similar: to "form statesmen,

---

[22]   Samuel Willard, *A Compleat Body of Divinity* (Boston: Printed by B. Green and S. Kneeland for B. Eliot and D. Henchman, 1726), 15.

[23]   Miller, *New England Mind*, 199.

[24]   *The Papers of Thomas Jefferson*, vol. 2, *2 January 1777 to 18 June 1779, including the Revisal of the Laws, 1776–1786*, ed. Julian P. Boyd (Princeton, NJ: Princeton University Press, 1950), 526–27. A much-revised version was finally passed into law in 1796 as an "Act to Establish Public Schools." On December 4, 1779, while action on the bill was pending, William and Mary's Board of Visitors, under the leadership of Jefferson – who was by then governor of Virginia as well as a member of the Board – adopted resolutions that were endorsed by the faculty and supported by the Reverend James Madison, the College President. These resolutions, which incorporated some, but not all, of Jefferson's plans for the College, came to be known as the Jeffersonian Reorganization.

legislators and judges"; "expound the principles and structure of government"; and otherwise instill precepts of order and virtue in youth.[25] In the fledgling nation, there was proper concern that colleges produce a sufficient number of men – both civically virtuous and trained in principles of governance – for leadership in the courts and the legislature.

If the colleges in the initial colonial period were "schools of the reformation" in mindset and purpose, by the other side of the Revolution colleges were "schools of the Republic." In a narrower sense, the colleges were schools of the *American* Republic. National self-sufficiency was important. The poet and diplomat Joel Barlow (1754–1812), for instance, engaged his friends Thomas Jefferson, James Monroe, and James Madison in an attempt to create a domestic university to fulfill all of America's educational and research needs.[26] Dependence on Europe was sufficiently frowned upon for the Georgia legislature to penalize students who attended institutions beyond American shores.[27] In a broader sense, however, the colleges were schools of the American *Republic*. "The liberal sciences," Barlow said, were of republican character: delighting in "reciprocal communication," cherishing "fraternal feelings," and leading to "a freedom of intercourse," which "combined with the restraints of society" would contribute to the improvement of governance and society.[28] American and republican, education was to forge the leaders needed for the flourishing of a new nation.

As had been true of the colonial colleges, the Revolutionary colleges were vocational in their focus; they fitted and directed men toward functions and stations in life to which God or Providence or their talents called them, and, increasingly, work in the professions. By the mid-eighteenth century, indeed, colleges were becoming "pre-professional schools."[29] At the College of New Jersey, for instance, seventy-five percent of the students in twenty-one graduating classes became lawyers, ministers, or doctors.[30] A 1770 faculty statement at

[25] [Thomas Jefferson, James Madison, et al.], "Report of the Commissioners Appointed to Fix the Site of the University of Virginia. 4 Aug 1818" in *The Founders' Constitution*, ed. Philip P. Kurland and Ralph Lerner (Chicago: University of Chicago Press, 1986), Chapter 18, Document 33.

[26] Joel Barlow, *Prospects of a National Institution to Be Established in the United States* (Washington City [DC]: Printed by Samuel H. Smith, 1806).

[27] Oscar Handlin, *The American University as an Instrument of Republican Culture* (Leicester, UK: Leicester University Press, 1970), 6.

[28] Barlow, *Prospects*, 5.

[29] James McLachlan, "Classical Names, American Identities: Some Notes on College Students and the Classical Tradition in the 1770s," in *Classical Traditions in Early America: Essays*, ed. John Eadie, 81–95 (Ann Arbor, MI: Center for Coordination of Ancient and Modern Studies, 1976), 85.

[30] McLachlan, "Classical Names," 85.

William and Mary declared the college's purpose as "training up Youth, who are intended to be qualified for any of the three learned Professions" of divinity, law, and medicine.[31]

Indeed, colleges sometimes provided the context for specific study of the law. John Witherspoon (1723–94), the President of the College of New Jersey, urged degree-holders to return to Princeton for independent study and thereby

> fit themselves for any of the higher Branches to which they will think proper chiefly to devote further application, whether those called learned Professions, Divinity, law, and Physic, or such liberal Accomplishments in general as fit young Gentlemen for serving their Country in Public Stations.[32]

James Madison was among those who accepted the invitation.[33]

THE MORAL PHILOSOPHY COURSE

A new course in moral philosophy gave shape to the American college curriculum from the late eighteenth century through the middle of the nineteenth.[34] "Moral philosophy" – also called "moral science" or "metaphysics and ethics" – was taught by the college president as a capstone course, and integrated the curriculum.[35] Its overall content, in the words of a prominent textbook of 1795, was "that science which gives rules for the direction of the will of man in his moral state, or in his pursuit after happiness."[36]

---

[31] "Journal of the Meetings of the President and Masters of William and Mary College: May 1770," *William and Mary Quarterly* 13, no. 3 (1905): 148–157, 151.

[32] Robson, *Educating Republicans*, 60.

[33] "I intend myself to read Law occasionally and have procured books for that purpose … The principles and Modes of Government are too important to be disregarded by an Inquisitive mind and I think are well worthy of a critical examination by all students that have health and Leisure." *The Papers of James Madison*, vol. 1, *16 March 1751 – 16 December 1779*, ed. William Hutchinson and William Rachal (Chicago: University of Chicago Press, 1962), 100–102.

[34] For introductions, see D. H. Meyer, *The Instructed Conscience: The Shaping of the American National Ethics* (Philadelphia: University of Philadelphia Press, 1972); Henry May, *The Enlightenment in America* (New York: Oxford University Press, 1976); Douglas Sloan, *The Scottish Enlightenment and the American College Ideal* (New York: Teachers College, Columbia University, 1981); Mark Noll, *Princeton and the Republic, 1768–1822: The Search for a Christian Enlightenment in the Era of Samuel Stanhope Smith* (Princeton, NJ: Princeton University Press, 1989). For its decline, see Sara Paretsky, *Words, Works, and Ways of Knowing: The Breakdown of Moral Philosophy in New England before the Civil War* (Chicago: Chicago University Press, 2016).

[35] George Schmidt, *The Old Time College President* (New York: Columbia University Press, 1930), Chapter IV, "The Bearer of the Old Tradition," 108–45.

[36] John Daniel Gros, *Natural Principles of Rectitude* (New York: T. and J. Swords, 1795), 10.

In an important sense, a specific moral philosophy course was a continuation of a century of broader instruction. As we have seen, the earliest curriculum at Harvard included moral philosophy in the fourth year. Likewise, the spirit of the Revolutionary colleges' moral philosophy course followed in the logic of Ramus and the colonial colleges' insistence on the unity of truth. Even the new epistemic priority of humanity and nature – now treated before God and revelation – while in distinction to the general spirit of colonial education, was in continuity with Christian apologetic teaching that had developed earlier in the eighteenth century. Instruction in so-called controversies against heretics had been the subject of a course, for instance, at William and Mary in 1736. Throughout the colonies, Bishop Butler's *Analogy of Religion, Natural and Revealed* had been popular, as too was William Paley's *View of the Evidences of Christianity.*[37] If the colleges were no longer schools of the reformation, through direct appeals to nature they nonetheless employed the most modern means available to defend the truth of Christian religion.

Logic had dominated and grounded the colonial curriculum. By the middle of the eighteenth century, systematic ethics had taken its place.[38] And morals were now taught at least partially independent of theology. Moral philosophy's starting points, instead, were physical, sociological, or psychological.[39] Nonetheless, teachers still assumed that this humanistic approach tracked divine laws in nature, such that nothing they might find would contradict the teachings of Christianity.

Of particular importance was the so-called common sense philosophy, which had started life as the "Scottish" philosophy, but in the New World amalgam of the thought of its principal authors truly became "the American philosophy," and remained that way well into the nineteenth century.[40] The writings of Francis Hutcheson (1694–1746) and Thomas Reid (1710–96) – also James Beattie, Adam Ferguson, Dugald Stewart, with Butler and Paley – were read together by Americans and taken to form a unity.[41] This common sense

---

[37] Jospeh Butler, *Analogy of Religion, Natural and Revealed* (London: Printed for James, John and Paul Knapton, 1736); William Paley, *View of the Evidences of Christianity* (London: Printed for R. Faulder, 1794).

[38] Willis, *Growth*, 169–70.

[39] G. Stanley Hall, "On the History of American College Text-Books and Teaching in Logic, Ethics, Psychology and Allied Subjects," *Proceedings of the American Antiquarian Society* 9 (1893–94): 137–74, 145.

[40] James McCosh, the Scottish president of Princeton from 1868 to 1888, first wrote its history: *The Scottish Philosophy* (London: Macmillan, 1875).

[41] As these authors were treated as authorities, instruction often took the form of commentary on their work. But as the art of commentary entails, instructors made distinctions and criticisms,

philosophy married enlightenment ideas with the assumptions of the moderate party of the Scottish Church.[42]

Human morality, said the common sense philosophers, was grounded in universally self-evident, commonsensical principles; there are starting points to our thought for which there can be no further explanation. Mind and matter exist, as does good and evil. Human beings can choose actions and possess a moral faculty, a capacity akin to sense perception.[43] True happiness is the goal of morality.[44]

Common sense philosophy as practiced in the Revolutionary colleges assumed that these principles were not only rational and scientific, but also congruent with Christian morality. Common sense was undergirded by the conviction that God is revealed in nature, and that nature's law is consistent with true revelation in Scripture. Accordingly, the philosophy of common sense appealed in its moment as properly rationalistic, yes, but also moralistic and theistic.[45]

NATURAL LAW AND CIVIL LAW IN THE CURRICULUM

The colleges of the new Republic, we have seen, engaged modern natural law and the common sense tradition. But they also taught the statutes and common law of their political community, albeit in conversation with broader topics. The collegiate study of ethics, law, and politics was well embedded by the time King's College, New York – renamed Columbia in 1784 – and Dartmouth College published their first curriculums.[46] In New York in

---

as well as offering appreciation. Accordingly, curriculums changed through the period. For example, while Paley's *Moral and Political Philosophy* (1785) was an early text in wide use, later Dugald Stewart's *Philosophy of the Active and Moral Powers* (1828) took its place, and thereafter Francis Wayland's *Elements of Moral Science* (1835). See Willis, *Growth*, 171.

[42] Marsden, *Soul*, 90–93. Unlike its anti-clerical French counterpart, the Scottish Enlightenment was broadly supportive of the established Scottish church, and many of its principal figures were clergymen. David Hume is the exception that proves the rule.

[43] In Julie Reuben's description, Witherspoon, for instance, "maintained that the human mind worked through related processes or faculties: the understanding, the will, and the affections. These faculties included the capacity to perceive moral qualities. Just as people could sense the hardness of an object, they could sense the goodness of an act or idea"; *Making of the Modern University*, 19.

[44] Schmidt, *Old Time*, 57.

[45] This is the assessment of Wilson Smith in his *Professors and Public Ethics: Studies of Northern Moral Philosophers before the Civil War* (Ithaca, NY: Cornell University Press, 1956).

[46] Even at conservative Yale, the Reverend Thomas Clap – Yale's president from 1739 to 1766 – commended an increase in "publick Dissertations upon every Subject necessary to qualify young Gentlemen for those stations and Employments in civil life," with such commencement disputations a colorful part of the life of the colony as much as the college. Anna Haddow, *Political Science in American Colleges and Universities, 1636–1900* (New York: D. Appleton-Century, 1939), 14.

1755, a student's fourth year was principally devoted to "the Chief Principles of Law and Government," while at Dartmouth in 1796, juniors were assigned a course in "Natural and Moral Philosophy," with instruction in "Natural and Political *Law* and Moral Philosophy" reserved for seniors.[47]

The moral philosophy course was understood as preparatory for students' leadership in the colonies and early Republic.[48] A 1756 plan for the College of Philadelphia – a precursor to the University of Pennsylvania – called for a course that would give the student "a knowledge and a practical sense of his position as a man and a citizen ... embracing ethics, natural and civil law, and an introduction to civil history, law and government, and trade and commerce."[49] In Philadelphia, as at King's College and the College of Rhode Island – later know as Brown University – the central instructional text was Francis Hutcheson's *Short Introduction to Moral Philosophy*.[50] Hutcheson devoted the entirety of Book II of this *Short Introduction* to "Elements of the Law of Nature."[51]

As John Witherspoon taught the course in Princeton, moral philosophy emphasized the complementary nature of reason and revelation and the

---

[47] Reed, *Training*, 114 (emphasis added). In 1792, Columbia's Faculty of Arts consisted of the President and seven professors. John Daniel Gros – a minister in the German Reformed Church in America – was professor of moral philosophy. He taught a course divided into three sections: "1. The first explaining the Principles and Laws resulting from the nature of man, and his natural relations to God and his fellow creatures by which human conduct ought to be regulated in a manner becoming the dignity of human nature, and conformable to the will of God. This constitutes the Law of Nature, strictly so called ... 2. In the second part of the system those general principles are applied to the different states, relations and conditions of man, comprehending (a) Ethics ... (b) Natural Jurisprudence, laying down the principles of perfect and imperfect rights ... 3. The Law of Nations, as founded in nature." See Snow, *College Curriculum in the United States*, 98; James Fairbanks Colby, "The Collegiate Study of Law," *Report of the Nineteenth Annual Meeting of the American Bar Association* (Philadelphia: Dando, 1896), 525.

[48] John Witherspoon, President of the College of New Jersey – later known as Princeton – taught a notable version. President from 1768 to 1794, he set a pattern of teaching at Princeton broadly in the Scottish common sense tradition that lasted through the presidency of James McCosh (1868–88).

[49] Thwing, *American College*, 21 (emphasis on "trade and commerce" removed).

[50] *A Short Introduction to Moral Philosophy: In Three Books; Containing the Elements of Ethicks, and the Law of Nature*. Its first American edition printed the fifth edition of the Glasgow edition. (Philadelphia: Printed and sold by Joseph Crukshank, in Market Street, between Second and Third Streets, MDCCLXXXVIII [1788].)

[51] In this, Hutcheson followed the pattern set by his Glasgow predecessor Gershom Carmichael, and engaged the works of Hugo Grotius and Samuel Pufendorf. A recent overview of Hutcheson's thought is provided by Daniel Cary, "Francis Hutcheson's Philosophy and the Scottish Enlightenment: Reception, Reputation, and Legacy," in *Scottish Philosophy in the Eighteenth Century*, vol. 1, *Morals, Politics, Art, Religion*, ed. Aaron Garrett and James Harris, 36–76 (Oxford: Oxford University Press, 2015).

supremacy of an innate moral sense as a guide for action.[52] The object of applied common sense, he said, was virtuous conduct, defined as human duties to God, neighbors, and self. Witherspoon offered discourses on the state of nature, natural rights, "compact" as the basis of society, private property, and the right of rebellion. The lectures also covered general discussions of jurisprudence and the nature of contracts.[53]

In a later influential iteration, Mark Hopkins (1802–87), President of Williams College, taught a comprehensive class concerned with "Man, as he is in himself, and in his relations to his fellow creatures, and to God."[54] The imagined breadth of the course is striking to those accustomed to specialization:

> [W]e take up first the physical man, and endeavor to give … an idea of every organ and tissue of the body. We then take the intellectual man, and investigate, first, and classify his several faculties; then the grounds of belief and the processes of the mind in the pursuit of truth, with an explanation of the inductive and the deductive logic; then the moral nature, together with individual and political morality, comprising a knowledge of constitutional history and of the rights and duties of American citizens; then the emotive nature, as taste and the principles of the fine arts; then natural theology and the analogy of the natural to the moral government of God.[55]

---

[52] *An Annotated Edition of Lectures on Moral Philosophy*, ed. Jack Scott (Newark: University of Delaware Press, 1982). Jennifer Herdt offers an incisive treatment of the ways in which Witherspoon sought to hold together Reformed commitments with modern natural law. She concludes that he was not particularly successful in so doing. "Calvin's Legacy for Contemporary Natural Law," *Scottish Journal of Theology* 67, no. 4 (2014): 414–35.

[53] He offered the following suggestions for reading. On ethical matters, he suggested students read: Samuel Clarke, *Demonstration of the Being and Attributes of God, more particularly in answer to Mr. Hobbs, Spinoza, and their Followers* (London, 1705); Samuel Pufendorf, *De Officio hominum & civium* (London, 1673); Cicero, *De Officiis*; Lord Shaftesbury's *Characteristics of Men, Manners, Opinions, Times* (London, 1711); Henry Home, Lord Kames, *Essay on the Principles of Morality and Natural Religion* (Edinburgh, 1751). On "politics and government," Witherspoon suggested students read: Hugo Grotius, *Of the Law of War and Peace* (London, 1654); Pufendorf's *De Jure Naturae et Gentium* … (1st Eng. trans., London, 1710); Richard Cumberland, *A Treatise on the Laws of Nature*, trans. John Maxwell (London, 1727); the three volumes of legal scholar John Selden's *Works* (London, 1726); the two volumes of Jean Jacques Burlamaqui, *The Principles of Natural and Political Law* (London, 1748–52); James Harrington, *The Commonwealth of Oceana* (London, 1656); John Locke, *Two Treatises of Civil Government* (London 1690); Algernon Sidney, *Discourses on Civil Government* (London, 1698); Charles Louis de Secondat, Baron de Montesquieu, *The Spirit of Laws* (Eng. Trans., London, 1752); and Adam Ferguson, *An Enquiry on the History of Civil Society* (Edinburgh, 1767). Underlying all of Witherspoon's lectures was the work of Francis Hutcheson: *A Short Introduction to Moral Philosophy* (Edinburgh, 1747), and the two-volume *A System of Moral Philosophy* (Edinburgh, 1755).

[54] *Miscellaneous Essays and Discourses* (Boston: T. R. Marvin, 1847).

[55] Ibid.

Of course, teaching about the law – whether in New York's "Chief Principles of Law and Government" or Philadelphia's natural and civil law, and law and government – is not teaching the practice of the law. American colleges followed John Locke, who had urged the young to read Cicero's *De officiis*,[56] Pufendorf's *De officio hominis et civis*, and Grotius's *De jure belli ac pacis* or Pufendorf's *De jure naturae et gentium*, but not to bother with treatises on the practice of law. In reading Cicero, Pufendorf, and Grotius, Locke thought, students would be "instructed in the natural Rights of Men and the Original and Foundations of Society, and the Duties resulting from thence."[57] The focus for virtuous youths, accordingly, was the "Affairs and Intercourse of civilized Nations in general, grounded upon Principles of Reason," and not "the Chicane of private Cases."[58]

All gentlemen have an interest, Locke had argued, in knowing the law of their country, particularly as they might occupy offices of state. But the focus of their education should ever be seeking "the true measures of Right and Wrong" and not the "wrangling and captious part of the *Law*."[59] This distinction, however, was not to the exclusion of the facts of governing. So together with Cicero, Grotius, and Pufendorf, Locke urged the reading of the "*English Constitution*," "the ancient books of the *Common Law*," history, and statutes.[60] In the Revolutionary colleges, too, the focus was knowledge of right and wrong, *and* proper governance. Such knowledge formed the student for his expected position as "a man and citizen."[61]

---

[56] Locke uses the common eighteenth-century nomenclature "Tully's *Offices*."

[57] John Locke, *Some Thoughts Concerning Education*, ed. John Yolton and Jean Yolton (Oxford: Clarendon Press, 1989), 239, §186.

[58] Ibid.

[59] Ibid., 240, §187.

[60] Ibid.

[61] Other aspects of the curriculum – and particularly classics – were likewise understood to form the student not only for life but for the professions. "[T]he utility of a knowledge of the classics for the practice of the professions of law, medicine, and theology was taken for granted." Bruchbacher and Rudy, *Higher Education*, 14. See Richard Gummere, *The American Colonial Mind and the Classical Tradition* (Cambridge, MA: Harvard University Press, 1963).

Latin was the primary language of college instruction and the language of international scholarship. Study of ancient languages provided, too, aspects of the technical vocabulary for the professions, and functioned as a mark of learning and status. Less well appreciated today is that study of the classics was assumed to provide students with access to the body of ancient wisdom that "would definitely help in the training of leaders and in preparation for service to the community." Bruchbacher and Rudy, *Higher Education*, 14.

As ever, the classical world was interpreted within the thought world of the time. Whereas the Puritans read primarily through the lens of Scripture, by the Revolution, classical literature found interlocutors – explicitly or implicitly – in John Locke and other enlightenment writers, foundational writers in the common law, and their reception of New England Puritan thought. On this, see generally Robson, *Educating Republicans*; Caroline Robbins, *The Eighteenth-century*

The colleges, we have seen, taught law in combination with ethics and government, and as part of the moral philosophy course designed to prepare students for civic leadership. Specifically legal content also featured in the colleges' curriculum in *disputations*. These formal debates on a thesis formed one of the principal methods of early instruction. Looking to the changing form and content of the disputations we see the ways in which the traditional curriculum of the colonial colleges developed through the eighteenth century.

Disputations – first syllogistic in pattern, and later forensic in style – formed a pedagogically essential part of the undergraduate curriculum.[62] One specific link between the American colleges and Scotland was the prominent place of disputations at commencement exercises, major events in the lives of the colonies.[63] Students could be examined on any topic treated through their four years of study.[64] A list of disputation theses was printed for distribution to those in attendance. Broadsheets with a hundred or more Latin propositions covered the breadth of the curriculum.[65]

Commonwealthman: Studies in the Transmission, Development and Circumstance of English Liberal Thought from the Restoration of Charles II until the War with the Thirteen Colonies (New York: Atheneum, 1959); Trevor Colbourn, *The Lamp of Experience: Whig History and the Intellectual Origins of the American Revolution* (Chapel Hill: University of North Carolina Press, 1965); Bernard Bailyn, *The Ideological Origins of the American Revolution* (Cambridge, MA: Belknap Press of Harvard University, 1967); Gordon Wood, *The Creation of the American Republic, 1776–1787* (Chapel Hill: University of North Carolina Press, 1969); and J. G. A. Pocock, *The Machiavellian Moment: Florentine Political Thought and Atlantic Republican Tradition* (Princeton, NJ: Princeton University Press, 1975).

With the Revolution came a new focus on the political wealth to be mined in the classical tradition. Lawyers came to study, and speak with, classical erudition, developing practices that had previously been limited to the clergy. James Kent urged lawyers to mastery of Greek and Latin, indeed "the whole circle of the arts and sciences" together with "the general principles of Universal Law." See Robert Ferguson, *Law and Letters in American Culture* (Cambridge, MA: Harvard University Press, 1984), 28.

In the guise of the Ciceronian orator, lawyers, from the mid-1700s onward, newly contributed to the broader political and literary cultures of the era. McLachlan, *Classical Names*, 85. The lawyer was to be a statesman, and classical literature spoke to contemporary politics. Words were to provoke action. For this tradition, see Anthony Kronman, *The Lost Lawyer: Failing Ideals of the Legal Profession* (Cambridge MA: Harvard University Press, 1995).

62   Mark Garrett Longaker, *Rhetoric and the Republic: Politics, Civic Discourse, and Education in Early America* (Tuscaloosa: University of Alabama Press, 2007).

63   David Potter, *Debating in the Colonial Chartered Colleges: An Historical Survey, 1642 to 1900* (New York: Teachers College, Columbia University, 1944), 12.

64   Pryde, *Scottish Universities*, 5.

65   James Walsh, *Education of the Founding Fathers of the Republic: Scholasticism in the Colonial Colleges; A Neglected Chapter in the History of American Education* (New York: Fordham University Press, 1935). Cotton Mather's *Magnalia* talks about the principal part of commencement being the public act where theses were disputed. Book IV, §7, 20.

Logic was ever central to college education, but it was particularly so in the earliest years of the colonial colleges. "Logic is the most general of all arts," read one proposition at 1643 and 1708 commencements.[66] The advancement of the ideas of modern natural law resulted in the students' expected ability to debate propositions such as: "Ethics is equally capable of demonstration as mathematics" (Harvard, 1767).

Commencement disputations, however, also increasingly spoke of the law of nations, and questions of government and law.[67] A Harvard thesis of 1743 read: "Are we bound to observe the mandates of kings, unless they themselves keep their agreements?"[68] And five years later: "Is it lawful to resist the supreme magistrate, if the commonwealth cannot otherwise be preserved?" At the College of New Jersey in 1759, a thesis read: "Is it right to resist by force and arms kings who invade the rights of the people?" Likewise in Philadelphia: "Is it allowed to resist the supreme magistrate if the commonwealth cannot be otherwise preserved?" (1761).

Indeed, at Philadelphia there was an entire "division" of theses on "*De jurisprudentiale naturali*": "The will of God revealed by the light either of nature or of Sacred Scripture is an adequate rule and norm of conscience" (1762); "Almost all laws especially natural laws refer to the whole human race or to all of a certain class"; "All men are by nature equal"; "Whatever is opposed to the common good is also opposed to the law of nature."[69] But theses probing the legal and political limitations of natural-law reflection were found across the colleges: "Subjects are bound and obliged, according to the law of nature, to resist their king and defend their liberty when he is acting with inhuman ruthlessness or overthrowing the laws of the state" (College of New Jersey, 1770), for instance, and "Ex post facto laws are not binding" (College of Rhode Island, 1786).[70]

---

[66] Potter, *Debating*, 16.

[67] Twentieth-century commentators broadly dismissed the Puritan curriculum as remaining profoundly medieval, and, as such, unable to integrate new developments in science. This view is, at least, partially mistaken. The curriculum did change with the integration of the "new learning" of mathematics and natural science, and with this, the reading of texts in English. And, of course, the scholastic curriculum brought from the Old World was not that of 1400, but had already been transformed by the humanism of the preceding centuries. If the broad contours of the scholastic curriculum remained, the works engaged, the reasoning undertaken, and the presumed purpose of this study, had changed.

[68] In Potter, *Debating*, 23. All the examples that follow are likewise from Potter unless otherwise cited.

[69] Walsh, *Education*, 229.

[70] Ibid., 135. The lists of these theses prove fascinating. Other relevant examples include the following. "The rights of the people are as divine as those of their rulers" (College of Philadelphia, 1763). "All power of maintaining laws and inflicting penalties is derived from

COLLEGIATE PROFESSORS OF LAW

With the Revolutionary War, college study of law gained new import. The Declaration of Independence begins by invoking the "Laws of Nature and of Nature's God," justifying the fight for independence as flowing from British denial of "certain unalienable rights," granted not by men but by God.[71] This language is found too in the Federalist Papers and other writings of the founding fathers.[72] But while these works often sought to justify "a right of rebellion," natural law was also increasingly invoked in the colleges to inculcate good citizenship and a love of liberty. The college curriculums, in other words, continued to connect law and government, together with cultivation of man and citizen, within the framework of the natural-law tradition.

But there were institutional changes afoot. Yale's president Ezra Stiles called upon "the several States" to endow professorships of law, "[r]emembering that it is scarcely possible to enslave a Republic where the Body of the People are Civilians [citizens], well instructed in their Laws, Rights, and Liberties."[73] Teaching the law was an education for free men, training in the necessary conditions for liberty. Distinctly practical outcomes were intended: the equipping of students for roles in Congress, for instance, and

---

the people; therefore, for a legislative body to impose taxes upon people who are not represented in that legislature is unjust" (College of Rhode Island, 1769). "Are the people the sole judges of their rights and liberties?" (Harvard, 1769). "A well equipped but unsalaried militia is the best defense for a commonwealth" (College of Rhode Island, 1773). "A defensive war is permissible" (College of Rhode Island, 1774). "All men are born free, and it is glorious to meet death in securing their liberty by force and arms" (College of Rhode Island, 1776).

[71] The relationship between the Declaration and discourse on natural law and natural rights is well treated by Dieter Grimm, "Europäisches Naturrecht und Amerikanische Revolution," *Ius commune* 3 (1970): 120–51.

[72] R. H. Helmholz, for instance, points to the example of *The Federalist* No. 43 and its invoking of a right to self-defense premised on "the transcendent law of nature." See *The Federalist*, ed. Jacob Cooke (Middletown, CT: Wesleyan University Press, 1961), 297. Helmholz also provides references to state constitutions invoking natural law and the writings of twenty-three "leading lights" in the new Republic. *Natural Law in Court: A History of Legal Theory in Practice* (Cambridge, MA: Harvard University Press, 2015), 130n16–39.

[73] As quoted in Edmund Morgan, *The Gentle Puritan: A Life of Ezra Stiles* (New Haven, CT: Yale University Press, 1962), 323. On December 3, 1777, Stiles recorded in his diary: "I drafted a Plan of an University, particularly describing the *Law* & *Medical* Lectures: at the Desire of the Corpor of Yale to be by them laid before the Committee of the General Assembly of Connect. appointed to consider among other Things where it be expedient to found these 2 Professorships." *The Literary Diary of Ezra Stiles*, ed. Franklin Bowditch Dexter, vol. II (New York: Charles Scribner's Sons, 1901), 233. The full address can be found in Charles Warren, *History of the American Bar* (Boston: Little, Brown, 1911), 563–66.

to "conduct[] the public arrangements of the military, naval & political Departments & the whole public administration."[74]

Stiles proposed sets of lectures ranging over Roman law, English common law – insisting, however, that "neither this nor any other foreign Law will ever be in force in America" except by its "derivative use, Custom & Adoption" – the codes of the thirteen states, and lectures on the world governments, especially those of Europe and China. His focus was practical, if not professional; "the Spirit & Governing Principles" of the law were to be taught, not matters "officinal," better learned "at the Bar & by living with a Lawyer."[75]

Such college study of the law, therefore, would teach students to sift from history and international practice what was worthy of America's attention, and help students learn to repel dangers to liberty. College study of the law was still to cultivate character, but character was now understood as necessarily connected to the continuance of American liberty. The emphasis had shifted from the good of moral law, as such, to the flourishing of political community: Proper knowledge of law and politics, said Stiles, would "transfuse a spirit among the body of the people in America."[76] Indeed, in the shaky days of the new Republic, this spirit, claimed Stiles, would be Americans' "only security of Liberty under Providence," necessary to "effect that public Virtue" required if the new Republic were to flourish.[77]

Despite Stiles's efforts at Yale, however, the first dedicated chair in law in America was at William and Mary, where George Wythe was appointed

---

[74] Warren, *History*, 565.

[75] Ibid., 564. In its now obscure sense, "officinal" is an adjective, meaning: "of, belonging to, or characteristic of a shop or shopkeeper."

[76] Ibid., 566. Law was taught as an act of patriotism: a means to build political leadership. See, Paul Carrington, *The Revolutionary Idea of University Legal Education*, 31 Wm. & Mary L. Rev. 527 (1990).

[77] Warren, *History*, 566. There was a realization that structures of government and law were worthy of significant study in the new Republic. This was true in Joel Barlow's influential, if unsuccessful, proposal to found a national university. Barlow, *Prospects*. The federal system, he argued, operates if not with new principles of government, then with "at least new combinations of principles, which required to be developed, studied and understood better than they have been." Ibid., 17. He commended the study of the science of government within a natural law sensibility: "we regard it as founded on principles analogue to the nature of man, and designed to promote his happiness" . . . [and] "believe our government to be founded on these principles." Ibid., 8. "The science of morals connects itself so intimately with the principles of political institutions." Ibid., 11. He notes the opportunity to distinguish American practice from European. Eminent men who have studied government and law in Europe had not, he noted, been included among the learned societies: "Locke, Berkeley, Pope, Hume, Robertson, Gibbon, Adam Smith, and Blackstone," he says, for example, "were never admitted into the Royal Society." Ibid.

professor of law and police in 1779.[78] Specialization – a process begun fifty years earlier – would increasingly separate study of the American legal system from ethics and philosophy, but Wythe's appointment marks a smaller separation than it first appears: In the eighteenth century, "police" referred to the complete organizational scheme of government.[79]

By 1792, William and Mary awarded two degrees: a Bachelor of Arts and a Bachelor of Law. The substance of both degrees represents a shift in the curriculum to an emphasis on "law, politics, and science."[80] Both degrees included study of natural law and the law of nations, and principles of politics alongside other subjects. The Bachelor of Law curriculum additionally included studies of civil history both ancient and modern, together with municipal law and the principles of public policy.[81]

The study of law remained a study in government such that James Wilson – an Associate Justice of the U.S. Supreme Court – could announce his 1790 lectures in Philadelphia as furnishing "a rational and useful entertainment to gentlemen of all professions, and in particular to assist in forming the legislator, the Magistrate, and the 'Lawyer.'"[82] Knowledge of "those rational principles on which the law is founded," he argued, "ought, especially in a free

[78] Jefferson studied law under Wythe from 1762 to 1767, and later wrote a brief sketch of his life. *Notes for the Biography of George Wythe, The Writings of Thomas Jefferson*, ed. Andrew Lipscomb and Albert Bergh (Washington, DC: Thomas Jefferson Memorial Association of the United States, 1903), 1:166–70.

[79] At the beginning of the colonial era, college tutors taught all subjects to a group of students. But in 1722 Harvard founded the Hollis professorship of divinity – dedicating a position to a particular field of study – and in 1766 abolished its tutorial system, with all instructors assigned to teach particular classes. Kraus, *Development*, 69. "What the German would call *Polizeiwissenschaft*, and what the Greeks termed πολιτεία was taught for nearly a century at the college of William and Mary under the head of '*police*.' That name would probably suggest nothing but constabulary associations to most college faculties in these modern days." Herbert Baxter Adams, *The College of William and Mary: A Contribution to the History of Higher Education with Suggestions for National Promotion. Circulars of Information of the Bureau of Education No. 1–1887* (Washington, DC: Government Printing Office, 1887), 39n1.

[80] Ernest Earnest, *Academic Procession: An Informal History of the American College, 1636 to 1953* (Indianapolis, IN: Bobbs-Merrill, 1953), 54.

[81] *Statutes of the University of William and Mary*, 1792. Reprinted in: The William and Mary Quarterly 20, no. 1 (1911): 52–59, 57–58. Thomas Jefferson was decidedly complimentary. "They hold weekly courts and assemblies in the capitol. The professors join in it; and the young men dispute with elegance, method and learning. This single school by throwing from time to time new hands well principled and well informed into the legislature will be of infinite value." "From Thomas Jefferson to James Madison, 26 July 1780," in *The Papers of Thomas Jefferson*, vol. 3, *18 June 1779 – 30 September 1780*, ed. Julian P. Boyd (Princeton, NJ: Princeton University Press, 1951), 506–508.

[82] Reed, *Training*, 122. In 1790, Wilson began a proposed three-year course on law in Philadelphia, then the nation's capital, with lectures given three times a week at six in the evening.

government, to be diffused over the whole community."[83] Wilson's successor Charles Hare planned a three-year program of teaching, beginning with "Natural Jurisprudence," next "International Jurisprudence," and only in the final year, "Jurisprudence of the United States and Pennsylvania."[84]

At Columbia, James Kent likewise spoke of the "singular obligations" of American citizens, given the nature of their government, "to place the Study of the Law at least on a level with the pursuits of Classical Learning."[85] He was convinced that the "Science of Civil Government" could be "stripped of its delusive refinements, and restored to the plain Principles of Reason"[86]

Nonetheless, specialization, together with the vicissitudes of funding, increasingly separated law from ethics. At the University of Virginia – the other significant site of post-revolution college legal education – lack of funds resulted in the appointment of two instead of the three professors in human conduct that Thomas Jefferson had proposed, one in Ethics and Moral Science, another in Law and Politics. As at William and Mary, with specialization came the continued combination of law with practical politics, but not, as before, moral philosophy.[87]

* * *

Out of a population of two and a half million in America, there were only 5,000 college graduates by the outbreak of the Revolution.[88] And yet, as the colonial colleges had taught the colonial elites, so too college graduates would

---

[83] *The Works of James Wilson*, ed. Robert Green McCloskey (Cambridge, MA: Belknap Press of Harvard University, 1967), 73.

[84] Ibid., 122–23. See also C. Stuart Patterson, "The Law Department" in *Benjamin Franklin and the University of Pennsylvania*, ed. Francis Newton Thorpe (Washington, DC: Government Printing Office, 1893).

[85] James Kent, *An Introductory Lecture to a Course of Law Lectures, delivered November 17, 1794* (New York: Published at the request of the trustee, printed by Francis Childs, 1794), 4.

[86] Ibid.

[87] Thomas Jefferson's 1818 plans for the university included ten schools. Three were to be concerned with human conduct: private ethics, combined with general grammar, rhetoric, and belles-lettres and the fine arts under a professor of Ideology; a professor of Government to give instruction in the Law of Nature and Nations, Political Economy, and History being interwoven with politics and law; and a professor of Municipal Law, that is domestic law (federal and state laws), in distinction to international law. Thomas Jefferson, "Report for the Commissioners for the University of Virginia, August 4, 1818" in Merrill Peterson, ed., *Thomas Jefferson: Writings*, 457–73 (New York: Literary Classics of the United States, 1984).

[88] James D. Teller, *A History of American Education* (New York: Macmillan, 1973), 213–14. Three thousand of these men had graduated from the American colleges, while a further 2,000 held degrees from British institutions.

form an absolute majority at the 1787 Constitutional Convention and in the early administrations of the new Republic.[89]

By the mid-eighteenth century, the college curriculum had gained a new emphasis: Reason alone was now sufficient for true knowledge. In college teaching, at least, reason took priority over revelation, even as reason was used to offer additional arguments for the veracity of God's law. Still, the intellectual worlds of Puritans and Revolutionaries alike held to the unity of the truth: The universe was orderly, even divinely ruled, with human knowledge promising an ever-expanding vision of the various laws governing the universe.[90] Only in the late nineteenth century, or even twentieth century, were these connections sundered, when scholars increasingly accepted a distinction between fact and value. Knowing the true would no longer mean – as it had done for the Puritan and Revolutionary alike – knowing, *ipso facto*, the good.[91]

Scholarly treatments of the Revolutionary period and, particularly, the moral philosophy course have often occluded colleges' relationship to the study of law. By equating natural law solely with its modern form, some scholars herald the moral philosophy course as the beginning of natural-law reflection in America, thereby cutting off continuities with the colonial colleges.[92] Others, by accepting the twentieth-century consensus on the nature of law, anachronistically split ethics from politics and law.[93] Both accounts are incomplete, if not entirely mistaken.

[89] Of the fifty-five men who attended, thirty-one were college graduates. James McLachlan, "Classical Names, American Identities: Some Notes on College Students and the Classical Tradition in the 1770s," in *Classical Traditions in Early America*, ed. John W. Eadie, 81–95 (Ann Arbor, MI: Center for the Coordination of Ancient and Modern Studies, 1976), 85. Sixty-three percent of the higher civil service appointees of John Adams attended college. Fifty-two percent of Jefferson's appointees were college educated. Sidney H. Aronson, *Status and Kinship in the Higher Civil Service: Standards of Selection in the Administrations of John Adams, Thomas Jefferson, and Andrew Jackson* (Cambridge, MA: Harvard University Press, 1964), 124–25.

[90] This intellectual vision continued through much of the nineteenth century. Certainly it was the vision of Noah Porter (1811–92), Yale's president. Veysey, *Emergence of the American University*, 26. Recognizing this intellectual vision, of course, does not entail valuing it. "This curriculum really cohered around nothing but tradition. But it did assume, almost subliminally, the unity of knowledge: all truth flowing, it was supposed, from God." James Turner, *Language, Religion, Knowledge: Past and Present* (Notre Dame, IN: University of Notre Dame Press, 2003), 51.

[91] Moral "truth," therefore, became only emotional or nonliteral. Science became the only arbiter of truth. Reuben, *Making of Modern University*, 3.

[92] "Natural law, the realm of reason, the realm of nature were in the ascendency. The supernatural was in decline." Rudolph, *American College and University*, 40.

[93] This is true even of supporters of natural-law reflection who make a distinction between moral education and political and policy ideas undertaken. Robson's emphasis, for instance, is on finding "politics" in the education of the founding fathers. Thus, when they read Jean Jacques Burlamaqui's *Principles of Natural and Political Law* they found material "related to politics,"

From their colonial roots through the Revolution, American colleges taught law. They did not often teach the details of common-law rules, at least before the establishment of college law professorships – although Witherspoon taught broadly on contracts – yet neither was the study of law separated from the practicalities of the moral life or government. Through their continued adherence to natural law – however changed in its details through the years – American colleges provided the intellectual tools for future leaders to justify, even critique, law and government. Morality and law were commensurable ideas. For most Americans, indeed, both remained equally God's law.

in Robson's estimation. But in Pufendorf's *De Officio Homines et Cive*, the "emphasis was more on the moral than the governmental facet of politics." Educating Republicans, 83–84.

3

Organizing Common Law

William Blackstone in America

Any history of the American legal tradition – let alone any story of natural-law thinking in the law – must account for the transplant, growth, and withering in New World soil of the influence of William Blackstone (1723–80) and that "legendary fount of knowledge for lawyers and statesmen in American history," his *Commentaries on the Laws of England*.[1] Based on lectures delivered at Oxford and published from 1765 to 1769, Blackstone's *Commentaries* present a systematic treatment of English law in four volumes: *The Rights of Persons, The Rights of Things, Of Private Wrongs*, and *Of Public Wrongs*.[2] A touchstone of American law over two-and-a-half centuries, the *Commentaries* equipped Abraham Lincoln for legal practice,[3] and still today furnish constitutional originalists with a trusted repository of founding-era jurisprudence.[4]

In the previous two chapters, we looked to early American collegiate education and the broader intellectual cultures – Puritan, Revolutionary, and Republican – that the colleges inhabited and cultivated. The colleges,

---

[1] Jessie Allen, "Reading Blackstone in the Twenty-First Century and the Twenty-First Century through Blackstone," in *Re-Interpreting Blackstone's Commentaries: A Seminal Text in National and International Contexts*, ed. Wilfred Prest (Oxford: Hart, 2014), 215.

[2] Blackstone was fully involved in eight editions of the *Commentaries*. Among the changes in subsequent editions, Blackstone offered a more rigorous examination of equity (fourth edition), and a defense of why he focused on the good of the English Constitution and not its imperfections (eighth edition). The variations between the first eight editions are noted in W. G. Hammond's edition of the *Commentaries* (San Francisco: Bancroft-Whitney, 1890).

[3] For a nuanced account of Lincoln's legal education, see Mark E. Steiner, *Abraham Lincoln and the Rule of Law Books*, 93 Marq. L. Rev. 1283 (2010).

[4] Originalists treat as authoritative the Constitution's understood meaning at the time of its promulgation. For an introduction, see *Originalism: The Quarter-Century of Debate*, ed. Steven Calabresi (Washington, DC: Regnery, 2007); and Robert Bennett and Lawrence Solum, *Constitutional Originalism: A Debate* (Ithaca, NY: Cornell University Press, 2011).

we saw, were sources of natural-law reasoning in America, and sites for natural law's negotiation with common law. In Blackstone's *Commentaries* we turn to the other pre-eminent source and site. Blackstone, we shall see, organized the common law. He gave it structure and order through natural law. In doing so, he commended common law at a time when both its disorderliness offended the Enlightenment minds of the builders of a new Republic and its English origin rendered its survival in America uncertain. Concise yet comprehensive, Blackstone's *Commentaries* provided American students and practitioners with a much-needed tool, and well into the nineteenth century remained a prominent and – with some judicious editing – relevant guide. The *Commentaries* shaped the assumptions of generations of Americans that the common law is fundamentally in accord with natural law.

BLACKSTONE AND HIS *COMMENTARIES*

Few would have predicted William Blackstone's influence. True, he achieved conventional success in England during his lifetime, as a university reformer (Oxford University Press owes much to his reorganization), a member of parliament (for Hindon, 1761–68, and Westbury, 1768–70), and a seemingly undistinguished judge of the Court of Common Pleas.[5] But his fame today rests almost solely on two interrelated achievements. First, through his lecturing, latterly as the inaugural holder of Oxford's Vinerian Chair (1758–66), he established English common law as a university discipline. Before Blackstone, only the Church's canon law and Rome's civilian law had been taught in English universities. Second, in writing his *Commentaries on the Laws of England*, Blackstone organized English common law's seemingly ad hoc collection of forms and precedents into a comprehensive system.

Blackstone pleads his case for the university study of law in the opening pages of the *Commentaries*. "Law," he begins, is the "most useful and most rational branch of learning"; it is "built upon the surest foundations, and approved by the experience of the ages."[6] As a *useful* science, indeed, common

---

[5] Biographies of Blackstone include: Ian Doolittle, *William Blackstone: A Biography* (Haselmere, UK: Ian Doolittle, 2001); David A. Lockmiller, *Sir William Blackstone* (Chapel Hill: University of North Carolina Press, 1938); Wilfrid Prest, *William Blackstone: Law and Letters in the Eighteenth Century* (Oxford: Oxford University Press, 2008); and Lewis C. Warden, *The Life of Blackstone* (Charlottesville, VA: Michie, 1938).

[6] William Blackstone, *Commentaries on the Laws of England*, vol. 1, *Of the Rights of Persons* (1765; repr. Chicago: University of Chicago Press, 1979), *3, *5. The *Commentaries* are standardly cited to the page of the original edition (known as the star page). Most later editions include the star page in the margin or text. Where necessary for ease of reading, I have sparingly modernized Blackstone's punctuation and spelling.

law's neglect by the universities, says Blackstone, has had practical consequences. Future politicians and men of property, he says, have been robbed of
constitutional wisdom developed through the centuries.[7] And would-be lawyers, excluded from the benefits of "liberal education," have been forced to
endure "a tedious lonely process to extract the theory of law from a mass of
undigested learning," or attempt by "assiduous attendance on the courts to
pick up theory and practice together."[8]

Whether speaking to future politicians, men of property, or would-be
lawyers, Blackstone self-consciously organized common law. He offered his
readers "a general map of the law, marking out the shape of the country, its
connexions and boundaries, its greater divisions and principal cities."[9] In an
introduction and four further books, Blackstone works methodologically
through the nature of law, its application, and its study; the "rights of the
person," what today would be called public or constitutional law;[10] the law of
property; civil procedure and remedies; and criminal law. English law, thus
marshaled by Blackstone, was rendered elegant and clear – to be understood
through his exposition and examples and admired as the fruit of the rational
order of nature and the specific history of the English people.

THE *COMMENTARIES* AND NATURAL LAW

Natural law undergirds the structure of the *Commentaries* and governs the
content of some of its most important concepts. Blackstone was far from the
first English lawyer to describe natural law as either a component of English
common law or its source.[11] But new with Blackstone's age were the application of modern natural-law's suppositions to common law, and – contempor-
aneously to the first edition of the *Encyclopædia Britannica* (1768–71) – the
comprehensive exposition of common law. One count of the *Commentaries'*

---

[7] Commentaries 1, *7.
[8] Ibid., *31; ibid., *32.
[9] Ibid., *35.
[10] For Blackstone and his initial readers, "constitutional" did not refer to a document or body of
     higher laws, but rather *all* the laws, institutions, and conventions of government "as consti-
     tuted." See Bernard Bailyn, *The Ideological Origins of the American Revolution* (Cambridge,
     MA: Belknap Press of Harvard University, 1967), 68. His "constitutional" concerns accordingly
     are not our own. He assumes that the courts and legislature do not clash. His attention, instead,
     is on the balance of the executive (the Crown) and the legislature (Parliament), and not on
     citizens' relationship to the executive or the legislature. See Edwin S. Corwin, *The "Higher
     Law" Background of American Constitutional Law*, 42 Harv. L. Rev. 149 (1928); and 42 Harv.
     L. Rev. 365 (1928).
[11] For a list of previous exponents, see R. H. Helmholz, *Natural Law and Human Rights in
     English Law: From Bracton to Blackstone*, 3 Ave Maria L. Rev. 1, 5–11 (2005).

references to "natural law" or "law of nature" found eighty-one.[12] And this number does not tally the occurrence of distinct but related terms in the *Commentaries*, such as "natural rights" or "natural justice." Nor does it include those places where descriptive and normative conceptions of nature come together, such as Blackstone's discussion of natural duties toward children, natural liberty, the natural foundations of justice, and natural equity, let alone more implicit treatments of nature.[13]

"OF THE NATURE OF LAWS IN GENERAL"

Most scholarly treatments of the *Commentaries* restrict their attention to Blackstone's most sustained discussion of natural law, which occurs in "Of the Nature of Laws in General," the second section of his Introduction.[14] The section begins: "Law, in its most general and comprehensive sense, signifies a rule of action."[15] In this broad sense, people speak of "laws of motion, of gravitation, of optics, of mechanics, as well as the laws of nature and of nations."[16] However, to speak of "law" proper, says Blackstone, is to speak of a rule of action that involves a superior and an inferior: A law is "prescribed by some superior . . . which the inferior is bound to obey."[17]

Natural Law as Precept

While Blackstone thus includes brief treatments of "law" as it pertains to inanimate, vegetable, and animal life, his attention is on *precepts*.[18] To speak of law proper, on Blackstone's account, is to speak of free and rational beings that can recognize and follow commands given by a superior. In this understanding of law, Blackstone follows the modern natural lawyers we met in

---

[12] R. H. Helmholz, *Natural Law in Court: A History of Legal Theory in Practice* (Cambridge, MA: Harvard University Press, 2015), 133.

[13] Commentaries 1, *436 (duties toward children); e.g., ibid., *53 (natural liberty); ibid., *42 (natural foundations of justice); William Blackstone, *Commentaries on the Laws of England*, vol. 2, *Of the Rights of Things* (1766; repr. Chicago: University of Chicago Press, 1979), *162 (natural equity).

[14] "Of the Nature of Laws in General" is preceded in Blackstone's Introduction by "On the Study of Law," and followed by "Of the Laws of England" and "Of the Countries subject to the Laws of England."

[15] Commentaries 1, *38.

[16] Ibid.

[17] Ibid. Blackstone supposes that laws of motion, etc., are commands imposed by God upon matter. Today, when scientists speak of "laws" they mean that particular phenomena always occur under certain conditions, *irrespective of any lawgiver*.

[18] Ibid., *38–39.

discussing early American colleges – Hugo Grotius (1583–1645) and Samuel Pufendorf (1632–94) among them – and through them the Spanish late scholastic Francisco Suárez (1448–1617). Thus, in Blackstone's account, "law" *for human beings* denotes "the precepts by which man, the noblest of all sublunary beings, a creature endowed with both reason and freewill, is commanded to make use of those faculties in the general regulation of his behavior."[19]

Will and Reason

Blackstone offers different treatments of the relation between will and reason. At first he stresses that the content of the law of nature for (reasonable and free) human beings is God's *will*: the "will of his maker," he says, "is called the law of nature."[20] As for Grotius, Pufendorf, Suárez, and their ilk, Blackstone's attention, then, is on God's ability and choice to "regulate[] and restrain[]" human will, by laying down "certain immutable laws of human nature."[21]

Given what God has chosen – the constitution of the universe as it is, and human beings as *rational* – humans can "discover the purpose of those laws" laid down by God.[22] Accordingly, even if in one sense God "establishes at his own pleasure certain arbitrary laws," nonetheless the subject of such laws "answers the end of its formation."[23] God may choose arbitrarily, but human beings so created fulfill the ends of their creation through exercise of the reason God has chosen to (arbitrarily) impart.

Blackstone, it is fair to say, is neither philosopher nor theologian. His overall account of natural law has internal tensions. Having stated the seemingly arbitrary grounds for God's choices, Blackstone quickly suggests that, given God's "infinite wisdom," God has:

> laid down only such laws as were founded in those relations of justice, that existed in the nature of things antecedent to any positive precept. These are the eternal, immutable laws of good and evil, to which the creator himself in all his dispensations conforms; and which he has enabled human reason to discover, so far as they are necessary for the conduct of human actions.[24]

[19] Ibid., *39.
[20] Ibid.
[21] Ibid., *39–40.
[22] Ibid., *40.
[23] Ibid., *38.
[24] Ibid., *4.

It seems that God is not the arbitrary lawmaker after all, but a ruler who chooses the good.

There are ways, perhaps, to account for Blackstone's differing treatments of the relationship of *will* and *reason* in his depiction of natural law. For good reason through the centuries great minds have agonized over how to affirm simultaneously God's utter freedom yet goodness. It is most straightforward, perhaps, to think that Blackstone presents a not-entirely-worked-out conglomerate of the standard positions of his day. Blackstone traverses the overall structure of natural law solely in order to speak of law as it applies to human beings. His focus is not – as it must be for philosophers and theologians – God's nature, then, except as it pertains to human knowledge of natural law. Indeed, all that is needed for the coherence of his account is that human beings possess the ability to rationally reflect on their nature, that there are "laws of good and evil," and that reflection on human nature brings some knowledge of these laws.[25] The metaphysics of why all this is so has little import for the arguments in the nearly 2,000 pages that follow.

Knowledge of the First Principles of Natural Law

The principles of good and evil that are discoverable by humans, Blackstone suggests, are that "we should live honestly, should hurt nobody, and should render to everyone its due."[26] It is to these three, he notes, that Justinian reduced the whole of the law.[27] Knowledge of these principles is available through the exercise of right reason, says Blackstone, although indolence and ignorance disrupt their discernment. Happily, he says, "we should want no other prompter to enquire after and pursue the rule of right, but our own self-love, that universal principle of action."[28] With Grotius and Pufendorf, Blackstone affirms that human beings are so constituted that self-interest by itself can reveal the first principles of natural law. With John Locke (1632–1704), however, Blackstone also emphasizes *happiness*: "[T]he laws of eternal justice" and "the happiness of each individual," he says, are so interwoven "that the latter cannot be attained but by observing the former."[29] And while Blackstone speaks at times, then, of "man's *real* happiness" – and thereby suggests that human beings can wrongly identify the objects of their happiness, or wrongly act to obtain them –

---

[25] Ibid.

[26] Ibid.

[27] *Juris praecepta sunt haec, honeste vivere, alterum non laedere, suum cuique tribuere.* Blackstone cites this to Justinian's *Institutes* 1.1.5. In modern editions, the usual citation is 1.1.3.

[28] *Commentaries* 1, *40.

[29] Ibid.

happiness, as he describes it, nonetheless consists in pleasure, not perfection.[30] Blackstone follows modern natural law, not its scholastic forebear. For modern natural lawyers, human beings know, and are induced to follow, the first principles of natural law because of our experience as vulnerable people who live in society, not as subjects ordered to the common good of all creation. And human beings know, and are induced to follow, the first principles of natural law not in relation to ultimate goodness, but because the principles both accord with and further what we experience or anticipate as desirable or good for us.

While Pufendorf was sure that human beings in their current state can know the first principles of natural law, Blackstone seemingly follows the later thought of Locke, for whom human reason is sufficiently weakened that it needs the support of the revealed law of Scripture. For "every man" finds "that his reason is corrupt, and his understanding full of ignorance and error."[31] And thus, because of human frailty, God "hath been pleased, at sundry times and in diverse manners," to make knowledge of divine and natural laws available to humanity "by an immediate and direct revelation."[32]

The content and obligatoriness of the natural law known either through reason or through revelation is the same, however, says Blackstone, because reason and revelation share the same source.[33] Yet "humanly speaking," as to knowledge of that law, the revealed law of Scripture is truly "the law of nature, expressly declared so to be by God himself," whereas, apart from Scripture, we have "what, by the assistance of human reason, we imagine to be that law."[34]

Human Laws and Natural Law

Blackstone is clear that, "[u]pon these two foundations, the law of nature and the law of revelation, depend all human laws; that is to say, no human laws should be suffered to contradict these."[35] But the relationship he traces between human law and the natural and divine laws is distinctly variegated. In a state of nature, the laws of nature and God would be sufficient to govern human life, he says. But because of our drive to sociability, human beings need human laws.[36] Indeed, Blackstone cites Pufendorf's famous claim that

---

[30] Ibid., *41, my emphasis.
[31] Ibid.
[32] Ibid., *42.
[33] Divine *positive* law can nonetheless create obligations beyond natural law.
[34] Commentaries 1, *42.
[35] Ibid.
[36] Ibid., *43. Although, he argues that in a state of nature, the laws of nature and God would be sufficient.

"the fundamental natural law is this: that every man must cherish and maintain sociability, so far as in him lies."[37]

Human laws are necessary, then, on account of the need of self-interested but weak human beings to live in society. But the situations in which human law is enacted, and its relationship thereby to natural and divine laws, differ. There are circumstances, for instance, where human law pertains but natural and divine laws are indifferent: circumstances neither good nor bad in themselves.[38] In such circumstances, human beings, in Blackstone's view, are left to their "own liberty," save the restraints set by society through human laws.[39]

There are other circumstances, however, to which the natural and divine laws are *not* indifferent. In these circumstances, human laws "are only declaration of, and act in subordination to," their foundations. Murder, for instance, is "expressly forbidden" by divine law, and is an offense "demonstrabl[e] by natural law."[40] It is the divine and natural laws, then, that establish murder's "true unlawfulness," and not the words of judges or the text of legislation.[41] Human laws in such cases do "annex a punishment" to the crime.[42] They do put the law, and the consequences of its breach, into action. But in so doing they "do not at all increase [a crime's] moral guilt, or superadd any obligation *in foro conscientiaie* to abstain from its perpetration."[43] Blackstone, however, is not interested in the question of the *existence* or otherwise of human laws. His is not the analytical approach of nineteenth- and twentieth-century legal philosophers. So in this discussion where purported human "laws" offend divine and natural law, Blackstone is not careful to strip the nomenclature of "law" from them. He does not quote the famous maxim associated with Augustine and Thomas Aquinas, and later Martin Luther King, Jr., *an unjust law is not a law at all*. Instead, Blackstone says that human beings would be "bound to transgress a human law" that enjoined committing murder, lest they "offend both the natural and the divine [laws]."

And there are situations, too, where "the thing itself has its rise from the law of nature" but "the particular circumstances and mode of doing it become right or wrong, as the law of the land shall direct."[44] In other words: There are

---

[37] Ibid.
[38] Brian Tierney explores 700 years of discussion on natural law and indifference in his *Liberty and Law: The Idea of Permissive Natural Law, 1100–1800* (Washington, DC: Catholic University of America Press, 2014).
[39] Commentaries 1, *42.
[40] Ibid.
[41] Ibid.
[42] Ibid.
[43] Ibid., *42–43.
[44] Ibid., *55.

situations where human law specifies the details of natural law. Blackstone's example is civil duties: A certain obedience to superiors, he says, is shown by divine and natural laws, but "who those superiors shall be, and in what circumstances, or to what degrees they shall be obeyed" is a matter for legislation.[45]

The Law of Nations and Municipal Law

Blackstone's work is on the law of England, but for completeness his discussion of "the nature of laws in general" includes the law of nations. In the relations between states, he says, natural law forms the default. Each state recognizes no superior, so each relies upon natural law as the law "to which [all] communities are equally subject."[46] That much is straightforward.

Less straightforward is Blackstone's treatment of *municipal* law – that is, the law of a particular state, as distinguished from the law between states – which has confused his interpreters, and not without reason. He first defines municipal law clearly enough as "the rule by which particular ... nations are governed," and cites Justinian: "[T]he civil law is that which every nation has established for its own government."[47] However, shortly thereafter he offers a further definition, this time within quotation marks: "Municipal law, thus understood, is properly defined to be 'a rule of civil conduct prescribed by the supreme power in a state, commanding what is right and prohibiting what is wrong.'"[48]

But what does it mean to command what is right and wrong? The answer divides Blackstone's contemporary readers. Some proponents of natural-law thinking read this second definition as taking for granted Blackstone's earlier articulation of natural and divine laws as foundational to human law. This is true, for instance, of Hadley Arkes, who presents the second definition as exemplary of the idea that human law should "seek to embody principles of right and wrong."[49] The second definition, therefore, is descriptive: the lawmaker can, and would only, command that which is in accord with natural law.

Some later editors of the *Commentaries*, however, add notes to the text suggesting that Blackstone's second definition is superfluous given his first,

---

45 Ibid.
46 Ibid., *43.
47 Ibid., *44. *Jus civile est quod quisque sibi populus constituit.*
48 Ibid.
49 Hadley Arkes, *First Things: An Inquiry into the Principles of Morals and Justice* (Princeton, NJ: Princeton University Press, 1986), 26.

and, indeed, that the second sits in some tension with Blackstone's general treatment of natural law.[50] Others propose – to their delight or disdain – that the second definition reveals Blackstone to be a positivist. Indeed, not only is Blackstone revealed as a *legal* positivist, for whom the law is whatever the sovereign says it is, but Blackstone, the seeming *moral* positivist, suggests that "right" and "wrong" too are defined by the sovereign lawgiver. In other words, Blackstone's references to natural law amount to a pious gloss on a Hobbesian vision.[51]

The proponents of the natural-law position, then, read Blackstone's words before the second definition but not those that follow, while the proponents of the positivist position read only the bare statement, not the surrounding discussion. What makes more sense in context is to read Blackstone as working with different valences of "right" and "wrong" in his two definitions.

Unlike in his first definition of municipal law, in Blackstone's second his attention is not on the moral meaning of right and wrong, but rather on *right* as the legal ability to do something and *wrong* as the violation or transgression of the law. This distinction becomes clearer as Blackstone distinguishes "civil conduct" from "moral conduct."[52] And, indeed, when he shortly after treats the nature of obligations, Blackstone offers both a "non moral" account, which presents an obligation as a reason to act in a particular way (including simply to avoid punishment), and a "moral" account, in which laws "are binding upon men's consciences."[53] Importantly, the non-moral account adds to the moral. The non-moral account captures the ways in which the bad man receives additional motivation to follow the law. This pattern continues. Blackstone, for instance, repeatedly distinguishes between things that are *mala in se* ("bad in themselves") and those that are *mala prohibita* ("wrong because prohibited" by positive law). "Conscience," he suggests, is engaged with the former, but not the latter.[54]

In his treatment of the nature of municipal law, then, Blackstone suggests that moral conduct pertains to human duties to God, self, and neighbor, but that "municipal or civil law regards [the human being] also as a citizen, and

---

[50] See, e.g., *Commentaries on the Laws of England in Four Books, with Notes Selected from the Editions of Archibold, Christian, Cole, Ridge, Chitty, Stewart, Kerr, and Others; And in Addition Notes and References to All Text Books and Decisions Wherein the Commentaries Have Cited and All the Statutes Modifying the Text*, ed. William Draper Lewis (Philadelphia: J. B. Lippincott, 1893), volume 1, *44.

[51] Paul Lucas, *Ex Parte Sir William Blackstone, "Plagiarist": A Note on Blackstone and the Natural Law* 7 Am. J. Legal Hist. 142 (1963).

[52] Commentaries 1, *45.

[53] Ibid., *57.

[54] Ibid.

bound to other duties toward his neighbour, than that of mere nature and religion."[55] Blackstone thus sees the civil realm of municipal law as imposing duties *additional* to the law of nature. Human beings, *as citizens*, must "contribute, on [their] part, to the subsistence and peace of the society."[56] In short, when solely concerned with the civil realm – in situations *indifferent* to natural law, or where *specification* by human legislation is needed – municipal law declares actions *right* (permitted or empowered by law) or *wrong* (prohibited by law). Blackstone gives the example of a woman's goods becoming her husband's on their marriage. This, he says, "has no foundation in nature; but . . . [in England was] merely created by law, for the purposes of civil society."[57]

NATURAL LAW IN THE *COMMENTARIES* BEYOND "OF THE NATURE OF LAWS IN GENERAL"

Most contemporary critics of Blackstone's natural law stop their analysis here. In so limiting their attention, some positivists seek to excuse Blackstone's natural-law sensibilities: They treat Blackstone's introductory words as merely an eighteenth-century nicety without broader import, or as a failure to follow through on his broader logical commitments. Blackstone's Old Whig political commitments, they say, prevent him from embracing the consequences of parliamentary sovereignty, the English doctrine that Westminster's human lawmakers have the right to make or unmake any law, regardless of content.[58]

Other positivists reject the value of the *Commentaries* precisely because of Blackstone's expressly stated natural-law position.[59] Daniel Boorstin, for one, portrays Blackstone's work as disturbingly circular. Blackstone's natural-law beliefs lead him to assume that the law should be reasonable, says Boorstin, and – *poof!* – the *Commentaries* make English law reasonable. Whatever the assessment of contemporary critics, few consider the overall frame of the *Commentaries*. This is a mistake.

---

[55]   Ibid., *45.
[56]   Ibid.
[57]   Ibid., *55.
[58]   Stanley H. Katz, "Introduction to Book I" in *Commentaries* 1, iv; Holdsworth, *History of English Law*, 10:529; A. V. Dicey, *Introduction to the Study of the Law of the Constitution*, 8th ed. (Indianapolis, IN : Liberty Fund, 1982), 3.
[59]   Daniel J. Boorstin, *The Mysterious Science of the Law: An Essay on Blackstone's Commentaries* (Chicago: Chicago University Press, 1941). Moreover, the "rationality" on which this depends, says Boorstin, relies on foundational, yet indemonstrable, values at the heart of existing social arrangements.

The Structure of the Commentaries

Limiting analysis of Blackstone's views on natural law to his explicit discussion at the beginning of the *Commentaries* misses the fundamental contribution of natural law to his project. As David Ibbetson notes: "In the course of the eighteenth century, many areas of [English] law came to be redefined in terms of natural lawyers' principles."[60] Henry Ballow (1707–82), for instance, "plagiarized from Pufendorf" to present an organized English law of contract.[61] The general rule of liability for negligence, first stated in England in 1767, likewise drew from the German jurist and philosopher.[62] New treatments of the law of trusts and the first work on corporate law were likewise explicitly based on natural-law grounds. And most of all, Blackstone organizes *all* of English law in its image. Given the influence of Blackstone's approach, we can easily miss that, in his time, organization was itself innovation. English law had been formed through the development of particular writs or procedural actions.[63] With Blackstone's eighteenth-century adoption and adaptation of natural-law concepts, he transformed a list of writs into a system of concepts and categories. Blackstone did not order his work through discussion of particular writs to be pleaded – from the *writ of aiel* through the *writ of mesne* to the *writ of waste*[64] – or by discussing an ad hoc collection of terms.

---

[60] David Ibbetson, "Natural Law." In *The Oxford International Encyclopedia of Legal History*. New York: Oxford University Press, 2009. See also David Ibbetson, *Natural Law and Common Law*, 5 Edin. L. Rev. 1 (2001); and Julia Rudolph, *Common Law and Enlightenment in England, 1689–1750* (Woodbridge, UK: Boydell, 2013), "Common Law Jurisprudence and the Philosophy of Natural Law," 164–200.

[61] Ibbetson, *Natural Law* (Encyclopedia). See also Warren Swain, *The Law of Contract 1670–1870* (Cambridge: Cambridge University Press, 2015), 275–78. Blackstone is widely regarded as offering a poor treatment of contract. See Stephen Waddams, *Principle and Policy in Contract Law: Competing or Complementary Concepts?* (Cambridge: Cambridge University Press, 2011), 1–21.

[62] Ibbetson, "Natural Law" *(Encyclopedia)*.

[63] The common law that Blackstone sought to organize primarily grew, from the medieval period, through the use and development of writs: legal orders of the King's courts that directed or enjoined their addressees to do, or refrain from, a specified act. The writ of habeas corpus ("produce the body"), for instance, is a formal order by a court to a person or agency to deliver to the court a person currently held by that person or agency.

To bring a case to a common law court a party needed to find an appropriate writ in order to plead his case: the *form* of the legal action having priority over the *cause*. For a short introduction, see F. W. Maitland's *The Forms of Action at Common Law: A Course of Lectures*, ed. A. H. Chaytor and W. J. Whittaker (New York: Cambridge University Press, 1989). *Forms of Action* was first published together with Maitland's *Equity* in 1909.

[64] Writs are highly specific. The *writ of aiel* was an action by a party based on the seisin (possession of land by freehold) of a grandfather for the recovery of land of which that party had been dispossessed. The *writ of mesne* was an action by which a tenant could recover damages from a mesne lord (intermediate feudal lord) whose failure to perform services owed to a superior lord had led the latter to distrain (seize) chattels on the tenant's land. The *writ of*

Rather, he divided his work into larger questions of rights and duties. He begins the second volume of the *Commentaries*, for instance, by noting that the volume considers *"jura rerum,* or those rights which a man may acquire in and to such external things as are unconnected with his person. These are what the writers on natural law style the rights of dominion, or property."[65] Principle was to shape the common law.

Justifying Laws

In addition to providing the frame and conceptual basis for the *Commentaries*, natural law undergirds, explains, and justifies specific laws or defenses. For instance, in volume four, concerning crimes, Blackstone explains – with reference to Grotius and Pufendorf – that the justification for punishing certain crimes such as murder is that they are "crimes against the law of nature."[66] Meanwhile, in volume three, concerning private wrongs, Blackstone suggests that the best justification of self-defense is the prompting of nature.[67] Self-defense, indeed, is "justly called the primary law of nature," he says, because of its direct relationship to the human drive to survival.[68]

If laws are to be justifiable, however, they must have a principled basis on which arguments can be advanced. Natural law, then, also provides Blackstone with a means to criticize laws and policies that do not possess such a basis. And yet Blackstone is rarely considered a critic. It is true that in instincts and conviction Blackstone was a conservative. He sought to conserve the values, ideas, and institutions foundational to the British Constitution, which he thought admirable. Thus, while some scholars assess Blackstone's political and legal vision as "moderate and realistic," the *Commentaries* was strongly criticized from its initial publication.[69] Most profoundly, Jeremy Bentham (1748–1832) launched an assault on Blackstone's natural-law arguments, his defense of the British Constitution, and, beyond Blackstone's

---

waste was an action commanding a sheriff to inhibit a tenant from an act of waste. (Waste being the unauthorized act of a tenant for a freehold estate not of inheritance, or for any lesser interest, which tends to the destruction of the tenement, or otherwise to the injury of the inheritance.)

[65]   Commentaries 2, *1.

[66]   See Grotius, de j.b.&. p.l.2.c.20. Puffendorf, L. of Nat. and N. b.8.c.3; William Blackstone, *Commentaries on the Laws of England*, vol. 4, Of Public Wrongs (1769; repr. Chicago: University of Chicago Press, 1979), *7.

[67]   William Blackstone, *Commentaries on the Laws of England*, vol. 3, Of Private Wrongs (1768; repr. Chicago: University of Chicago Press, 1979), *3–4.

[68]   Ibid., *4.

[69]   Doolittle, *William Blackstone*, 15.

account alone, the very probity of common law.[70] Bentham's successors have agreed, at least with his first criticism. H. L. A. Hart and Duncan Kennedy are only two of the more famous critics who have suggested that Blackstone was an apologist for the status quo, and that his recourse to natural law stifles rightful criticism of the law.[71]

Blackstone's adversaries, however, usually neglect the *Commentaries*' not infrequent criticisms of *specific* laws, from military law to laws on gambling.[72] And importantly, they neglect Blackstone's arguments on the rightful bounds of the state, including its use of the death penalty. Divine and natural laws, says Blackstone, suggest that capital punishment may be appropriate for crimes that are *mala in se*; that is, the death penalty may be acceptable, or even required, for crimes "bad in themselves," such as murder and rape.[73] But there is no natural sanction for inflicting capital punishment "at will and discretion of the human legislature."[74] For "no individual has, naturally, a power of inflicting death."[75] In an era when theft and forgery were capital offenses, Blackstone critiques the practice of his age and undermines the supposed right of the state to determine, without limitation, the punishment of crimes.[76]

[70]   Jeremy Bentham, *A Fragment on Government*, ed. J. H. Burns and H. L. A. Hart (Cambridge: Cambridge University Press, 1988). First published in 1776, Bentham criticizes Blackstone for his apathy to reform and casts legislation – and not common law – as rational and reforming.

[71]   Duncan Kennedy, *The Structure of Blackstone's Commentaries*, 28 Buff. L. Rev 209 (1979); H. L. A. Hart, *Blackstone's Use of the Law of Nature*, 3 Butt. S. Afr. L. Rev. 169 (1956). For Hart's broader statement of the moral grounds for separating law and morality, see "Positivism and the Separation of Law and Morals," 49–87 in *Essays in Jurisprudence and Philosophy* (Oxford: Clarendon Press, 1983). Daniel Boorstin suggests that Blackstone's conservatism relied on unsubstantiated beliefs that the law is "witness to the power of man's reason, to the beauty of English institutions, and, ultimately, to the Intelligence of God." *Mysterious Science*, 23.

[72]   Blackstone discusses military law at *Commentaries* 1 *413–16, 421, and gambling laws at *Commentaries* 4 *171. It is certainly true that Blackstone did not criticize the legal system as a whole. Nonetheless, he condemned statutes relating to the poor as inadequate and imperfect. Such is "the fate that has generally attended most of our statute laws," he says, "when they have not the foundation of the common law to build on." *Commentaries* 1, *365. In general, indeed, Blackstone was strongly aware of the inadequacies of criminal law. "Those who still believe in the legend spread by Bentham, that Blackstone was an uncritical optimist who defended all things established, should read the Fourth Book of his Commentaries." Holdsworth, *History of English Law*, 11:579.

[73]   "With regard to offences mala in se, capital punishments are in some instances inflicted by the immediate command of God himself to all mankind; as, in the case of murder, by the precept delivered to Noah, their common ancestor and representative, 'whoso sheddeth man's blood, by man shall his blood be shed.' In other instances they are inflicted after the example of the creator, in his positive code of laws for the regulation of the Jewish Republic; as in the case of the crime against nature." Commentaries 4, *9.

[74]   Ibid.

[75]   Ibid.

[76]   See, Commentaries 4, *9–12, *17–19.

Distinguishing Natural Law and Common Law

Believing natural law to structure the law of England, and to serve, with divine law, as one of its foundations, Blackstone devotes little time to distinguishing natural law from English common law.[77] In his treatment of laws, penalties, and procedures, natural law and common law are combined or separated depending on immediate context. For instance, he suggests that the measure of human punishments "can never be absolutely determined by any standing invariable rule," and therefore it should be left to human legislators to consider what is "warranted by the laws of nature and society."[78] But when considering the adjudication of municipal law, he suggests that, while offenses arise from breach of "the revealed law of God, others against the law of nature, and some ... against neither," in the common-law legal system it is best to consider all offenses as punishable based solely on "the law of man."[79] By this he seems to mean that, while the *source* of an offense's illegality is the natural law (or human law where natural law is indifferent), courts administer all laws, irrespective of source, as part of the municipal, human processes of justice.

The interwoven relationship of natural law and common law, however, does find sustained, if indirect, exposition as Blackstone considers the nature of property in *Of the Rights of Things*, book two of the *Commentaries*. The right of property, he suggests, is "that sole and despotic dominion which one man claims and exercises over the external things of the world, in total exclusion of the right of any other individual in the universe."[80] Few people, however, care to think too hard about the origins of property, he says, and when they do, they tend to think about the most immediate origin of a particular thing. They ask: From whom did I inherit this land? And, perhaps, if pushed, they consider the positive law and its rules of inheritance.

Few consider, however, that "accurately and strictly speaking ... there is no foundation in nature" for receiving property on the basis of words in the last will and testament of a previous owner, or in following the general rules for inheritance.[81] Following Pufendorf, Blackstone affirms instead that the right to property comes from *possession*, with that right accruing to "he who first

---

[77] See John Finnis, *Blackstone's Theoretical Intentions*, 12 Am. J. Jurs. 163 (1967). Richard Cosgrove argues, alternatively, that Blackstone looks "backwards" to natural law and "forwards" to positivism. *Scholars of the Law: English Jurisprudence from Blackstone to Hart* (New York: New York University Press, 1996), 21–49.

[78] Commentaries 4, *12.

[79] Commentaries 4, *42.

[80] Commentaries 2, *2. See Carol A. Rose, *Canons of Property Talk, or, Blackstone's Anxiety*, 108 Yale. L. J. 601 (1998).

[81] Ibid.

began to use it," and continuing "for the same time only that the act of possession lasted."[82]

But why should possession or occupancy determine ownership? For an answer, Blackstone surveys the positions of a number of modern natural lawyers. In Grotius and Pufendorf's thought, he says, a right of possession or occupancy "is founded upon a tacit and implied assent of all mankind."[83] "Barbeyrac, Titus, Mr. Locke, and others," in contrast, hold the view that there is no implied assent, but that "the very act of occupancy, alone, being a degree of bodily labour, is from a principle of justice ... sufficient of itself to gain title."[84] Blackstone the lawyer, however, suggests that any dispute on this point "favours too much of nice and scholastic refinement!"[85] For his legal purposes, it is enough to say that occupancy is the grounds for property.

Having established the grounds for property in possession by harmonizing the views of modern natural lawyers, Blackstone recognizes, however, that human positive law stands in tension with natural law. If possession is indeed the key to property in Blackstone's account, then it makes sense that "on the death of the possessor the estate should again become common" to the mass of humanity.[86] But Blackstone notes that, "for the sake of civil peace," the positive laws of "almost every nation (which is a kind of secondary law of nature)" provide for rules of inheritance to property.[87] Nonetheless, such rules are "creatures of the civil polity, and juris positivi merely."[88]

In considering the law of property, then, Blackstone does not treat the first principles of natural law as a trump card; the first principles do not override other justifications for laws.[89] Positive law wins out in practice. True, rules for inheritance receive support from the widespread practice codified in the laws of nations, a "secondary natural law," but tensions remain. We should not think of Blackstone as blind to this problem, however. While some contemporary natural law proponents expect to derive timeless precepts from the operation of human reason, would-be natural lawyers through the centuries

---

82   Commentaries 2, *3, citing "Barbeyr, Puff. 1. 4. C. 3." (Barbeyrac's preface notes to, and his translation of, Pufendorf's *Of the Law of Nature and Nations*.)

83   Commentaries 2, *8.

84   Ibid.

85   Ibid.

86   Ibid., *9.

87   Ibid., *13,*10. There remain types of property subject to the law of nature directly, says Blackstone. These include: unclaimed land, certain kinds of right of water, and wild animals. Ibid., *18, *390.

88   Ibid., *211.

89   See Ronald Dworkin, "Rights as Trumps," in *Theories of Rights*, ed. Jeremy Waldron (Oxford: Oxford University Press, 1984), 153.

have repeatedly posited situations in which law will part company with the ideals of natural law. Private property, indeed, has long been the primary locus of this discussion. Seemingly scripturally warranted, and affirmed by the leading authority of their age, for scholastic natural lawyers private property was an accommodation to human society necessary because of the effects of sin: Given our fallen nature, they said, it is now impossible for human beings to follow natural law's ideal of property in common.[90]

What Blackstone's position entails is that the law of property requires defending; precisely because the law of property deviates from natural law, arguments must be made on its behalf. Even if, as Pufendorf suggests, modification to the doctrine of occupancy is "very justly and reasonably" done, and does not take away any present property rights – but merely "abridges ... one means of acquiring a future property" – the laws of society nonetheless still deprive citizens of a natural right.[91] Natural law, therefore, may establish a right to property, says Blackstone. But the details require civil enactment. And such details are sometimes worked out in tension with natural rights, or even contradiction. With such enactment comes uncertainty, and the temptation to claim for nature decidedly human policies. For "we often mistake for nature what we find established by long and inveterate custom."[92] Natural law may explain and stabilize human laws, then, but it likewise renders them contingent and revisable.

BLACKSTONE'S RECEPTION IN AMERICA

As we have seen, Blackstone's *Commentaries* organized and explicated the law of England through the structure of modern natural law. Most straightforwardly the *Commentaries* asserted that English law was in conformity with natural law. More importantly, natural law, with its attention to rights and duties and its deployment of concepts (not particular procedure) structured Blackstone's text and its discussion of important crimes, practices, and principles.

The *Commentaries'* natural-law presentation of English common law, we shall see, found an audience in America. It met Americans' natural-law expectations for law and governance, justified continued adherence to the

---

[90] See Jean Porter, *Natural and Divine Law: Reclaiming the Tradition for Christian Ethics* (Grand Rapids, MI: Eerdmans, 1999), 253–55.

[91] *Commentaries* 2 *412.

[92] Ibid., *11.

common-law tradition, and served as a guide for legal practice in the new nation.

There is some irony that the chief legacy of Blackstone, the English conservative, is in America.[93] Certainly, the success of the *Commentaries* came despite and not because of William Blackstone the man. As a member of parliament, he was not sympathetic to the colonials' cause. He opposed the repeal of the Stamp Act of 1765, and in the *Commentaries* he denies that the American colonists share the liberties of Englishmen. The American colonies, he insists, are not part of the mother country, but dominions.[94] And yet – if Edmund Burke is correct – by the time of the Revolution, nearly as many copies of the *Commentaries* had been sold in the American colonies as in England.[95] Certainly, 1,000 English copies had been sold in the colonies prior to the publication of Robert Bell's first American edition of 1771–72.[96] To date, a further 139 American editions have been printed, together with 141 abridgments and extracts.[97]

Blackstone reached an influential audience. Subscribers to the first American edition included John Adams and John Jay.[98] Justices and judges

---

[93] Blackstone's influence in England was soon diminished: first by Jeremy Bentham's attacks on his conservatism; and next by John Austin and other students of an emerging legal positivism, who rejected Blackstone's appeals to nature. Meanwhile, in the United States, one in thirteen cases before the U.S. Supreme Court from 2000 to 2012 referenced Blackstone. Allen, "Reading Blackstone," 218.

[94] Writing of *The Countries subject to the Laws of England*, Blackstone suggests: "But in conquered or ceded countries, that have already laws of their own, the king may indeed alter and change those laws; but, till he does actually change them, the antient laws of the country remain, unless such as are against the law of God, as in the case of an infidel country.

OUR American plantations are principally of this [] sort, being obtained in the last century either by right of conquest and driving out the natives (with what natural justice I shall not at present enquire) or by treaties. And therefore the common law of England, as such, has no allowance or authority there; they being no part of the mother country, but distinct (though dependent) dominions." Blackstone, Commentaries 1, *105.

[95] "Speech on Moving His Resolutions for Conciliation with the Colonies (March 22, 1775)" in *The Works of the Right Honorable Edmund Burke*, rev. ed., vol. 2 (Boston: Little, Brown, 1865), 125. Burke concluded that the study of law was one of the circumstances that had engendered the colonists' "fierce spirit of liberty." Ibid., 120, 127.

[96] David Lockmiller, *Sir William Blackstone* (Chapel Hill: University of North Carolina Press, 1938), 170. Bell's Philadelphia edition reprinted the fourth Oxford edition of 1770.

[97] Ann Jordan Laeuchli, *A Bibliographical Catalog of William Blackstone*, ed. James Mooney (Buffalo, NY: William S. Hein for Yale Law Library, 2015). In comparison, there were fifty-seven English editions, and seventy-three abridgments and extracts.

[98] As Dennis Nolan notes: "In all, 16 of the subscribers became signatories of the Declaration of Independence, six were delegates to the 1787 Constitutional Convention, one was elected President of the United States and another became Chief Justice of the Supreme Court." *Sir William Blackstone and the New American Republic: A Study of Intellectual Impact*, 51 N.Y. U L. Rev. 731, 743–44 (1976).

in the new Republic acknowledged their reliance on the *Commentaries*, not least John Marshall (1755–1835) and Joseph Story (1779–1845).[99] And if ordinary American lawyers could have avoided Blackstone in the various legal treatises of their day, they would have been surely negligent if they missed him in the cases: from 1789 to 1915, Blackstone's *Commentaries* were cited some 10,000 times. Indeed, beyond the law proper, across all literature in the "founding era" from 1760 to 1805, Blackstone was the second most cited secular author, after Montesquieu and before John Locke.[100]

A list of names and numbers cannot suffice as a history of the *Commentaries'* reception. Care is needed. Claiming too much for Blackstone is a tempting, if familiar, trap. With more or less evidence, a litany of voices has lauded him as "the prime influence on the Declaration of Independence, the United States Constitution, the reception of the common law in America and the development of American legal education."[101] Today, Blackstone functions for many as the authoritative recorder of the law at the time of the Constitution's writing. But more than this, he is an *idea*. For some, Blackstone is usefully invoked for antiquarian reasons – a piece of Anglo-American nostalgia – but for other mostly conservative voices, he is the claimed authority for the necessary congruence of state and federal laws with the founders' ideals, or even the law of God.[102]

But neither should too little be claimed for Blackstone. The *Commentaries* found fertile ground in the American colonies and new Republic for good reason. Its volumes were the needed repository and organizer of the law Americans had known.[103] A common-law system requires precedent. Even when making determinations based on statutes, judges must provide answers

---

[99] Ibid., 756.
[100] Indeed, Locke is a poor third, cited two and a half times less frequently than Blackstone. Donald Lutz, "The Relative Influence of European Writers on Late Eighteenth-Century American Political Thought," *Political Science Review* 78, no. 1 (1984): 189–97. See also the Liberty Fund's account of the founding fathers' libraries, last modified April 16, 2016, http://oll .libertyfund.org/pages/founding-father-s-library.
[101] This is the "popular mind" on Blackstone that Dennis Nolan seeks to disrupt. *Blackstone*, 731–32.
[102] Blackstone, after all, claimed that human law's validity comes from the law of nature, and that the law of nature is God's will. Commentaries 1, *39. Myriad conservative political and legal groups are named for, or invoke, Blackstone. One example is the Blackstone Legal Fellowship – a program of the Alliance Defending Freedom – founded to respond to the successes of the "progressive" American Civil Liberties Union. The fellowship coordinates and funds legal strategies to protect what the Alliance Defending Freedom understands to be religious freedom, the sanctity of human life, and traditional family values.
[103] One reason that Blackstone's influence in America was greater than in England was simply that a broader range of material was available in England; Mary Ann Glendon, *Rights Talk: The Impoverishment of Political Discourse* (New York: Free Press, 1991), 23. For busy

in circumstances not treated by the bare text of legislation. Colonial history had bred common-law minds in American lawyers and officials: They looked for precedent and analogy, and as no official American law reports were available until 1789, in the young Republic they found in Blackstone a sound, accessible guide to the common law as it stood.[104]

American Natural-Law Assumptions

The *Commentaries'* successful transplant to American soil was possible because of widely held, commonsensical assumptions about natural law. In the background culture of many Americans, irrespective of education – although made evident with more precision through collegiate education, or heard more clearly in the debates of statesmen and the sermons of preachers – was a distinction between those rights bestowed by nature and those bestowed by men.[105] Early Americans knew that freedom of speech was a natural right, existing in a state of nature, whereas habeas corpus and jury rights were acquired, as rights put into law in civil society for the purpose of restraining government. Blackstone both contributed to this natural-law common sense and was received as authoritative because his *Commentaries* accepted and reflected it.[106]

More precisely, both Blackstone's work and the thought-world of the early American Republic were pervaded by *modern* natural law, best known to us, as to them, in the writings of Hugo Grotius, Thomas Hobbes, Samuel Pufendorf, and John Locke. If most Americans were unaware of the differing details of the

---

practitioners, "[t]he easiest course to pursue" was to follow Blackstone "where constitutions or legislatures had not spoken." Alfred Zantzinger Reed, *Training for the Public Profession of the Law: Historical Development and Principal Contemporary Problems of Legal Education in the United States* (New York: Carnegie Foundation for the Advancement of Teaching, 1921), 111.

[104] Ephraim Kirby, *Reports of Cases Adjudged in the Superior Court of the State of Connecticut from the year 1785, to May 1788* (Litchfield, CT: Collier & Adam, 1789). Informal reports had circulated prior to independence. See Erwin Surrency, *Law Reports in the United States*, 25 Am. J. Legal Hist. 48 (1981). R. H. Helmholz reports that the colonies of Maryland and Pennsylvania had printed law reports prior to independence, and that the State of Connecticut was joined by Delaware, New Jersey, New York, North Carolina, South Carolina, Vermont, and Virginia in having printed reports prior to 1800. Printed federal reports began in 1789–90. *Natural Law in Court*, 22on4.

[105] Philip Hamburger examines the "simplified, generalized theory" of natural law and natural rights that "Americans often learned in school, [. . .] repeated and had reinforced in sermons and secular political arguments," and which therefore functioned as unexplained assumptions for many Americans in the eighteenth century. *Natural Law, Natural Rights, and American Constitutions*, 102 Yale L.J. 907, 915 (1993).

[106] By "common sense" I mean here simply the sociological reality of the general views within a community, held widely and usually unreflectively. Or, rather, more particularly: I mean the conglomeration of sense, feeling, and judgment underlying such generally held views.

various positions held by the modern natural lawyers – and Blackstone, we have seen, elided them – the common sense of the age embraced modern natural law's basic shared claim that, amid the conflict of competing personal interests, adherence to the natural law secures self-preservation and maintains the social order. Americans knew that adherence to the natural law was to their mutual advantage: keeping them safe in their beds and cooperative in the civic square and marketplace.

Anti-British Feeling

This natural-law common sense, then, was the cultural background to Blackstone's initial success in America. Nothing about this success, however, was inevitable. Indeed, the political circumstances militated against it. While the Revolutionary War was many things, in popular sentiment, at least, it was a repudiation of British rule and the various apparatuses of that rule, English law included.[107]

And yet the colonists were, with their British rulers, co-inheritors of a common-law tradition, and heirs to the previous century's debates on the so-called ancient constitution understood as ensuring Englishmen's liberty.[108] The famous *Dr. Bonham's Case* was invoked in the colonies, for instance, to argue that Acts of Parliament could be void if offensive to natural reason. Edward Coke, Chief Justice of the King's Bench, had said after all that:

> [I]n many cases, the common law will control Acts of Parliament, and some times adjudge them to be utterly void: for when an Act of Parliament is against common right and reason, or repugnant, or impossible to perform, the common law will control it, and adjudge such Act to be void.[109]

The 1657 Boston case of *Giddings* v. *Brown* is but the first clear evidence of an American court declaring a particular legislative act invalid on the strength

---

[107] "In the first flush of enthusiastic independence from the mother country, there was a strong movement to repudiate all traces of the English common law." Reed, *Training*, 110. Indeed, Reed suggests that because of the extent of the repudiation of common law in the new Republic "[i]t is hardly an exaggeration to say that what we actually took over from England was simply Blackstone." Ibid., 111.

[108] A now classic treatment is J. G. A. Pocock, *The Ancient Constitution and the Feudal Law: A Study of English Historical Thought in the Seventeenth Century* (Cambridge: Cambridge University Press, 1957).

[109] *Dr. Bonham's Case* (C.P. 1610); Coke, Reports 8:118a (modernized spelling). The right interpretation of the case is much debated.

of Coke's words.[110] A century later, James Otis in the *Writs of Assistance* case could argue that "an Act against natural Equity is void."[111] And John Adams, who recorded Otis's words, could later contend that "Reason & the Constitution are against this Writ"; "[n]o Acts of Parliament can establish such a writ; Though it should be made in the very words of the petition it would be void, AN ACT AGAINST THE CONSTITUTION IS VOID."[112]

As late as 1766, indeed, George Mason explained to London merchants that it was "the liberty and privileges of Englishmen" that properly undergirded the colonists' reactions to the taxation imposed by the Sugar Act of 1764, Stamp Act of 1765, and Quartering Act of 1765.[113] Nonetheless, in the new American Republic, factions sought to repudiate the remaining traces of British rule, particularly those, like the common law, considered lacking in principled reason. Seeking to begin America's story afresh and make America's laws accord with reason, state legislators in Kentucky, Pennsylvania, and elsewhere passed "noncitation acts" forbidding state judges from recourse to English precedents.[114]

However, the Enlightenment sensibility that animated opposition to the adoption or retention of the seemingly chaotic and tradition-laden English common law was the same sensibility Americans found in the writings of Blackstone, the common law's champion. His *Commentaries* commended the common law to them as an organized system governed by principle and not the ad hoc collection of rules they thought they knew. True, states adopted

---

[110] See, Thomas Hutchinson, *Hutchinson Papers* (Albany, NY: Printed for the Prince Society by J. Munsell, 1865), 2:1–15.

[111] *Petition of Lechmere* (Feb. 1761) in *Legal Papers of John Adams*, ed. L. Kinvin Wroth and Hiller B. Zobel (Cambridge, MA: Belknap Press of Harvard University, 1965), 2:127.

[112] See M. H. Smith, *The Writs of Assistance Case* (Berkeley: University of California Press, 1978); and Philip Hamburger, *Law and Judicial Duty* (Cambridge, MA: Harvard University Press, 2008), "Colonial Departures," 255–80.

[113] George Mason, "Letter to the Committee of Merchants in London (June 6, 1766)" in *The Life of George Mason, 1725–1792, Including His Speeches, Public Papers, and Correspondence*, ed. Kate Mason Rowland (New York: G. P. Putnam's Sons, 1892), 1:387.

[114] Nathan Isaacs examines the noncitation acts by looking at: *Turnpike Co. v. Rutter*, 4 Serg. and R. (Pa.) 6 (1818); Morehead and Brown (Kentucky), Statutes, 613 (1807); *Hickman v. Boffman*, Hardin's Rep (Ky) 348, 356, 364; and *Gallatin v. Bradford*, Hardin's Rep. 365, note (1808). "The Merchant and His Law," *Journal of Political Economy* 23, no. 6 (1915): 529–61, 541.

Thomas Jefferson's antipathy toward the practice of Lord Mansfield provided him a further, pragmatic, reason to shift Americans' eyes from Westminster and its courts. "I hold it essential in America to forbid that any English decision should ever be cited in a court, which has happened since the accession of Ld. Mansfield to the bench. Because tho' there have come many good ones from him, yet there is so much sly poison instilled into a great part of them, that it is better to proscribe the whole." "From Thomas Jefferson to John Brown Cutting (October 2, 1788)," in March-October 7, 1788, vol. 13 of *The Papers of Thomas Jefferson*, ed. Julian Boyd (Princeton, NJ: Princeton University Press, 1956).

written, codified constitutions – when Britain had none – but Americans did not, after all, opt for the statutory codes that formed European civil law.[115] Americans kept the common law.

Blackstone as Guide

The formal and principled coherence of Blackstone's work, the coherence that rendered the common law acceptable to Enlightenment minds, also made it a straightforward guide for students and practitioners in the new Republic. The success of the *Commentaries*, therefore, was not predetermined by the work's legal quality or literary grace, although Blackstone was praised for both. Providing principle and structure to the legal system, the *Commentaries* met the concerns of the time for intellectual coherence and the practical needs of students and practitioners. Indeed, when required, they could turn quickly to chapter XVI of the first volume, *Of the Rights of Persons*, to learn the law "Of PARENT and CHILD," or to chapter XII of the third volume, *Of Private Wrongs*, for the law "Of TRESPASS."

If Blackstone's work was to continue to function as a repository of the content of the law, however, it needed re-presentation. Even if based in principle, the common law develops through the refinement of cases. With his 1803 edition, St. George Tucker was just the first to keep the *Commentaries* up to date. Tucker rendered its volumes more fully American by adding 1,000 footnotes emending and contextualizing Blackstone's text.[116] A pattern was set. Well into the nineteenth century, Americans offered, in effect, commentaries on the *Commentaries*. When updating and annotating the text finally proved too cumbersome – and James Kent (1763–1847) and Joseph Story (1779–1847) came to offer home-grown alternatives – the *Commentaries* slipped from the prescriptive to the historical: a book consulted for what the law *is* became a record of what the law once *was*.

Yet what the law *was* is of no small interest in a system predicated on precedent. And if one subscribes to theories of constitutional interpretation that treat as authoritative the Constitution's understood meaning at the time of

[115] Reed, *Training*, 111. Debates about replacing the common law with a written civil code were not over, however, and were particularly fierce in the decades following the Civil War. The desire for codification continued, and found twentieth-century expression in the Uniform Commercial Code and Restatement projects, which seek to harmonize legal rules across the states. See Lewis Grossman, *Langdell Upside-Down: James Coolidge Carter and the Anticlassical Jurisprudence of Anticodification*, 19 Yale J.L. & Human. 149, 152–56 (2013).

[116] *Blackstone's Commentaries: With Notes of Reference to the Constitution and Laws, of the Federal Government of the United States, and of the Commonwealth of Virginia*, 5 vols. (Philadelphia: William Young Birch and Abraham Small, 1803).

its promulgation, Blackstone's importance is greater still.[117] With the exception of 1801 to 1810, *today* the U.S. Supreme Court cites the *Commentaries* more often than at any time since the founding of the Republic.[118]

* * *

Blackstone organized the common law. He did so by structuring the law around rights and principles known in the natural-law tradition. This hitherto unknown cohesion commended common law to Americans at a Revolutionary moment when the rejection of common law – intellectually and politically – was possible, even likely.

Recognizing today that a common-law legal system can be outlined and explained in reference to natural law is, itself, an achievement (given the broadly positivistic terrain of analysis of the common law).[119] Blackstone offers an example, then, for how natural law can serve to describe the ultimate sources or justifications for human law as a system. But he does more. He offers natural-law tools for structuring the body of law and justifying or critiquing common law's specific enactments, defenses, and punishments.

We have seen, however, that Blackstone does not merely apply natural law to common law. Whether we like the result or not, he suggests that, *in matters of legal determination*, human law is in conversation with natural law. And this conversation, he suggests, is not one in which natural law necessarily has the final word. One result is that natural law may explain and stabilize human laws while simultaneously rendering them contingent and revisable. Given the realities of sin, says Blackstone, human reason must be suitably modest in its claims to track natural law's revelation of God's reason and will.

---

[117] For just one recent use of Blackstone – as representative of the thought of the U.S. founders – see then-Judge Neil Gorsuch, *Williams* v. *Trammell*, 782 F.3d 1184, 1220 (10th Cir. 2015). In fact, in appealing to a variety of common law sources (including Matthew Hale and Francis Bacon), Gorsuch is more sophisticated in his use of Blackstone than most of his peers on the bench. For the range of sources known to the founders, see *The Founders' Constitution*, ed. Philip Kurland and Ralph Lerner (Chicago: University of Chicago Press, 1987).

[118] Allen, "Reading Blackstone," 218.

[119] In her *Law's Virtues*, Cathleen Kaveny offers one contemporary model for what can thereafter be achieved. She treats commitments to autonomy and solidarity as fundamental to the contemporary shape of American law. (Washington, DC: Georgetown University Press, 2012).

4

Subsuming Natural Law into Common Law

Joseph Story

For most of America's history, becoming a lawyer has required "purely practical training" with little time or attention given to the principled content of
the law, common or natural.[1] To practice law in America, first you appren-
ticed. Professional legal education – with few exceptions – consisted of learning the ropes with a local judge or practicing lawyer.[2] The tasks and
expectations of these apprenticeships, even their basic structure, differed
significantly across counties and states, but it was the diligence, or otherwise,
of the "master" that most determined the content and quality of education.
Some apprenticeships were primarily an exercise of observation, with apprentices picking up rules of thumb and basic procedure along the way.[3] Other
masters set their apprentices structured programs of reading. In his "rules to be
observed by students of law" from the 1820s, Massachusetts Chief Justice
Lemuel Shaw required weekly reports from his apprentices on their reading
over the last seven days.[4] Whatever the form of the apprenticeship, however,

[1] Josef Redlich, *The Common Law and the Case Method in American University Law Schools:
A Report to the Carnegie Foundation for the Advancement of Teaching* (New York:
The Foundation, 1914), 7. For a brief overview of the role of natural law in American legal
education, see R. H. Helmholz, "Legal Education in the United States," in his *Natural Law in
Court: A History of Legal Theory in Practice*, 127–41 (Cambridge, MA: Harvard University Press,
2015).

[2] Before the Revolution, some Americans trained at London's Inns of Court. For brief overviews
of apprenticeship, see Lawrence Friedman, *A History of American Law*, 3rd ed. (New York:
Simon & Schuster, 2005): 226–50; and William Johnson, *Schooled Lawyers: A Study in the
Clash of Professional Cultures* (New York: New York University Press, 1978), 42–58. For a case
study, see Charles McKirdy, *The Lawyer as Apprentice: Legal Education in Eighteenth-Century
Massachusetts*, 28 J. Legal Educ. 124 (1976).

[3] Roscoe Pound, *The Place of Justice Story in the Making of American Law*, 1 Mass. L.Q. 135, 140
(1916).

[4] Frederick Hathaway Chase, *Lemuel Shaw, Chief Justice of the Supreme Court of
Massachusetts, 1830–1860* (Boston: Houghton Mifflin, 1918), 120–21.

local judges or practicing lawyers, irrespective of the jurisdiction, almost always administered examinations for entry into the profession.[5] It was this combination of "on-the-job" training and examination by leaders at the bar that formed the norm for most American lawyers until the end of the nineteenth century, and, indeed, to this day, it is possible in several states to qualify for practice by undertaking supervision under an experienced attorney.[6]

By the final decades of the 1700s, though, those at the pinnacle of the profession sought more consistently high quality legal education. Educators at the College of New Jersey in Princeton, we saw earlier, endeavored to transform the college into a site of legal training. President John Witherspoon (1723–94) urged graduates – including James Madison – to return to Princeton to "fit themselves for any of the higher Branches to which they will think proper chiefly to devote further application."[7] Witherspoon promised, moreover, to offer lectures on "Composition, and the Eloquence of the Pulpit and Bar," and the possibility of an independent study program, in effect, in which the student was to "chuse his own Studies" in tandem with "Lists and Characters of the Principal Writers on any Branch" of higher learning.[8]

Whatever its merits, this model of self-directed study, however, did not rival the apprenticeship system. It would take the creation of the new institutions of the proprietary and university law schools to do so.

PROPRIETARY SCHOOLS

Following the Revolution, the increasing technical complexity of the laws of the new states and the emerging federal government – products of changing economic and social structures, not least urbanization and industrialization – provoked a shift in legal education. Elite would-be lawyers looked for more systematic instruction, and entrepreneurial attorneys set up schools for this

[5]   For a very brief overview see Robert Stevens, "Once Upon a Time," in *Law School: Legal Education in America from the 1850s to the 1980s*, 3–19 (Chapel Hill: University of North Carolina Press, 1983).
[6]   California is the most significant jurisdiction in which it is possible to qualify for legal practice by apprenticeship. The requirements for admission are contained in the *Rules of the State Bar of California*, Title 4 – Admissions and Education Standards, Division 1, Chapter 3, Rule 4.29. Rule 4.29 adopted effective September 1, 2008; amended effective November 14, 2009.
[7]   See his December 1, 1773 letter to William Bradford in 16 *March 1751–16 December 1779*, vol. 1 of *The Papers of James Madison*, ed. William Hutchinson and William Rachal (Chicago: University of Chicago Press, 1962), 100–102.
[8]   "For the Information of the Public. By Order of the Trustees of the College of New-Jersey," in *Extracts from American Newspapers, Relating to New Jersey, 1768–1769*, vol. VII of *Documents Relating to the Colonial History of the State of New Jersey*, ed. William Nelson (Paterson, NJ: Call Printing and Publishing, 1904), 306.

purpose. The product, a "proprietary school" – owned by a lawyer-teacher – functioned as "essentially a specialized and elaborated law office," such that apprentices were only somewhat recast as students.[9] This form of professional education left to the colleges the teaching of philosophy or government as it pertained to law. And yet, in their attention to the details of common-law practice, the proprietary schools operated within a framework that assumed, and perhaps even required, natural law. We see this clearly when we look to the most famous of the proprietary schools: the Litchfield Law School.

Set up in Litchfield, Connecticut, in 1784, the Litchfield Law School was not the first law school in America, but it was the first to teach students from all across the new nation and the first to gain a national reputation.[10] Tapping Reeve (1744–1823), its founder, owner, and teacher, exercised a national influence on legal education, particularly through his presentation of the common law as a principled system.

The curriculum at Litchfield would have been "unthinkable," says John Langbein, without Blackstone's *Commentaries*.[11] What allowed Reeve to teach students beyond the local Connecticut context was Blackstone's cosmopolitanism. The conflation of common law and natural law in Blackstone's work gave universality to the seemingly parochial rules he outlined. At the Litchfield School, said Yale's president Timothy Dwight IV, "[l]aw is taught ... as a science; and not merely, nor principally, as a mechanical business; not as a collection of loose, independent fragments, but as a regular, well-compacted system."[12] Based on the evidence of student notebooks of the 1790s, we can see that Reeve taught sequences of lectures under distinct headings: nine lectures on the law of husbands and wives, for instance,

---

[9]   Alfred Zantzinger Reed, *Training for the Public Profession of the Law: Historical Development and Principal Contemporary Problems of Legal Education in the United States* (New York: Carnegie Foundation for the Advancement of Teaching, 1921), 49, 128. See Charles McManis, *The History of First Century American Legal Education: A Revisionist Perspective*, 59 Wash. U. L.Q. 597 (1981); Rosco Pound, *The Achievement of the American Law School*, 38 Dicta 269 (1961).

[10] See Marian McKenna, *Tapping Reeve and the Litchfield Law School* (New York: Oceana, 1986). From the roughly 1,000 students who attended, two became vice presidents of the United States, fourteen became governors, and more than 10 percent served in Congress. Three joined the bench of the United States Supreme Court, and at least thirty-four were members of their states' highest courts. Samuel Fisher, *Litchfield Law School, 1774–1833: Biographical Catalogue of Students* (New Haven, CT: Yale University Press, 1946).

[11] John Langbein, "Blackstone, Litchfield, and Yale: The Founding of the Yale Law School," in *History of the Yale Law School: The Tercentennial Lectures*, ed. Anthony Kronman (New Haven, CT: Yale University Press, 2004), 27.

[12] "Learning, Morals, &c. of New-England, Letter II" in *Travels in New-England and New-York*, vol. 4 (New Haven, CT: Timothy Dwight, 1821–22), 306.

and nineteen on contracts. Students heard lectures, yes, but they also copied essays and drew charts comparing English law with the law of Connecticut. Student Asa Bacon's notebook contains a comparison chart running 117 pages.[13]

The natural-law framework of Reeve's common law instruction allowed the Litchfield School to teach students from across various jurisdictions, despite differences in the states' legal rules. And continuities between English law and law in America remained possible – despite the political break – because precedents in common law can always be distinguished: In the common law, the judicial decisions, which constitute authoritative examples or rules for subsequent cases, are only binding in analogous situations.[14] New Americans, then, could at once accept English law as authoritative, yet – like Asa Bacon with his comparison table – could determine whether on-the-ground American facts rendered English precedents sufficiently disanalogous to be inapplicable.

Accordingly, America's first law treatise – *A System of the Laws of the State of Connecticut* – could mold its presentation of Connecticut's laws into the English pattern identified and laid out by Blackstone.[15] And the Litchfield curriculum – which set the standards for law school teaching long after the school's closure in 1833 – followed Blackstone's *Commentaries* too, albeit with notable changes, including the deletion of Blackstone's treatment of the English Constitution and public law.[16] Reeve was eulogized precisely for "refining our jurisprudence, by embodying the best principles and maxims of the English system, and rejecting such as were inapplicable in our local circumstances, or ill-adapted to the texture of our government."[17] While some parts of English law were just simply discarded, then, on the whole natural law and history justified the retention of English common law. And common-law

---

[13] Whitney Bagnall, Yale Law School Library Document Collection Center, Litchfield Law School Sources, "Composite Curriculum at Litchfield Law School Based on Lectures of Tapping Reeve, 1790–1798," published September 30, 2013, https://documents.law.yale.edu/litchfield-law-school-sources/composite-curriculum-litchfield-law-school-based-lectures-tapping-reeve-1790-1798.

[14] See Bryan Garner, et al., *The Law of Judicial Precedent* (St. Paul, MN: Thomson Reuters, 2016). For a discussion of the philosophy of the common law, see Neil McCormick, *Legal Reasoning and Legal Theory* (Oxford: Clarendon Press, 1978).

[15] Langbein, "Blackstone, Litchfield, and Yale," 27; Zephaniah Swift, *A System of Laws of the State of Connecticut: In Six Books* (Windham, CT: Printed by John Byrne for the author, 1795).

[16] Bagnall, "Litchfield Law School Sources."

[17] Lyman Beecher, *A Sermon Preached at the Funeral of the Hon. Tapping Reeve: Late Chief Justice of the State of Connecticut, Who Died December Thirteen, Eighteen Hundred and Twenty-Three, in the Eightieth Year of His Age, with Explanatory Notes* (Litchfield, CT: S. S. Smith, 1827), 5fn*.

judges' capacity to follow or distinguish precedents – through attention to the particularities of each individual case – allowed natural law-inflected common law to make continued sense in America.

UNIVERSITY LAW SCHOOLS

Proprietary schools like Tapping Reeve's in Litchfield embedded and perpetuated a common-law professional education that relied upon natural-law foundations. With the development of university law schools, however, arose possibilities that American professional legal education might explicitly engage the content of common law and natural law: treating the law in a liberal manner by interrogating the law humanistically, and seeking to advance the content of the law, not solely train its practitioners.[18]

Just such plans were imagined in New York in 1784. A University of New York was to be founded by adding faculties to the undergraduate King's College, now to be renamed Columbia College. A law faculty would have three professors: one concerned with "the Law of Nature and Nations"; another with "Roman Civil Law"; and the third with "Municipal Law" (that is, American domestic law).[19] A lack of funds stalled the project, however, and the scheme for a University of New York failed.

In the end, it was in Cambridge, Massachusetts, that the first recognizable university law school emerged when, in 1817 at Harvard, Asahel Stearns, a distinguished Boston lawyer, was appointed Professor of Law to teach students pursuing a degree of bachelor of laws.[20] Like the College of William and Mary and the University of Virginia, Harvard had a tradition of *college* professors of law, but 1817 saw something new: a separate school with its own separate faculty and degree program.[21]

---

[18] See Nolan, "Blackstone," 760.

[19] Reed, *Training*, 120.

[20] See Daniel Coquillette and Bruce Kimball, *On the Battlefield of Merit: Harvard Law School, The First Century* (Cambridge, MA: Harvard University Press, 2015); *The Centennial History of the Harvard Law School, 1817–1917* (Boston: Harvard Law School Association, 1918); Samuel Eliot, ed., *The Development of Harvard University since the Inauguration of President Eliot, 1869–1929*, (Cambridge, MA: Harvard University Press, 1930); and Arthur Sutherland, *The Law at Harvard: A History of Ideas and Men, 1817–1967* (Cambridge, MA: Belknap Press of Harvard University, 1967).

[21] Harvard determined in 1816 to allocate funds left in 1781 by Isaac Royall, Jr. to found a college professorship in law. Isaac Royall, "Will & Codicils," dated May 16, 1778, Harvard Law School Library, Cambridge, MA. See also Janet Halley, *My Isaac Royall Legacy*, 24 Harv. Blacklett. J. 118, 120n18 (2008).

The founding of Harvard Law School was partly the product of a campaign by Isaac Parker, the first holder of Harvard College's Royall chair in law. In 1816, in his inaugural address, Parker advocated that Harvard found "a school for the instruction of resident graduates in jurisprudence."[22] In his speech, Parker traced the development of law and the legal profession in America from its earlier "low state," as "a trade rather than a science," to his present day, suggesting that great nineteenth-century lawyers understood law to be "a comprehensive system of human wisdom, derived from the nature of man in his social and civil state, and founded on the everlasting basis of natural justice and moral philosophy."

This conception of law, Parker thought, was "worthy to be taught" at Harvard in "fellowship with its sister sciences." Law's "fundamental and general principles," he argued, were rightly to be treated as a "branch of liberal education in every country, but especially in those where freedom prevails and every citizen has an equal interest in its preservation and improvement." Parker's vision for Harvard, like Ezra Stiles's for college education at Yale and Reeve's for the training of lawyers at Litchfield, combined universal appeals to natural justice and a vision of law as a science with the particularities of the American experience and its traditions of liberty.

In the assessment of later generations, at least, early university legal education had a "dogmatic character."[23] Recitation of content was a central component. As at Litchfield, Blackstone's *Commentaries* "formed the almost exclusive basis of the work."[24] Students gained a systematic coverage of the content of the law, with the central subjects and principles of common law and equity expounded for their memorization. As too at Litchfield, in its earliest days Harvard Law School – despite the high-mindedness of Parker's vision – was a "glorified law office under the eaves of a university."[25] It sought to inculcate the craft of lawyering. If this was tedious work – seemingly involving little judgment or imagination – its systematicity promised students that in the common law they would find a unity of principles, reasonably organized under distinct heads.

---

[22] Isaac Parker, "Inaugural Address delivered in the Chapel of Harvard University," *North American Review & Miscellaneous Journal* 3, no. 7 (May 1816): 11–27.

[23] Redlich, *Common Law and the Case Method*, 8.

[24] Ibid., 6. The law school's early course of study was described by Stearns in 1825 as consisting of "[i]n the first place a reading of *Blackstone*, more or less particular, of the whole work. This practise has been found by experience to be highly useful. It aids the student in fixing his attention, enables him more readily to acquaintance with the technical terms and language of the law, and at the same time to obtain a more distinct view of that admirable outline of the science." "1825 Report of Professor Stearns to the Board of Overseers," in Warren, *History*, 333.

[25] Pound, "Place of Justice Story," 161.

Early advertisements for the new degree touted connections to college study of the law and Harvard's broader educational context. Students could "attend, free of expense," the various public lectures of the college's Royall Professor, private lectures designed for graduates on "Moral and Political Philosophy," and a whole host of public graduate lectures on "Theology, Rhetoric and Oratory, Philosophy, Natural and Experimental Philosophy, Astronomy, Chemistry, and Anatomy and Mineralogy."[26] Perhaps given its precursors in apprenticeship and the proprietary school, Harvard Law School struggled, however, to integrate such humanistic reflection on the law with study for professional practice. In 1825, Stearns distinguished between students heading to the bar and those who were not. "For those gentlemen who do not pursue the study of law as a profession," he offered an extended reading course on "the Civil Law, the Law of Nations, Constitutional Law and Political Economy" in the place of practice-related courses.[27]

The needs of "professional" students took priority, such that the province of law was seemingly trimmed at Harvard even under Joseph Story (1779–1845), the U.S. Supreme Court justice who penned an encyclopedia article on natural law, and whose judicial opinions made appeals to "eternal maxims of social justice."[28] Story's appointment as Dane Professor at Harvard Law School, nonetheless, revitalized the school.[29] His fame drew students. So too did shifts in legal and broader culture; for those with sufficient resources, education in Cambridge seemed more congenial than apprenticeship in a law office.[30] And for the more serious minded: No law office could compare with Harvard's libraries and their ever-increasing holdings of law reports and treatises. Story's nationalist outlook – prioritizing federal law over the states –

---

[26] "Boston Daily Advertiser, July 28, 1817," in Warren, *History*, 314–15. The law school itself was a lean operation confined to the lower north room of a low, two-story wooden building. Stearns's instruction was paid out of students' fees.

[27] "1825 Report of Professor Stearns to the Board of Overseers," in Warren, *History*, 333.

[28] See Story's opinion in *La Jeune Eugenie*, 26 F.Cas., 832, 846 (C.C.D. Mass. 1822); and also Christopher Eisgruber, *Justice Story, Slavery, and the Natural Law Foundations of American Constitutionalism*, 55 U. Chi. L. Rev. 273 (1988). The Harvard Corporation first invited Story to occupy a chair in 1820. Story declined. However, in 1829, Nathan Dane – author of the nine-volume *General Abridgment and Digest of American Law* – proposed that he would gift $10,000 of his publishing profits to Harvard on the condition that Story take up a chair. Story was convinced, and the school reorganized, with Story as Dane Professor and John Hooker Ashmun as Royall Professor. From 11 students in 1819, the school reached 163 by 1844. See Reed, *Training*, 143.

[29] Coquillette and Kimball, "The School Saved," 131–156, and "Joseph Story's Law School in the Young Republic," 157–188, in *On the Battlefield of Merit*.

[30] Friedman, *History of American Law*, 241; and R. Kent Newmeyer, *Supreme Court Justice Joseph Story: Statesman of the Old Republic* (Chapel Hill: University of North Carolina, 1985), 240.

fit too with the aspirations of Harvard and the legal profession for prestige across the Republic.

Story adhered to a view of common law as a collection of principles, indeed as a science, and taught "the Law of Nature" and "the Law of Nations" as two of the five "federal" courses of study.[31] These five, he thought, were in force across the Republic. Story deliberately focused on the common law developed by courts at the expense of statutes passed by legislatures. Despite his commitment to natural law, however, by 1832 the regular two-year course of legal study consisted solely of standard common law subjects and federal constitutional law to the exclusion, it seems, of broader reflection on the nature and purpose of law.[32]

What was true at Harvard was true elsewhere: Initial plans for the broad study of the law quickly gave way to practitioner-focused instruction. Columbia's 1857 plan for a law school, for instance, included courses in "Modern History, Political Economy, the Principles of Natural and International Law, Civil and Common Law, and the study of Cicero, Plato, and Aristotle."[33] Within a couple of years, however, the school claimed "a special emphasis on real estate law," with natural-law reflection confined to a solitary "Moral Philosophy" course taught by a professor borrowed from Columbia College.[34]

Not that the educational dream of directly connecting law with universal justice had dissipated. At regular intervals, in various institutions, there were

---

[31] The five were: "the Law of Nature, the Law of Nations, Maritime and Commercial Law, Equity Law, and, lastly, the Constitutional Law of the United States." *A Discourse pronounced upon the Inauguration of the Author, as Dane Professor of Law in Harvard University: on the Twenty-Fifth Day of August, 1829* (Boston: Hilliard, Gray, Little, and Wilkins, 1829), 41. And see Louis Brandeis, *The Harvard Law School*, 1 Green Bag 10, 14 (1880).

[32] "Under the lead of this most successful of American law schools the orthodox province of law school teaching was now defined. Politics and law were no longer to be joined." Reed, *Training*, 148–49.

[33] *A History of the School of Law, Columbia University, by the Staff of the Foundation for Research in Legal History, under the Direction of Julius Goebel, Jr.* (New York: Columbia University Press, 1955), 28.

[34] Columbia University School of Law, "Announcement," 1859; reference found in David Forte, *On Teaching Natural Law*, 29 J. Legal Educ. 413 (1978). His inaugural address offers a treatment of natural theology, and includes discussion of human nature and reason: "man is distinguished from the lower animals, and connected with the nature of angels and of God, by the reasoning faculty; and that, in the use of this faculty, all mankind – from the child to the sage, from the barbarian to the philosopher – are doing precisely the same thing in the self-same way – namely, deducing conclusions from premises." "Inaugural Address by Charles Murray Nairne, Professor Literature and Philosophy, February 1858," in *Addresses of the Newly-appointed Professors of Columbia College* (New York: Trustees of Columbia College, 1858), 156.

calls to reform and renew. Theodore Dwight Woolsey at Yale called for a place of "sound learning relating to the foundations of justice, the doctrine of government ... all those branches of knowledge which the most finished statesman and legislator ought to know."[35] And new establishments, like the Lumpkin School of Law in Athens, Georgia, solemnly declared that law would be taught "as far as in us lies ... not as a collection of arbitrary rules, but as a connected logical system, founded on principles that appeal for sanction to eternal truth."[36]

So where, then, did natural law go at Harvard?

JOSEPH STORY

If only the titles of courses are considered, we might think that professional legal education – spearheaded by Joseph Story at Harvard – focused solely on common-law doctrine. The collegiate tradition of teaching law together with philosophy and government, we might conclude, was left behind for the practice of lawyering. To think that way, however, is to ignore the various assumptions and practices of Story's day that cast common law as incorporating or subsuming natural law. It is just this relationship of common law and natural law that we will see in Story's treatment of law in general, natural law, the limits of natural law, and the place of natural law in the details of common law. Natural law *simpliciter* receives explicit attention as a source of law, moreover, when Story considers international law.

Joseph Story was a busy man. He served on the U.S. Supreme Court from 1812, and headed Harvard's law school from 1829. He also wrote at least thirteen major books. Together with James Kent (1763–1847), he was recognized in his time, and is recognized still, as the foremost American legal scholar of the early nineteenth century.[37] Story and Kent each provided

---

[35] *Historical Discourse* (New Haven, CT: Law Department of Yale College, 1874).

[36] Quoted in Gwen Wood, *A Unique and Fortuitous Combination: An Administrative History of the University of Georgia School of Law* (Athens: University of Georgia Press for University of Georgia Law School Association, 1998), 6.

[37] Kent's standard biography is John Horton, *James Kent: A Study in Conservatism, 1763–1847* (New York: Appleton-Century, 1939). See also John Langbein, *Chancellor Kent and the History of Legal Literature*, 93 Columb. L. Rev. 547 (1993). In his course of lectures at Columbia, Kent sought to "present a comprehensive, plain, and practical view of the principles of our municipal law." He did so through a trifold scheme: first, a general outline of the principle and usages of the law of nature; second, constitutional law of the United States; and, third, law of New York State. *A Lecture, Introductory to a Course of Law Lectures in Columbia College, delivered February 2, 1824* (New York: The College, 1824), 3. Kent's endeavor was to "give the study of the law, in our own state, a more accurate and scientific character, than it has hitherto usually received." Ibid., 4. He thought that if legal education

accessible but comprehensive treatises on the main branches of American law. These made common-law rules and precedents readily accessible to lawyers at a time when, as we will shortly see, the common law was under threat from ignorance and populism. In Roscoe Pound's estimation Kent and Story "saved the common law" in America.[38]

The first threat to common law was eminently practical: American lawyers in the early nineteenth century had significant difficulties in accessing, and understanding, the precedents that form the basis of common law. There were few reported American court decisions. So through multiple volumes, Kent and Story each laid out the law, making known American decisions, whenever possible, and making those decisions understandable by outlining their principled relationship to earlier English precedents. Offering both selected English cases – suitably annotated and cited – and appeals to natural law, Story and Kent provided the principles that American common law lacked.[39]

The second threat to common law emerged from the populist political atmosphere of the early nineteenth century. Common law – codified by judges, not the people or their elected representatives – found little favor from those who distrusted elites. Story's defense and promotion of common law was part and parcel of his broader belief that lawyers and courts form a necessary corrective to the excesses of politicians and legislatures.[40] The law, as he saw it, is a bulwark against the tyranny of the majority.[41] On the bench, in the lecture hall, and in his treatises, Story made the argument for common law, propounded a national jurisprudence that opposed states' rights, and read

---

was to prepare a student to be a lawyer and statesman, "He must not only be properly instructed in moral science, and adorned with the accomplishments of various learning; he must not only have his passions controlled by the disciplines of Christian truth, and his mind deeply initiated in the elementary doctrines of natural and public law, but he must be accurately taught in every great leading branch of our own domestic jurisprudence." Ibid., 7. Considering Story and Kent together, Friedman suggests that "[b]oth were erudite teachers and judges. Both had enormous reputations in their day. Both have since suffered a decline in prestige, and an irretrievable decline in their readership. In their day, they had greater reputations, at home and abroad, than any other legal scholar in America." *History of American Law*, 246.

[38] "Place of Justice Story," 140.

[39] Newmeyer, *Story*, 68.

[40] See ibid., 63, 178.

[41] We should not be romantic, however, about Story's promotion of individual liberty. The tyranny threatening the individual in Story's mind was most often economic regulation. Story believed in economic progress as moral progress. An individual's right to contract, for instance, he held as sacrosanct. His support of laissez-faire economics is one reason Story's reputation diminished after his death. With increasing corporate power in the late nineteenth century, Story's defenses of property rights and the corporation seemed, at best, out of touch, as did his suspicion of state regulation.

the U.S. Constitution as granting extensive powers to the federal government.[42]

Story's ideal was uniformity of law across the states, an ideal formed from his studies of legal history and comparative jurisprudence. Like Blackstone, and Reeve at Litchfield, Story did not hold a parochial view of common law. To be clear, this did not mean that Story understood common law to exist apart from its particular history. History and principle went together. He thus looked to English law to understand American law, but also to the civil law of continental Europe, Roman law, and even other ancient legal systems. Common law could draw from the tradition of natural-law reflection Story found in English common law, but also the work of the great European civilians. Truth has no boundaries.

LAW, HISTORY, AND REASON

Story relates history and reason in ways that find few proponents today. Few today believe, as Story does, that law holds together history and reason. Even twentieth-century admirers of Story, then, downplayed Story's natural-law commitments, or set them aside (believing, it seems, that his account of natural law is insufficiently robust for the purposes to which they want to put it).[43]

Certainly, Story sometimes offers a recognizably historicist view of the nature of law: "Laws are the very soul of a people," he says.[44] Laws, then, are "not merely those which are contained in the letter of [a people's] ordinances and statute books, but still more those which have grown up of themselves from their manners, and religion, and history."[45]

---

[42]   In his interpretation of Article VII of the U.S. Constitution, moreover, he concluded that the authority for the Constitution's ratification came from the "express authority of the people alone." *Commentaries on the Constitution of the United States: With a Preliminary Review of the Constitutional History of the Colonies and States, before the Adoption of the Constitution* (Boston: Hilliard, Gray, 1833), 3:710. If *the states* also possessed authority then the Constitution was, in effect, a treaty, and parties to a treaty can declare other parties in breach and dissolve it. Story strongly refuted such an interpretation.

[43]   Newmeyer downplays Story's account of natural law, while James McClellan laments that it deviates from scholastic natural law. See James McClellan, *Joseph Story and the American Constitution: A Study in Political and Legal Thought* (Norman: University of Oklahoma Press, 1971).

[44]   "Laws, Legislation, Codes," in *Encyclopedia Americana*, ed. Francis Lieber (Philadelphia: Lea & Blanchard, 1844), 7:576. Available in *Joseph Story and the Encyclopedia Americana*, ed. Morris L. Cohen (Clark, NJ: Lawbook Exchange, 2006), 94.

[45]   Ibid.

We might balk today at the ethnic and cultural uniformity assumed by members of the nineteenth-century historical school.[46] Nineteenth-century historicists too would have balked, however, at Story's apparent elision of enacted law – the letter of ordinances and statute books – and law as the "ways" of a particular nation. Story, of course, recognizes that there is a difference. But he thinks that customs are the seedbed of positive law. In other words, he thinks that it is from a people's ways that positive law properly selects, specifies, enacts, and protects. Story, then, has conservative instincts. Legislatures rightly follow the people. The "duty of the skilful legislator" in Story's estimation, is *not* to create new laws, "but only develop those which existed prior to any express recognition."[47]

Story, however, does not think that the customs of the people are always right. But here too an appeal to history is illuminating: Anomalous or even wrong aspects of the common law are the results of accidental or political circumstances, or even ignorance, all of which, Story trusts, can be gradually ameliorated by the processes of common-law adjudication.[48]

Story likewise confuses interpreters in his treatment of human rights. (A domain, indeed, where many expect the most congruence between American legal thought and the natural-law tradition.)[49] He says that history, not nature, provides the substance of rights. If Story is a natural lawyer of sorts, then his immediate appeals are not trans-historical or -cultural. The rights sought (and achieved) by the American Revolution, he thought, were *the rights of Englishmen*.

Story, for instance, points to the First Continental Congress, and the declaration and list of resolutions it issued on October 14, 1774.[50] These

[46] There are ways to imagine that laws might emerge from heterogeneous communities. Luke Bretherton, for instance, imagines a *sensus communis* emerging from the practices of broad-based community organizing. See Luke Bretherton, "Civil Society as the Body Politic," in *Resurrecting Democracy: Faith, Citizenship, and the Politics of a Common Life*, 179–218 (Oxford: Oxford University Press, 2014).

[47] Story, "Laws, Legislation, Codes," 7:576; available in Cohen, *Story*, 94.

[48] See Newmeyer's discussion in *Story*, 254–55.

[49] For instance, the Witherspoon Institute – a conservative research institution in Princeton, New Jersey – has an online "archive for and a commentary and study guide" for documents relating to natural law and rights: "Natural Law, Natural Rights and American Constitutionalism," www.nlnrac.org. For a view stressing the importance of natural law and rights in American history, but their limited domain, see Philip A. Hamburger, *Natural Rights, Natural Law, and American Constitutions*, 102 Yale L.J. (1993).

[50] For an accessible history of the Continental Congress, see Jack N. Rakove, *The Beginnings of National Politics: An Interpretive History of the Continental Congress* (New York: Knopf, 1979). The best source for understanding its details are the 23,000 letters contained in the 26 volumes of Paul H. Smith, ed., *Letters of Delegates to Congress, 1774–1789* (Washington, DC: Library of Congress, 1976–2000).

resolutions proceed from the claim that "our ancestors, who first settled these colonies, were at the time of their emigration from the mother country, entitled to all the rights, liberties, and immunities of free and natural-born subjects, within the realm of England."[51] In Story's reading, then, the revolutionaries sought specific rights with a particular lineage. They did not appeal abstractly to natural law or justice. When asserting a right of participation in government, they claimed that such participation was a "foundation of English liberty, and of all free government." Likewise in their resolutions on the legal system, they insisted that "the respective colonies are entitled to the common law of England" and, especially, the practice of trial by a jury of one's peers.

We can see, however, that the "English liberty" of political participation is also the liberty of "all free government." In the text of their declaration, the Continental Congress, before enumerating rights, suggests that the basis for these rights is "the immutable laws of nature, the principles of the English Constitution, and the several charters or compacts" that shaped the government of the colonies. Can all three – nature, constitution, and compact – be that government's basis? We might think that the wording betrays that its drafters were divided in their beliefs, or that they pulled upon anything at hand to help justify their resolutions. As is true for Story's thought, however, the delegates to the Continental Congress worked from the assumption that natural law, significant aspects of the English Constitution (developed through the centuries), and the specific liberties afforded by the express mechanism of charters together formed a cord of three strands. They did not assume that history and reason are necessarily contradictory.

Story, then, understood himself to stand in continuity with those American revolutionaries who protested the failure of the British authorities to treat the American colonists as subjects of the English Constitution. Like the delegates to the first Continental Congress, however – and unlike paradigmatic legal historicists – Story did not take history itself to be the source of laws. Indeed, he criticized prominent members of the European historical school of his day for forgetting that "the objects of their veneration, the juridical classics of Rome, owed their greatness to a perpetual habit of reverting to the maxims of natural law (their *aequitas*)."[52]

---

[51] "Declaration and Resolves of the First Continental Congress. October 14, 1774." This is available online through Yale Law School's Avalon Project, http://avalon.law.yale.edu/18th_century/resolves.asp.

[52] "Laws, Legislations, Codes," 7.579; available in Cohen, *Story*, 97.

Story thought that laws somehow come from history, more specifically from the history of a people's moral reflection. Laws are established in communities' considered "ways," their thought-out practices. It is such an account that explains why Story can say that a law "exists prior to all positive legislation." Indeed, Story goes so far as to suggest that law "is founded, not upon any will, but on the discovery of a right already existing." The laws of the United States, accordingly, are at once completely the product of its history, and yet these laws are somehow discovered not created. The U.S. Constitution may set down and determine particular rights, but its language of inalienability and indefeasibility, thought Story, is an acknowledgment that the Constitution "is a solemn recognition and admission of those rights, arising from the law of nature, and the gift of Providence."[53]

Even astute commentators have struggled with Story's position on the nature of law, and its implications for the practice of law. Kent Newmeyer suggests that, as a judge and treatise writer, "Story never stopped to ponder whether he was 'finding' law or 'making' it. The two were not mutually exclusive at this stage in the development of American common law."[54] But in this assessment Newmeyer is wrong. As we have just seen, Story certainly pondered the difference between finding and making the law. In his nonjudicial writings, he insists that law is properly found, not made. And, accordingly – and with no access to Story's internal psychology – it is most straightforward to assume that in his judicial writings Story sought to "find" the law. In other words, the "found" law put down in his judicial opinions was, he believed, the law "made" by, and expressed through, the history, morals, and religion of Americans. Newmeyer does descriptively capture in his assessment that, in a particular sense, to "find" the law is always to "make" the law. In an era with few authoritative legal resources, with each recorded decision or entry in a treatise Story set down and defined hitherto unwritten aspects of American common law.

STORY'S NATURAL LAW

Story speaks of natural law variously in his many writings. "In the largest sense," he says, natural law is the "philosophy of morals."[55] He writes in his

---

[53] *Commentaries on the Constitution*, 1:309.

[54] Newmeyer, *Story*, 70.

[55] A *Discourse Pronounced upon the Inauguration of the Author, as Dane Professor of Law in Harvard University: on the Twenty-fifth day of August, 1829* (Boston: Hilliard, Gray, Little, and Wilkins, 1829), 43. In this sense, the study of natural law exceeded his duties as a professor of law: "In the course of the academical instruction in this university already provided for, the subjects of ethics, natural law, and theology are assigned to other professors." Ibid., 45.

article on "natural law" for the *Encyclopedia Americana* that natural law
"comprehends natural theology, moral philosophy, and political philosophy;
in other words, it comprehends man's duties to God, himself, to other men,
and as a member of political society."[56] Or, more succinctly, and invoking
William Paley: Natural law, he says, is "the science, which teaches men their
duty and the reasons for it."

The *legal* face of natural law, however, receives greater attention in Story's
inaugural address as Dane Professor. He quotes the *Institutes of Justinian*,
which equates natural law with justice, "the set and constant purpose which
gives to every man his due."[57] Justice so defined was the business of the
"national jurisprudence," which Story advocated. (This favored the application of consistent laws across the whole of America, at the expense of "states'
rights.") Linking natural law to justice, justice to national jurisprudence, and
national jurisprudence to the law school allowed Story to present the motivat-
ing purpose of the school as "knowledge of things divine and human, the
science of the just and the unjust" (*[Iuris prudentia est] divinarum atque
humanarum rerum notitia, justi atque iniusti scientia*). Natural law, then, on
Story's account, not only forms the "foundation of all laws," but also "constitutes the first step in the science of jurisprudence."

Depending on context and generality, "natural law" to Story could mean
the whole system of morals or just that part of morality that pertains to justice.
Story does not remain, however, at this level of abstraction. In his treatise, for
instance, on the conflict of laws – the relationship of non-state actors in the
international context – Story commends James Kent's definition of natural law
in the case of *Wightman* v. *Wightman* (4 John, Ch. R. 343):

> by the Law of Nature, I understand, those fit and just rules of conduct, which
> the Creator has prescribed to Man, as a dependent and social being; and which
> are to be ascertained from the deductions of right reason, though they may be
> more precisely known, and more explicitly declared by Divine Revelation.[58]

To put it more straightforwardly, for Story natural law is the rules of conduct
that fit humans as dependent and social beings, which may be understood by
the exercise of reason, yet are better known through revelation.

---

[56] "Natural Law," in *Encyclopedia Americana*, ed. Francis Lieber (Philadelphia: Lea &
    Blanchard, 1844), 9.150. Available in Cohen, *Story*, 122.
[57] *Discourse Pronounced upon the Inauguration of the Author*, 43. Moyle's translation of Iustitia
    est constans et perpetua voluntas ius suum cuique tribuens, J. B. Moyle, *The Institutes of
    Justinian*, 3rd ed. (Oxford: Clarendon Press, 1896), 3.
[58] In Joseph Story, *Commentaries on the Conflict of Laws, Foreign and Domestic: In regard to
    Contracts, Rights, and Remedies, and especially in regard to Marriages, Divorces, Wills,
    Successions, and Judgments*, 3rd ed. (Boston: Little, Brown, 1846), 200n2.

Rules of Conduct Known as Dependent and Social Beings

In Story's account, from reflecting on natural law a human being gains rules to "form his character, and regulate his conduct."[59] Story does not offer a moral psychology that links compliance with rules with the formation of character. What he does suggest, though, is that by following natural law a human being ensures his "permanent happiness."[60] Like Blackstone and Locke, Story offers a eudaemonist account where human beings' "love of happiness" is the "end and aim" of life, and the content of natural law is, accordingly, the "duty of preserving that happiness."[61] What makes for distinctly *human* life is possession of "intellectual powers, and the freedom of [the] will."[62] Or as Story puts it in one of his encyclopedia articles, "[God] has given to man the power of discernment between good and evil, and a liberty of choice and the use of those means which lead to happiness or misery."[63]

So Story takes human nature and human faculties as lying behind human responsibilities: Humans possess reason to know the natural law, a will to follow it, and an instinct to seek their happiness. But Story also takes human *sociability* to be constitutive of human nature. The heart of natural law, as Story outlines it, is the regulation of a person's conduct "in all his various relations."[64] The human being, accordingly, has particular duties pertaining to life "as a solitary being, as a member of a family, as a parent, and lastly as a member of the commonwealth."[65] Story is concerned with human responsibility not only in "private relations as a social being," but also – most especially in his work on public laws and the Constitution – in the human being as "subject and magistrate, called upon to frame, administer, or obey laws, and owing allegiance to his country and government, and bound, from the profession he derives from the institutions of society, to uphold and protect them in return."[66] Rightly included in the discussion of the legal domain of natural law, then, is the very nature and purpose of government, marriage, property rights, social liberties, civil and political rights, the authority of laws, and the legitimacy of political institutions.

---

[59] *Discourse Pronounced upon the Inauguration of the Author*, 42.
[60] Ibid.
[61] Ibid., 44.
[62] Ibid.
[63] "Natural Law," 150–51; available in Cohen, *Story*, 123.
[64] Ibid., 150; available in Cohen, *Story*, 122.
[65] *Discourse Pronounced upon the Inauguration of the Author*, 44.
[66] Ibid., 42.

Understood by the Exercise of Reason

From human faculties and sociability Story thinks it possible to outline significant details of human responsibilities. Despite what we have seen, Story does not simply identify natural law either abstractly as an endpoint (justice) or minimally as the mere possession of human capacities of moral reflection. Instead, through reflection on human facilities and sociability, Story thinks there can be specification of particular rights and duties. The distinctly legal content of these rights and duties will be treated shortly – through discussion of different branches of common law – but it is helpful at this stage to attend to their moral analogs.

First, Story thinks we have duties toward God, namely *piety* or *devotion*.[67] As God is our creator, we "owe" God our worship and reverence. As God is our benefactor, we owe God gratitude. As God is lawmaker and judge, we are to obey God's commands. Even prayer is a duty for Story, emanating from human frailty and dependence. We need assistance and forgiveness, he says, and prayer tends to our improvement through self-reflection, the bringing together of divided affections, the spiritual elevation of our thoughts, and the more lively sense of our duties. Story provides similar reasons for a duty of public worship and the maintenance of religious institutions. In his writings on the Constitution, he makes clear that he does not think that government should impose religion or favor one sect over another, but nonetheless it should "foster and encourage the Christian religion generally, as a matter of sound policy as well as of religious truth."[68] For if proper piety cultivates a motivation to fulfill our duties, then religion is the foundation of a stable moral society.

Second, Story thinks we have duties toward ourselves.[69] Human beings should seek true happiness. They should maintain personal holiness, temperance, and humility, and should seek to improve in their knowledge, wisdom, and virtue. In short, human beings should preserve "a conscience void of offense towards God and towards man."

Third, Story thinks we have duties toward others. These *relative* duties flow from the rights of others. Story has a whole vocabulary of different rights, which are not exhausted by natural law.[70] But *natural* rights, in his terms,

---

[67] "Natural Law," 151; available in Cohen, *Story*, 123.
[68] *Commentaries on the Constitution*, 3:724.
[69] "Natural Law," 151; available in Cohen, *Story*, 123.
[70] For instance: "*Adventitious* Rights are those, which are accidental, or arise from peculiar situations and relations, and presuppose some act of man, from which they spring; such as the rights of the magistrate, of a judge, of electors, of representatives, of legislators, &c. we call those rights *alienable*, which may be transferred, by law, to others, such as the right to property,

belong to all of humanity, and result from the human constitution, and so include "man's right to life, limbs, and liberty, to the produce of his personal labor, at least to the extent of his present wants, and to the use, in common with the rest of mankind, of air, light, water, and the common means of subsidence."[71]

Better Known through Revelation

While Story thinks that rational reflection on human capabilities and sociability sufficiently provide the content of natural law, he also maintains that Christian revelation gives natural law a "higher sanction."[72] Most straightforwardly, the Christian faith helps illuminate the duties found in natural law. We might think of it this way: Christian faith provides a thick narrative and set of commitments that suppose that human beings are created with particular powers and faculties enabling the pursuit of happiness. Human beings, that is to say, have sufficient reason and agency to act for good or ill. Christian faith likewise accounts for human equality in creation – through its narrative and anthropological suppositions – and therefore checks the arrogance of power.[73]

Revelation, however, on Story's account, provides individuals not only with illumination of natural law but also with additional motivation to fulfill the duties that arise therefrom. Story is not a systematic theologian. But he contends that in the Christian faith's hope of life after death – what he calls "the doctrine of the immortality of the soul" – human beings gain a sense of the importance of their motivations and actions, and the connection between the two, irrespective of immediate consequences. Christian faith, therefore,

---

to debts, houses, lands, and money. We call those rights *unalienable*, which are incapable, by law, of such transfer, such as the rights to life, liberty and the enjoyment of happiness. We call those rights *perfect*, which are determinate, which may be asserted by force, or in civil society by the operation of law; and *imperfect*, those which are indeterminate and vague, which may not be asserted by force or by law but are obligatory only upon the consciences of parties. Thus a man has a perfect right to his life, to his personal liberty, and to his property; and he may by force assert and vindicate those rights against every aggressor. But he has but an imperfect right to gratitude for favors he bestowed others, or to charity, if he is in want, Or to the affection of others, even if he is truly deserving of it." "Natural Law," 151–52; available in Cohen, *Story*, 123–24.

[71] Ibid., 151; available in Cohen, *Story*, 123.

[72] *Discourse Pronounced upon the Inauguration of the Author*, 43.

[73] In a more restricted sense, Story thought that tendencies toward equality in the history of the common law attest to this understanding. Thus, Story thought that Thomas Jefferson was wrong in his contention that Christianity is not part of the common law. Jefferson's position, well known in private, was made public in a letter of 1824 to John Cartwright, the English radical. The letter was published in the *Boston Daily Advertiser*.

exhorts the practice of virtue and awakens hope.[74] God – infinite in power, knowledge, wisdom, benevolence, justice, and mercy – makes it possible, perhaps despite appearances, that the pursuit of virtue is connected "directly or ultimately" to happiness.[75]

For Story, revelation provides an account, too, of natural law's obligatoriness. "The obligatory force of the law of nature upon man is derived," thinks Story, "from its presumed coincidence with the will of his Creator."[76] Given God's nature, God's will accords with what is beneficial to human beings and their happiness. But natural law has force seemingly not as a result of its correspondence with reason, but rather through God's having the "supreme right to prescribe the rules, by which man shall regulate his conduct." While James McClellan can call Story's natural law "Thomistic" because of its close relationship to natural theology, Story's treatment of a human obligation to follow natural law places him more proximately in line with Francisco Suárez.[77] On Story's account, as it pertains to *moral* duties, natural law – as God's will – provides human beings with a reason for fulfilling imperfect duties. Laws may not prescribe the fulfillment of charitable obligations, for instance, but, as a result of God's commands, the conscience is obliged to meet them.

THE LIMITS OF NATURAL LAW

Despite his equation of natural law – in its broadest sense, at least – with the entire philosophy of morals, and despite his belief that natural law's precepts can be deduced from human capacities and sociability, and despite his view that natural law is morally obligatory (even its resultant imperfect duties), Story is nonetheless clear that there are limits to natural law.

Most obviously, he suggests, there are situations where reason cannot provide an answer. (Blackstone called these "matters indifferent.") In complex human societies, all sorts of regulations that make life more convenient have little connection in their specifics to the deductions of

---

[74]   *Discourse Pronounced upon the Inauguration of the Author*, 43.

[75]   "Natural Law," 151; available in Cohen, *Story*, 123. In his encyclopedia article he says that these things are assumed, "not because they are not susceptible of complete proof, but because, not being intended to be discussed in this place, they nevertheless form the basis of the subsequent remarks."

[76]   "Natural Law," 150; available in Cohen, *Story*, 122.

[77]   McClellan, 66. McClellan takes the non-Thomistic parts of Story as a "sad commentary on the intellectual confusion of the times." Ibid., 69. McClellan sees Story as caught up in the mistakes of Hobbes, Locke, and other moderns, rather than mining the resources of Cicero, say, and Thomas Aquinas.

human reason.[78] Americans drive on the right-hand side of the road, while the British drive on the left. Sometimes, decisions must be made for convenience, and where the decision (right or left) is one where moral or rational concerns are hardly engaged, the decision is arbitrary.

Less straightforward is Story's understanding of the way that "general rights of mankind" are instantiated in civilization. Story maintains that there are, indeed, rights to life, liberty, property, and the use of air, light, water, and the fruits of the earth.[79] But life, liberty, and property, he notes, can be justly taken away to prevent crimes, enforce others' rights, and maintain the safety and happiness of society. And, likewise, the use of air, light, water, and so forth are rightly regulated. The answer Story gives to all this is that the common law, through its historical (but principled) outworking of rules, has the authority to regulate even rights that derive from the natural law. In other words, common law – even when beginning from natural law, and seeking congruence with it – can admit of exceptions and modifications to natural law. In this, Story like-wise follows in the pattern of Blackstone.

Contemporary legal commentators have often equated natural law with the maxim *an unjust law is no law at all*, thereby dismissing natural law in the process as unworkable as a legal theory.[80] What such an equation does, however, is miss the ways in which someone like Story can at once accept natural law as binding, yet think that in its outworking it admits exceptions. Indeed, as is central to R. H. Helmholz's recent work, the history of self-conscious reflection on natural law *in the practice of the law* has allowed lawyers to explicitly recognize natural-law arguments, but reject them in place of other interests.[81] Slavery is the most notorious example.[82] But Story men-tions another. Natural law insists both on human equality and, partly as a result, on a right to be involved in the operation of government. Why, then, is this "not equally applicable to females, as free, intelligent, moral, responsible beings, entitled to equal rights, and interests, and protections, and having a vital stake in all regulations and laws of society?"[83] His answer is

---

[78] "Law of Nations," in *Encyclopedia Americana*, ed. Francis Lieber (Philadelphia: Lea & Blanchard, 1844), 9:141–42. Available in Cohen, *Story*, 113–14.

[79] "Natural Law," 9:152; available in Cohen, *Story*, 124.

[80] Lex iniusta non est lex. See, J. S. Russell, *Trial by Slogan: Natural Law and Lex Iniusta Non Est Lex*, 19 L. & Phil. 433 (2000).

[81] *Natural Law in Court: A History of Legal Theory in Practice* (Cambridge, MA: Harvard University Press, 2015).

[82] For an overview of the history, see David Boucher, "Slavery and Racism in Natural Law and Natural Rights," in *The Limits of Ethics in International Relations: Natural Law, Natural Rights, and Human Rights in Transition* (Oxford: Oxford University Press, 2009), 187–216.

[83] *Commentaries on the Constitution*, 2:54.

simply that, irrespective of whether or not this right has a fixed foundation in the laws of nature, the question of who gets to vote "has always been treated in the practice of nations, as a strictly civil right, derived from, and regulated by each society, according to its own circumstances and interests."[84] We may find this argument less than convincing. Story was a man of his time. His example, nonetheless, serves to show that, conceptually, recognizing the moral force of natural law need not necessarily result in its instantiation in positive law. We might add that Story fails to appreciate that natural-law thinking can critique present-day arrangements. A conflict between natural law and well-established practice need not always be resolved against natural law.

NATURAL LAW IN THE OPERATION OF COMMON LAW

Common law, we have seen, may sometimes specify legal results that oppose natural law. But in Story's several treatises and commentaries, the relationships he traces between natural law and common law are more often complementary than oppositional. What we find, indeed, is that there are often natural-law roots to common-law legal principles. Story's writings range across many volumes and tackle multiple branches of law. Something of the varied form these principles can take, however, are evident in the following five short examples.

Equity

The connections of natural law to "equity" are numerous, perhaps owing to the several meanings of the term.[85] To start, Story tells us, "equity" has general moral and legal meanings. In a moral sense, equity is that which is "founded in natural justice, in honesty, and in right, *ex aequo et bono*."[86] In a legal sense, at its highest level of generality, equity likewise suggests the connection between legal rules and justice. Quoting Blackstone, Story explains that equity "is the soul and spirit of the law; positive law is construed, and rational law is made by it. In this, equity is synonymous with justice."[87]

---

[84]   Ibid., 55.

[85]   Courts of equity once operated separately from the common-law courts in England and America. The body of laws known as "equity," therefore, may be contrasted with "common law." For our purposes, however, equity has a broader meaning than the distinction with common law. And, by the nineteenth century, courts of equity operated too with common-law reasoning.

[86]   "Equity," in *Encyclopedia Americana*, ed. Francis Lieber (Philadelphia: Lea & Blanchard, 1844), 4:560 . Available in Cohen, *Story*, 58.

[87]   Joseph Story, *Commentaries on Equity Jurisprudence: As Administered in England and America* (Boston: Hilliard, Gray, 1836), 1:7. Quoting William Blackstone, Commentaries on

More specifically, though, equity is also a body of laws, which, distinct from common law proper, possessed its own courts (Chancery), subject matter (trusts, most notably), and particular remedies (specific performance, for instance, and injunctions). But akin to common law, equity as a body of laws grew through the centuries in England to act on well-established principles (as opposed to, say, *de novo* recourses to abstract fairness).[88] So even as equity operated distinctly from, and in parallel with, the common law, in its decision-making it more and more resembled a principled system of precedent. Equity courts specified principles, even rules, and made decisions based on them.

Writing of the active body of law in his time, Story described "equity" as composed "partly of the principles of natural law, and partly of artificial modification of those principles."[89] Two short examples helpfully illustrate this bipartite character. Consider, first, the concept of "general average" in mercantile law. The general average is the contribution that all parties to an endeavor make when expenses are incurred or losses sustained in furtherance of the endeavor. (The classic example is the jettisoning of cargo in dangerous conditions at sea. In that situation, losses are proportionately shared, rather than shouldered by the merchant whose goods happened to be nearest at hand.)[90] Story notes that this principle is not founded on contract: Parties need not have specifically agreed that potential losses are to be treated in this way. Instead, general average "has its origins in the plain dictates of natural law."[91] But why not think that the principle is a matter of *convention*, rather than natural justice? Elsewhere, indeed, Story recognizes that since antiquity

---

the Laws of England, vol. 3, Of Private Wrongs (1768; repr. Chicago: University of Chicago Press, 1979), *429.

[88] Story therefore does not adopt the high position of Lord Kames that "a Court of Equity commences at the limits of the Common Law, and enforces benevolence, where the law of nature makes it our duty. And thus a Court of Equity, accompanying the law of nature, in its general refinements, enforces every natural duty, that is not provided for at Common Law." Quoted in *Commentaries on Equity Jurisprudence: As Administered in England and America* (Boston: Hilliard, Gray, 1836), 1:18. John Selden (1584–1654) famously complained of the variability of equity in his day: "Equity is a roguish thing. For Law we have a measure, know what to trust to; Equity is according to the conscience of him that is Chancellor, and as that is larger or narrower, so is Equity. 'T is all one as if they should make the standard for the measure we call a 'foot' a Chancellor's foot; what an uncertain measure would this be! One Chancellor has a long foot, another a short foot, a third an indifferent foot. 'T is the same thing in the Chancellor's conscience." Frederick Pollock, ed., *Table Talk of John Selden* (London: Quaritch, 1927), 43.

[89] *Commentaries on Equity Jurisprudence*, 2:preface.

[90] See, Richard Cornah, ed., *Lowndes & Rudolf: The Law of General Average and the York-Antwerp Rules*, 15th ed. (London: Sweet and Maxwell, forthcoming).

[91] *Commentaries on Equity Jurisprudence*, 2:468.

merchants have developed and practiced their own conventions because they navigate multiple jurisdictions and engage in fast-developing practices. What Story might reply is that, whether conventional or not, general average is itself grounded in a fundamental sense of *fairness*: Equity here, then, specifies a principle of natural law.

A second example of the way in which equity functions as natural justice is as a rule of interpretation in the administration of estates. Story thinks it uncontroversial that a debtor should pay her creditors. Equity accordingly has developed a rule of interpretation that, irrespective of what appears in the wording of a will, a testator – that is, the deceased – is given the "just and benignant interpretation" of fulfilling her "moral obligations in the just order, which natural law would assign to them."[92] Paying off debts comes before distributing bounty. Through recourse to an idea of natural justice, equity developed a rule that all testators would be taken as desiring to fulfill their duties, whatever their actual intentions.

Contract

A "contract," in Story's definition, is "an agreement or covenant between two or more persons, in which each party binds himself to do or forbear some act, and each acquires a right to what the other promises."[93] At first glance, a contract seems entirely the creature of the parties to it; it is, in other words, an exercise of the will of the parties. (Indeed, if a court needs to enforce a contract, legal orthodoxy holds that it does so simply by bringing about what the parties agreed.) Yet this bare structure of agreement, in Story's reckoning, is held up by the scaffold of natural law. At the most basic level: "Natural law requires that if one person accepts from another a service," says Story, "he should render to him something in return," whether this is known through express agreement or implied from the nature of the undertaking.[94] Built in to human sociability, in other words, is a fundamental sense of reciprocal fairness. Part of this sense is the importance of promises, which Story calls "essential to the existence of social intercourse among men."[95] Thought

---

[92] Ibid., 525.
[93] "Contract," in *Encyclopedia Americana*, ed. Francis Lieber (Philadelphia: Lea & Blanchard, 1844), 3:503. Available in Cohen, *Story*, 14.
[94] Ibid.
[95] Ibid. In the later twentieth century, legal scholarship on contracts mostly followed trends in the "law and economics" school of interpretation. However, some scholars did return to the idea of a *promise* as standing at the heart of contract. See Charles Fried, *Contract as Promise: A Theory of Contractual Obligation* (Cambridge, MA: Harvard University Press, 1981). The common law has traditionally required "consideration" as an essential part of a binding

through more fully, if contracts are to be the binding agreements of persons, they must be voluntary and founded in consent, involve mutual and reciprocal obligations, and be for the mutual benefit of the parties.[96]

Consent receives a classical if somewhat formal treatment from Story. It is "an act of reason accompanied with deliberation, the mind weighing, as in a balance, the good and evil on each side."[97] For more precision, Story turns to Pufendorf and his treatment of consent as a physical power, a moral power, and the serious and free use of both.[98] In the background of Story's thought is a particular understanding of human nature: A human being is a reasonable creature who can exercise a power, and thereby bind himself to promises.

How, then, does the positive law of contracts relate to natural law? First, Story is clear that the positive law of contracts must stay sufficiently close to natural law so that "the idea of justice implanted in the human mind should not be violated."[99] Practically, natural law insists that laws should stick close to our best instincts. But positive law specifies too; it can take care of special cases, establish particular forms and procedures, and – through the long experience of common law – create rules that give effect to promises.[100] Importantly, positive law might even withdraw from certain contracts their

---

contract. For a contract to exist, a party must receive something in recompense for undertaking her part of the contract. (This may itself be a promise.) Story skirts close to rejecting the need for consideration: "[C]onfidence in promises is so essential to the existence of social intercourse among men, that even the bare promise [i.e., a unilateral promise] of one of the parties, when given and received in earnest, that is, with the idea of its being binding, is not entirely destitute of the force of obligation," "Contract," 3:503; available in Cohen, *Story*, 14.

[96] These conditions are true, too, for other areas of the law that involve relations akin to contract: "In the civil and French law, as in our law, the principles, which regulate the contract of deposits, are the deductions from natural law, and do not depend upon any positive regulations." Joseph Story, *Commentaries on the Law of Bailments: With Illustrations from the Civil and the Foreign Law* (Cambridge, MA: Hilliard and Brown, 1832), 34. Partnership too "is also upon the like ground, that partnership is a contract founded purely upon the consent of the parties, that jurists are accustomed to attach to it the ordinary incidents and attributes of contracts. It is accordingly treated by them, as in its very nature and character a contract arising from and governed by the principles of natural law and justice." Joseph Story, *Commentaries on the Law of Partnership: As a Branch of Commercial and Maritime Jurisprudence: With Occasional Illustrations from the Civil and Foreign Law* (Boston: Little and Brown, 1841), 7–8. Accordingly, he says, partnership is founded in good faith, by the positive consent of the parties who are of legal age and competence, and for a lawful object and purpose.

[97] *Commentaries on Equity Jurisprudence*, 2:227.

[98] Ibid. Story points to Pufendorf's discussion in *De jure naturae et gentium* (1734), III.6.3. He later alludes to Grotius, "the use of reason is the first requisite to constitute the obligation of promise." *Commentaries on Equity Jurisprudence*, 2:228. Quoting *De jure belli ac pacis* (1646), II.XI.IV.3.

[99] "Contract," 3:503; available in Cohen, *Story*, 14.

[100] Ibid.

natural obligation. For instance, in Story's day if all the legal criteria were met, a bad bargain was enforced at law despite its offending conscience, morals, and religion.[101]

Story, then, does not treat natural law and common law as necessary competitors. Consider the question of the obligatoriness of contracts. Why are parties bound to a contract? Story first suggests that it is difficult to say more than *a contract is obligatory*.[102] What could be more intelligible? He does suggest, however, that the language of "right" helpfully illustrates what this means. We are under an obligation where, by our act of contracting, we give another a right to require something of us. The obligation of a contract is a conferred right or power over another's free will or actions. But how is this right or power to be measured? Story responds: Only by considering a combination of moral, natural, and positive law. He says: "[T]he moral law is explained, and applied by the law of nature, and both modified and adapted to the exigencies of society by positive law."[103] Positive law, in other words, gains its force from its relationship with moral law, which is known through natural law. But, particularly in advanced, complex societies, moral law requires specification through the enactments of positive legislation.

Marriage

Story argues that "[m]arriage is treated by all civilized nations as a peculiar and favored contract. It is in its origin a contract of natural law." In some countries, he notes, marriage has religious obligations and sanctions "superadded." This, Story suggests, has led to confusion. Not least, many persist in the "great mistake" of believing that if marriage is a religious contract, it is not a natural and civil contract as well. In the first edition of his *Commentaries on the Conflict of Laws* (1834), he posits, "the common law of England (and the like law exists in America) considers marriage in no other light than as a civil contract."[104] (Questions of its holiness, or otherwise, he suggests, are best left to religious authorities.) However, in the footnote of the revised

---

[101] The situation changed in the twentieth century often with the enactment of statutes ensuring consumer protections. However, there were also common-law fixes, including the rise of "unconscionability" (an equitable doctrine) as part of contract law. See Colleen McCullough, *Unconscionability as a Coherent Legal Concept*, 164 U. Pa. L. Rev. 779 (2016); and Anne Fleming, *The Rise and Fall of Unconscionability as the "Law of the Poor*," 102 Geo. L.J. 1383 (2014).

[102] His context here is discussion of the U.S. Constitution. See *Commentaries on the Constitution*, 3:243–44.

[103] Ibid., 243.

[104] *Conflict of Laws*, 100.

edition of 1841, he returns to the language of "contract" and suggests that it is perhaps not enough to think of marriage as merely a civil contract. "It is rather," he adds, "an institution of society, founded upon the consent and contract of the parties; and in this view it has some peculiarities in its nature, character, operation, and extent of obligations, different from what belongs to ordinary contracts."[105] Once again, natural law provides content – the societal basis for marriage – which positive law secures and enacts.

Story's encyclopedia article on the topic of marriage spells this out more fully. Marriage arises from natural law, in his account, for the "private comfort" of its parties, yes, but it furthers societal flourishing too: It best allows for the procreation of healthy citizens and their education, and secures the peace of society by, in words that might cause us to cringe, "assigning to one man the exclusive right to one woman."[106] Marriage promotes the cultivation of morals by cultivating domestic life – and the affections and virtues that follow – and distributes everyone into families, thereby creating permanent unions of interests and guardianships, and providing additional reasons for honest industry and good economy. Secured by positive law, "whatever has a natural tendency to discourage [marriage], or to destroy its value" can rightly be criminalized: "fornication, incest, adultery, seduction, and other lewdness."[107] So, from what is good, Story thinks, society can identify what is bad, and can justifiably take official action against it (although he is quick to suggest that "there are many independent grounds" for the criminality of fornication and the like).

Unsurprisingly, Story's logic that the law can criminalize acts that destroy institutions founded in natural law applies a fortiori to incest. Objections to incest, he says, are "founded in reason and nature."[108] Objections flow from the social relationships of human beings: the institution of families, and the "habits and affections flowing from that relation."[109] The arguments he offers, while empirically buoyed by references to cross-cultural "horror and detestation" of incest, focus most on the social institution of the family.[110] Incest

---

[105] Joseph Story, *Commentaries of the Conflict of Laws, Foreign and Domestic, in Regard to Contracts, Rights, and Remedies, and Especially in Regard to Marriages, Divorces, Wills, Successions, and Judgments*, rev. ed. (London: A. Maxwell, 32 Bell Yard, Lincoln's Inn, 1841), 170n3.

[106] "Natural Law," 9:152; available in Cohen, *Story*, 124.

[107] Ibid., 9:153; 125.

[108] *Conflict of Laws*, 201.

[109] Ibid.

[110] It is notable that Story's argument is not exhausted by reference to societal revulsion. For criticism of the cogency of moral and political arguments that rely on revulsion, see Martha Nussbaum, *From Disgust to Humanity: Sexual Orientation and Constitutional Law* (New York: Oxford University Press, 2010).

wrongly blends incompatible duties and feelings, he suggests, and therefore perplexes and confounds the various relations within the family. If legally acceptable, incest would impair the general perception of the purpose and goods of the family, and – as most people are socialized in their families – incest would broadly "corrupt the purity of moral taste."[111]

But, in the case of incest how are natural and positive laws specifically related? The prohibitions of natural law, Story says, are "of absolute, uniform, and universal obligation." Yet it is only through common law's adoption of natural law that the prohibition against incest becomes enforceable. And this adoption happens in a particular way, for common law "is founded in the common reason and acknowledged duty of mankind, [and] sanctioned by immemorial usage."[112] Common law, once again is not a positivist alternative to natural law in Story's thought, but a body of laws the proper content of which is natural law and history, where history itself is not value-free but the arbiter and refiner of morals.

Common law, nonetheless, does make definite what natural law cannot. The beginning and end points of incestuous relations, for instance, cannot be clearly ascertained by recourse to natural law or even the dictates of Christian faith.[113] But, as canon lawyers for centuries knew, courts or legislators' need for specification does not render natural law unhelpful. Indeed, when Story considers the practical issue of recognition of marriages across state lines, natural law marks an enforceable qualitative boundary, a limiting point.[114] The general rule is that courts will recognize as valid any marriage lawfully conducted under the laws where it was celebrated. However, if a foreign nation allowed, for example, marriage between a parent and child, American courts would not recognize it.[115] The law of nature forbids such a marriage despite the general acquiescence to the law of marriage of other jurisdictions. Yet, if the positive law in a court's own jurisdiction considered incestuous a particular relation which natural law does not clearly treat as incestuous – for instance, marriage between a man and his deceased wife's sister – the court should recognize this marriage, even if it could not be celebrated within the court's jurisdiction.[116]

---

[111] *Conflict of Laws*, 201.

[112] Ibid.

[113] Ibid., 104, 200.

[114] *Conflict of Laws*, 107.

[115] A form of this argument was used to support the Defense of Marriage Act. See, e.g., "Amici Curiae Brief of Robert P. George, Sherif Girgis, and Ryan T. Anderson in Support of Hollingsworth and Bipartisan Legal Advisory Group Addressing the Merits and Supporting Reversal" in *United States v. Windsor*, 570 U.S. 744 (2013).

[116] A similar logic holds for issues of comity in international law. Nations have equal sovereignty in international law, and so a nation cannot insist that its own laws have superior obligation to those of other nations. However, while U.S. courts most often will enforce contracts, say,

Property

In his discussion of title to land (the bundle of interests individuals can hold in a piece of property), Story notes that European nations based their New World claims to title on the "right of discovery," but argues that these claims do not properly pertain to land occupied by Native Americans.[117] It is "not easy to perceive," he says, "how, in point of justice, or humanity, or general conformity to the law of nature" Europeans could come to hold title to land "inhabited by the natives."[118] "Their right, whatever it was, of occupation or use stood upon original principles deducible from the law of nature, and could not be justly narrowed or extinguished without their own free consent."[119]

Story quickly retreats from the implications of his comments. He suggests that considering the "actual merits of the titles claimed by the respective parties" is not the purpose of his present work. And that even within the realm of the law of nature, there may be occasions where "civilized man may demand [title] from the savage for uses and cultivation different from, and perhaps more beneficial to, society than the uses to which the latter may choose to appropriate it."[120] And yet, despite his retreat, Story suggests there can be appeals to natural law that shore up Native Americans' rights to property.

Crime and Punishment

As Story presents it, natural law underpins a major classificatory and conceptual division in criminal law. Legal systems in both the civil and common law worlds distinguish between crimes understood as bad in themselves (delicta *juris naturalis* or crimes *mala in se*) and crimes where actions are ostensibly indifferent but where an authority has affixed a penalty for a particular reason (delicta *juris positivi* or crimes *mala prohibita*).[121] In the common-law world,

---

conducted in other nations, they will not enforce contracts that violate "the law of our own country, the law of nature, or the law of God." (He has in mind contracts of evasions, of fraud, that are against good morals or religion, or opposed to national policy.) Natural law, then, is among the limiting factors of the enforceability of law. *Conflict of Laws*, 44, 204. Story references the opinion of Mr. Justice Best in *Forbes* v. *Cochrane*, 2 B. and Cres. R. 448, 471; 101 Eng. Rep. 450, 459.

[117] For a helpful treatment of colonialist ideologies, see David B. Abernathy, *The Dynamics of Global Dominance: European Overseas Empires, 1415–1980* (New Haven, CT: Yale University Press, 2001).

[118] *Commentaries on the Constitution*, 1:5.

[119] Ibid.

[120] Ibid., 6.

[121] "Criminal law," in *Encyclopedia Americana*, ed. Francis Lieber (Philadelphia: Lea & Blanchard, 1844), 34. Available in Cohen, *Story*, 40.

natural law provides a justification for a right to punish crimes of the first type – murder, theft, and so forth – even where express laws do not exist, but it provides no similar justification for the second type. (Story's example of the latter is laws relating to trade in contraband.)

Story does recognize challenges to the right to punish without express laws. The influential jurist P. J. A. Feuerbach (1775–1833), for one, insisted on a purely deterrence-based theory of criminal law. In this telling only express laws, promulgated and known, can psychologically restrain would-be criminals, and thus justify punishment.[122] Story does not directly address such challenges. But his answer would likely appeal to a rationally accessible natural law, which prohibits killing except in self-defense. People do not need a statute book, he thought, to know that murder is wrong.

Story, however, does not think that natural law provides a clear guide to the proper punishments for crimes. Proper punishments cannot be discerned a priori, but instead "depend upon the particular circumstances of every age and nation."[123] Accordingly, the tariff of punishment "must be left to the exercise of a sound discretion on the part of the legislature." However, Story is clear that capital punishment is not prohibited by natural law or, indeed, by the norms of a Christian commonwealth. In fact, his view of the acceptability of capital punishment is bolstered by his belief in natural rights: "[I]t is often said," he reports, "that life is a gift of God, and therefore it cannot justly be taken away." But, he claims, "[l]ife is no more a gift of God than other personal endowments or rights." We have rights to personal liberty – for instance, freedom of movement – which imprisonment removes.[124] Just as freedom can be removed by civil society, so too can life be taken away.

We have seen in these examples from five branches of the law – equity, contract, marriage, property, and crime and punishment – that natural law affords Story distinct ways to explain and justify American common law.

---

[122] For a recent overview see Tatjana Hörnle, "PJA von Feuerbach and his *Textbook of the Common Penal Law*," in *Foundational Texts in Modern Criminal Law*, ed. Markus Dubber (Oxford: Oxford University Press, 2014), 119–40.

[123] "Death, Punishment of," in *Encyclopedia Americana*, ed. Francis Lieber (Philadelphia: Lea & Blanchard, 1844), 4:143. Available in Cohen, *Story*, 50.

[124] He does not seem to consider whether the permanency of capital punishment makes it different from other punishments. One could imagine casting (non-permanent) imprisonment as a *restriction* on a right, which is restored after the term of punishment has been served. The once-and-for-all nature of capital punishment does not allow for this.

THE *JEUNE EUGENIE* DECISION

In Story's many volumes of commentary on aspects of common law and equity, natural law plays a distinctive if variegated role. But it is in his treatment of international law that Story turns most directly to natural law as a source of law. This is seen best in his 1822 decision *La Jeune Eugenie*. In this decision, Story – presiding as a circuit justice on the U.S. circuit court for Massachusetts – held that federal courts have the authority to confiscate foreign ships employed in the African slave trade.[125] His principal justification was natural law.

The facts of the case are relatively straightforward. The crew of a ship of the U.S. Revenue-Marine captured the *Jeune Eugenie* off the coast of West Africa, suspecting that it was an American ship engaged in the slave trade. Under a U.S. law prohibiting the slave trade, the crew of the Revenue ship claimed the *Jeune Eugenie* as a prize.[126] The French consul in Boston and the French owners of the *Jeune Eugenie*, however, submitted claims for the return of the ship.

In his decision, Justice Story determined that the ship was, indeed, French-owned, but he nonetheless refused to return it to the owners, as it had clearly been involved in the African slave trade. He held that the federal courts have the authority to hear cases involving foreign citizens who participate in the international slave trade and to confiscate their property. Unless the slave trade were to be specifically protected by U.S. law, he said, then slavery's evident violations of natural law and international law give U.S. courts the authority to act. (Importantly Story treats natural law as a source of the law that U.S. courts can administer. Natural law is not merely an external moral judgment on the

---

[125] *La Jeune Eugenie*, 26 F.Cas., 832, 846 (C.C.D. Mass. 1822). For brief details, see Federal Judiciary Center, "*Amistad*: The Federal Courts and the Challenge to Slavery – Historical Background and Documents Legal Questions before the Federal Courts," www.fjc.gov/history/home.nsf/page/tu_amistad_questions.html. Story can hardly be viewed as a hero of abolitionism in today's terms. In his opinion in *Prigg* v. *Pennsylvania* he declared that the Fugitive Slave Act of 1793 was constitutional and that individual states could not prevent the recapture of runaway slaves from other parts of the United States.

[126] By an Act passed on March 2, 1807, the importation of slaves into the United States was prohibited after June 1, 1808. The Act also authorized the president to employ armed vessels to seize ships, including on the high seas, attempting to violate the Act. Previous Acts prohibited U.S. citizens or residents from being engaged in the international transportation of slaves. An Act of April 20, 1818, additionally provided that a defendant had to prove that the "negroes" he was charged with having brought into the United States were in the United States five years prior to the prosecution. An Act of March 3, 1819 provided that ships seized by armed U.S. vessels were to be sold, with the proceeds distributed as a prize to the crew. An Act of May 15, 1820 made it a capital offense to seize a "negro or mulatto" with intent to make him or her a slave.

law. Nonetheless, *other* sources of law – U.S. positive and constitutional law – can modify or override, he says, the provisions of natural law.)

Ultimately, the results were less dramatic than the decision. At the request of President Monroe, the *Jeune Eugenie* was delivered to the French government so that French courts could examine the owners' involvement in the slave trade. And the law did not stand still. In the 1825 case of *The Antelope*, the Supreme Court held – in an opinion written by Chief Justice John Marshall – that the federal courts must recognize a nation's right to engage in the slave trade if the law of that nation does not prohibit the trade. Whatever the promise of Story's decision in *Jenue Eugenie*, then, *The Antelope* restricted courts' ability to directly appeal to natural law as some form of "trump," as Ronald Dworkin would have it, over national laws, foreign or domestic.[127]

Twentieth-century legal commentators downplayed the role of natural law in Story's decision.[128] They focused, instead, on Story's discussion of the law of nations and, particularly, state practice as one of the sources of the law of nations. In other words, they focused on what has come to be called "customary international law." Customary international law is one part of international law, formed through the consistent practice of states (if accompanied by the conviction that the practice is obligatory).[129]

Newmeyer and other commentators who support the customary-international-law interpretation of the *Jeune Eugenie* case emphasize Story's treatment of state practice. The slave trade, Story noted, was banned in France, the United States, and the United Kingdom. And treaties condemning the slave trade and working for its global abolition had been signed in Vienna, Aix-la-Chapelle, and London.[130] Prioritizing state practice, they say, Story

---

[127] *The Antelope*, 23 U.S. 66 (1825). See John T. Noonan, Jr., *The Antelope: The Ordeal of the Recaptured Africans in the Administrations of James Monroe and John Quincy Adams* (Berkeley: University of California Press, 1977). Dworkin describes rights as "trumps" inasmuch as they permit rights-holders to act in a certain way even if society would be served better – on a utilitarian calculus, say – by doing otherwise. See his "Rights as Trumps" in *Theories of Rights*, ed. Jeremy Waldron, 153–67 (Oxford: Oxford University Press, 1984).

[128] See, e.g., Newmeyer, *Story*, 349.

[129] The Statute of the International Court of Justice (annexed to the Charter of the United Nations), for instance, treats "international custom, as evidence of a general practice accepted as law" as one of the sources of international law. Article 38(b). (New York: United Nations, 2005.)

It remains an open question in international jurisprudence whether *opinio juris* – the term used for the subjective sense that a custom is binding – is to be inferred inductively or deductively by a court. See Stefan Talmon, *Determining Customary International Law: The ICJ's Methodology between Induction, Deduction, and Assertion*, 26 Eur. J. Int. Law 417 (2015).

[130] *La Jeune Eugenie*, 26 F.Cas., 832, 846 (C.C.D. Mass. 1822).

"went on to consult the universal morality of natural law" for additional conceptual support or rhetorical potency.[131]

Story's twentieth-century interpreters are right to the extent that Story sought, and expected, the congruence of customary law and natural law. (We have seen this to be analogously true in Story's treatment of domestic law.) However, commentators fail to account for Story's indexing of positive law to natural law. The law of nations stands on natural law, in Story's telling, such that the international slave trade is not just illegal because of the "present state of nations" – state practice understood as obligatory – but also because the slave trade carries with it "a breach of all the moral duties, of all maxims of justice, mercy and humanity, and of the admitted rights, which independent Christian nations now hold sacred in their intercourse with each other."[132] Accordingly, after reviewing the horrors of the trade, Story concludes: "It is of this traffic, thus carried on, and necessarily carried on, beginning in lawless wars, and rapine, and kidnapping, and ending in disease, and death, and slavery, – it is of this traffic in aggregate of its accumulated wrongs, that I would ask, if it be consistent with the law of nations?" *Even if* each element of the trade (war, slavery, plunder, taking of life, selling human beings) could be shown to be lawful, Story continues: "It does not advance one jot to the support of the proposition, that a traffic, that involves them all, that is unnecessary, unjust and inhuman, is countenanced by the eternal law of nature, on which rests the law of nations."[133]

In deciding the case of the *Jeune Eugenie*, Story reviews the *basis* of the laws of nations. The sources of international law, he says, are: first, "general principles of right and justice"; second – when concerned with indifferent things – the "customary observances and recognitions of civilized nations"; and lastly, "the conventional or positive law, that regulates the intercourse between states."[134] The practice of states, therefore, can indeed change the content of international law. However, "no practice can obliterate the fundamental distinction between right and wrong."[135]

---

[131] Newmeyer, *Story*, 350.
[132] *La Jeune Eugenie*, 26 F.Cas., 832, 845 (C.C.D. Mass. 1822).
[133] Ibid., 846.
[134] Ibid. The Statute of the International Court of Justice includes these sources in Article 38: (a) international conventions, whether general or particular, establishing rules expressly recognized by the contesting states; (b) international custom, as evidence of a general practice accepted as law; (c) the general principles of law recognized by civilized nations; (d) subject to the provisions of Article 59, judicial decisions and the teachings of the most highly qualified publicists of the various nations, as subsidiary means for the determination of rules of law.
[135] *La Jeune Eugenie*, 26 F.Cas., 832, 864 (C.C.D. Mass. 1822).

What does this mean for the practice of adjudication? In Story's decision, the African slave trade clearly violates his first general principle: "It is repugnant to the great principles of Christian duty, the dictates of natural religion, the obligations of good faith and morality, and the eternal maxims of social justice."[136] But Story does not end his analysis with the first principle. The second principle (customary law) and the third (positive and treaty-based law) also provide good reasons for his decision. Importantly, Story assumes that the second and third principles are rightly in accord with the first.[137]

However, just as nineteenth-century American jurists could decry the international slave trade while countenancing its domestic operation, so too could Story speak of natural law as the first source of the law of nations while recognizing in theory – if not in the practice of this particular case – that he was bound to enforce "the universal law of society," *except* where slavery was "protected by a foreign government."[138] While Newmeyer and others might undervalue the role of natural law in Story's decision, we should not miss that slavery in 1822 was, in Story's telling, legally (if not morally) defensible. On Story's account, natural law provides all the presumptions that the slave trade is "altogether illegal" in international law. But this is to "throw on a claimant the burthen of proof, in order to shew, that by the particular law of his own country he is entitled to carry on this traffic."[139] Legally speaking, natural law is a rebuttable presumption. But it is a strange one. For, even if rebutted, natural law still (rightly) condemns the practice.

Story does not stop there. In closing, he offers a dictum – an authoritative but nonbinding statement of law – that "upon principles of universal law" those engaged in the international slave trade "cannot ... have a right to be heard upon a claim of this nature in any court."[140] This is a procedural

---

[136]   Ibid.
[137]   The 1814 treaty of peace between the United Kingdom and France, for instance, calls for universal abolition of the slave trade, given that its traffic is "repugnant to the principles of natural justice and of the enlightened age in which we live." Story quotes this at ibid., 847. For the full document, see Edward Baines, *History of the Wars of the French Revolution: From the Breaking Out of the War in 1792, to the Restoration of a General Peace in 1815; Comprehending the Civil History of Great Britain and France during That Period* (London: Printed for Longman, et al., 1817), 2:343–46.
[138]   *La Jeune Eugenie*, 26 F.Cas., 832, 847 (C.C.D. Mass. 1822).
[139]   Ibid., 848.
[140]   *La Jeune Eugenie*, 26 F.Cas., 832, 848 (C.C.D. Mass. 1822). The statement is nonbinding because the issue was not decided as part of the case before the court. (*Obiter dicta* are words said in passing, "by the way." *Ratio decidenti* – the reason for the decision – is binding.)

determination, he says, which receives support from the practice of other nations.[141]

Irrespective of these words – substantive or procedural, *ratio* or dicta – within three years, Chief Justice Marshall held in *The Antelope* that, whatever his personal belief that slavery violates natural law, the fact that many nations approve the trade means that the U.S. Supreme Court could not rule that the slave trade was a violation of international law.

* * *

Blackstone's *Commentaries* served as the primary educational basis for newly emerging proprietary schools and, from 1817, university law schools, such as Harvard's under the leadership of Joseph Story, professor, jurist, and judge. Yet, natural law quickly receded from instruction, even in the teachings and writings of Story, a champion of natural-law reasoning in the common law. As American common law was worked out in the early nineteenth century, natural law was subsumed into its details; except in rare circumstances – notably in the arena of international law – common law less frequently appealed to natural law, for judges and jurists could now turn to the developing body of principles and precedents constitutive of American common law. Not that this change entailed a rejection of natural law. Story's scholarly and judicial writings show that natural law could remain central to the animating vision and moral purpose of common law even when it was not explicitly invoked.[142]

This natural law, we saw, refers to the rules of conduct humans know from their status as dependent and social beings. It is understood by reason, but better known through revelation. In its legal treatment, however, it can admit of exceptions and even be passed over in favor of other interests. Unlike in its usual interpretation by contemporary critics and proponents, then, Story's natural law is exemplary of the ways in which natural law can be historicized

---

[141] In "trade contrary to the general law of nations," he says, the British High Court of Admiralty holds the same position. Ibid.

[142] Arguably, what Story offers is, in effect, a natural-law account of positive law. For more on this possibility, see Jeremy Waldron, "What is Natural Law Like?," in *Reason, Morality, and Law: The Philosophy of John Finnis*, ed. John Keown and Robert P. George, 73–92 (Oxford: Oxford University Press, 2013). For some, this portrayal of a historicized and relativized natural law will be contradictory, or, at least, a betrayal of the tradition. (The separation of legality from goodness, after all, is the very definition of positivism.) But what Story's account shows, however, is that natural law can meaningfully explain and account for aspects of a legal system, even when it is not employed as a *legal theory*. In other words, one might recognize the importance of natural law in the common-law legal system without thinking that natural law fully explains *legality* (what makes specific laws legally valid) or *normativity* (what makes us comply with laws).

and relativized, at least in its relationship to common law. Natural law was known in the historical details of the positive law: specifying duties; serving as a yardstick, from which positive laws can deviate only so far; acting as a limiting point; furnishing rights; classifying and justifying branches of the law; and forming a source of law, albeit one among several.

5

Law as Science

Christopher Columbus Langdell

High aspirations for university legal education did not lead to high achieve-ment. By the mid-nineteenth century, the site of most legal education remained far from university campuses in the offices and chambers of experi-enced lawyers and judges. The few university law schools that did exist were hardly the acme of excellence. Indeed, despite Joseph Story's fame and influence, following his death in 1845, Harvard Law Scho-ol still had no entry requirements and conducted no examinations; residence and the proper payment of fees sufficed to qualify students for degrees.[1] So it was that, in 1870, Oliver Wendell Holmes, Jr. could declare the school "almost a disgrace to the Commonwealth of Massachusetts."[2]

Partly as cause, partly as symptom: Low standards in the university law schools coincided with the obsolescence of the tools used by educated lawyers of the early and middle years of the nineteenth century. The various com-mentaries and other treatises – written by Joseph Story and others – which had profitably charted federal and state laws in the early nineteenth century were now out of date, and practitioners found the increasing volume of reported law cases unmanageable.[3]

[1] Alfred Zantzinger Reed, *Training for the Public Profession of the Law: Historical Development and Principal Contemporary Problems of Legal Education in the United States* (New York: Carnegie Foundation for the Advancement of Teaching, 1921), 145n1. C. C. Langdell, "The Law School," in *Annual Reports of the President and Treasurer of Harvard College. 1889–90* (Cambridge, MA: Published by the University, 1891), 131–32.

[2] This appeared in a "summary of events" anonymously written with Arthur Sedgwick in 5 Am. L. Rev. 177, 177 (1870).

[3] Joel Seligman, *The High Citadel: The Influence of Harvard Law School* (Boston: Houghton Mifflin, 1978), 45. In the preface of his casebook on contracts, Langdell writes of the "great and rapidly increasing number of reported cases in every department of law," and suggests that the case method provides a "satisfactory principle" to glean this material. *A Selection of Cases on the Law of Contracts with References and Citations ... Prepared for Use as a Text-Book in Harvard Law School* (Boston: Little, Brown, 1871), vi.

At Harvard Law School, these twin challenges of low standards and inadequate tools were met with the 1870 appointment of Christopher Columbus Langdell (1826–1906) as the school's first dean, and, more particularly, by his introduction the same year of the *case method*: a method of instruction and, it would seem, a legal way of thinking – a *Langdellian legal science* – which would eventually shape all of American legal education.[4]

To many, 1870 marks the birth of the modern American law school.[5] Under Langdell's influence, to study law meant to engage directly with reported legal opinions, almost entirely those of appellate court judges. Standard methods of instruction – the memorization of principles, rules, or maxims through rote learning, lectures, and textbooks – were replaced by the studied tracing of major legal doctrines through selected sets of the leading cases.[6] In the past, professors taught their students legal rules. Now, students were to divine the rules for themselves by reading the cases.

Consider just this one example. Both Story and Langdell treat the English case of *Chamberlain* v. *Agar*, both in their respective works on equity process and procedure.[7] In Story's *Commentaries on Equity Pleadings*, the case is discussed

---

4   In 1870, Harvard's President Eliot brought Langdell to serve as Dane Professor in the law school. Charles Eliot's presidency is now remembered for its broad and widely influential reforms, particularly the development of the college elective system, the improvement of professional education, and the strengthening of a research culture. See his "The New Education: Its Organization," a two-part essay in *Atlantic Monthly* (February and March 1869); *Educational Reforms: Essay and Addresses* (New York: Century, 1898); and *University Administration* (Boston: Houghton Mifflin, 1908).
      The case method first appears in the written record with Langdell's 1870–71 report to President Eliot, his first year as the first dean. "Professor Langdell's subjects of instruction were Contracts, Sales of Personal Property, and Civil Procedure at Common Law ... [i]n each of the two former subjects he used as a text-book a selection of cases which he had prepared for the purpose." *Annual Report to the President and Treasurer of the Harvard College 1870–71* (Cambridge, MA: University Press, 1872), 60.

5   Anthony Chase, *The Birth of the Modern Law School*, 23 Am. J. Legal Hist. 329 (1979); Robert Stevens, "Two Cheers for 1870: The American Law School," in *Law in American History*, ed. Donald Fleming and Bernard Bailyn (Boston: Little, Brown, 1971). For an important study on the shape of American legal education from Langdell through to the legal realists, which treats Langdell with unusual sympathy, see William LaPiana, *Logic and Experience: The Origin of Modern American Legal Education* (New York: Oxford University Press, 1994).

6   The standard approach was codified at Columbia Law School. Named for the school's dean, Theodore William Dwight (1822–92), this "Dwight Method" was highly influential across American law schools. See Thomas Fenton Taylor, *The Dwight Method*, 7 Harv. L. Rev. 203 (1893).

7   2 Ves. & B. 259. The case concerns a letter adding to a will (that is, a testamentary paper or codicil), which the plaintiff believed promised her an annuity of £200. On the death of the testator, his executors (his sons) claimed in a plea that the letter did not exist, and did not answer questions as to the circumstances surrounding the purported letter.

within a forty-five-page treatment of pleadings. (A "plea," in an equity suit, is "a special answer," given by a defendant, "showing or relying upon one or more things, as a cause why the suit should be either dismissed, delayed, or barred."[8]) The chapter begins with Story's treatment of the true nature, office, and frame of a plea. It is striking that, even in a treatise on the *practice* of the law, Story first provides a conceptual background before turning to the particular situations where pleas are an appropriate form of defense. When *Chamberlain* v. *Agar* appears, it is only in a footnote. It stands along with five other cases as authority for "a doctrine ... stated in a more general form."[9] It is one authority for a right of "discovery" – the compelled disclosure of relevant facts or documents – where a plaintiff's claim relies upon the existence of a document. If a defendant argues that a document does not exist, the defendant cannot avoid answering questions as to the circumstances surrounding the purported document. A plea to dismiss the suit for lack of documentation, in other words, cannot simply ignore the circumstances that might prove the document's existence.[10]

Langdell's treatment of *Chamberlain* v. *Agar* is quite different. It appears in his *Cases in Equity Pleading, Selected with Special Reference to the Subject of Discovery, Prepared for Use as a Text-Book in Harvard Law School.*[11] This casebook has no introduction apart from the title page and a list of cases. The report of *Chamberlain* v. *Agar* appears on pages 67 through 69. The entry includes a brief summary of the facts, a paragraph of each of the lawyers' arguments, and the judgment of Sir Thomas Plumer, Vice-Chancellor. Langdell adds no commentary. The only footnotes are internal citations to the cases mentioned in the judgment. Langdell's understanding of the law and editorial judgment are, of course, evident in the very selection of the texts, but the casebook is designed, nonetheless, to require its student readers to determine for themselves the importance of the selected cases by reading the judgments and considering the relationships between them. In short, unlike Story's treatise, Langdell's casebook gives its readers neither a general description of the subject matter nor an analytic treatment of how its components fit together. From its raw materials, (would-be) lawyers are to work out the law for themselves.

---

8   Joseph Story, *Commentaries on Equity Pleadings and the Incidents thereto, According to the Practice of the Courts of Equity of England and America* (London: A. Maxwell, Bell Yard, 1838), 406.
9   Ibid., 436.
10   Story also considers the case when discussing actual fraud as part of the substantive law of equity. *Commentaries on Equity Jurisprudence as Administered in England and America* (Boston: Hilliard, Gray, 1836), 1:259.
11   C.C. Langdell, Cases in Equity Pleading, Selected with Special Reference to the Subject of Discovery, Prepared for Use as a Text-Book in Harvard Law School (Cambridge, MA: Printed for the Author, 1878).

As dean, Langdell introduced meritocratic reforms at Harvard that were widely copied, and which continue, in some form, to this day: fixed entry standards, a systematic progression of courses, increased hours of instruction, and regular examinations.[12] These reforms, however, need not have accompanied the advent of the case method. Entry standards could have been raised under any regime of teaching. And yet, in time, the case method was identified both with the rise in educational standards that followed from Langdell's reforms and, more broadly, with the increasing prestige of university legal education, such that the case method and high-quality legal education came to seem inseparable.

THE CASE METHOD

The "entirely original creation" of the case method, as Langdell first imagined it, required students – aided by references given by their instructors – to use the library to find selected cases in the reports of English and American courts and, in reading these cases, to determine the law therefrom.[13] Put another way, the content of the law was to be found in reading the cases, not in principles provided by professors or found in treatises.[14] Directing many students to the same collections of cases, however, had the practical consequence of damaging the library books, and the limited number of copies available to students caused inconvenience and grumbling. Langdell's yearly reports to Harvard's President Eliot record the law school's response in some detail, including the purchase of more copies of case reports. Fortunately, though, Langdell already

[12]   "[A]ll of them who were not graduates of colleges had passed an examination for admission, either in Latin or French, and also in Blackstone's Commentaries." C. C. Langdell, "The Law School," in *Annual Reports of the President and Treasurer of Harvard College. 1889–90* (Cambridge, MA: Published by the University, 1891), 131. Likewise, a student's course of study was to be "regular, systematic and earnest, not intermittent, desultory or perfunctory," with three years of study "pursued in the prescribed order." See *The Harvard Law School*, 3 Law Q. Rev. 118 (1887). ("We reprint from the *Boston* (Mass.) *Weekly Advertiser* the speeches delivered by Mr. Justice Holmes and Prof. Langdell at the 'quarter-millennial' celebration of Harvard University on the 5th of November.") The new culture required additional weekly hours of instruction – an increase from ten hours to over thirty hours – and with that, the growth of the faculty from three professors in 1870 to five professors, one assistant professor, and three lecturers by 1890. Langdell, *Harvard Annual Reports 1889–90*, 132.

[13]   Josef Redlich, *The Common Law and the Case Method in American University Law Schools: A Report to the Carnegie Foundation for the Advancement of Teaching* (New York: Carnegie Foundation for the Advancement of Teaching, 1914),9.

[14]   M, *Correspondence to the Editors*, 1 Columb. L. Times 4 (October 1887). See also Bruce Kimball, *"Warn Students That I Entertain Heretical Opinions, Which They Are Not to Take as Law": The Inception of Case Method Teaching in the Classrooms of the Early C. C. Langdell, 1870–1883*, 17 Law & Hist. Rev. 57 (1999).

had an answer: the production of a new form of textbook that reproduced, in one volume, the relevant cases in any area of the law. In 1871, his volume on contract law was commercially published, and with *A Selection of Cases on the Law of Contracts*, the casebook – the dominant tool of legal study to this day – was born.[15]

Langdell's method of instruction was co-constituted with the casebook. No longer were law students to read treatises and listen to lectures about those treatises. Instead, students were to look at particular cases: digest their facts and decisions, consider the grounds for these decisions, and thereby trace a legal rule.[16] In the classroom, the "Socratic" method made this clear. Consider this example from the earliest days of case-method instruction. Samuel Batchelder, from the vantage point of 1906, recalled Harvard Law School:

> The class gathered in the old amphitheater of Dane Hall – the one lecture room of the School – and opened their strange new pamphlets, reports bereft of their only useful part, the head-notes![17] The lecturer opened his.
>
> > "Mr. Fox, will you state the facts in the case of Payne v. Cave?"
> > Mr. Fox did his best with the facts of the case.
> > "Mr. Rawle, will you give the plaintiff's argument?"
> > Mr. Rawle gave what he could of the plaintiff's argument.
> > "Mr. Adams, do you agree with that? . . . "[18]

In principle, students were to determine the law for themselves through direct engagement with the written authorities. The words of individual judges were to be assessed in reference to the development of legal doctrine

---

[15] *A Selection of Cases on the Law of Contracts: With References and Citations: Prepared for Use as a Text-book in Harvard Law School* (Boston: Brown, Little, 1871). If Langdell pioneered the common law casebook, canon law preceded him by centuries. In the Christian West, casebooks of "cases of conscience" had been prepared for use of confessors since at least the thirteenth century, and as textbooks for the training of priests since the sixteenth century. See Albert Jonsen and Stephen Toulmin, *The Abuse of Casuistry: A History of Moral Reasoning* (Berkeley: University of California Press, 1988), 141–43; John O'Malley, *The First Jesuits* (Cambridge, MA: Harvard University Press, 1993), 137, 146–47; Johann Theiner, *Die Entwicklung der Moraltheologie zur eigenständige Disziplin* (Regensburg: F. Pustet, 1970), 119–22; Louis Vereecke, *De Guillaume D'Ockham À Saint Alphonse de Liguori: Etudes d'histoire de la théologie morale moderne, 1300–1787* (Rome: Collegium S. Alfonsi de Urbe, 1986), 495–508.

[16] Samuel Batchelder, *Christopher C. Langdell*, 18 Green Bag 437 (1906).

[17] Headnotes appear at the top of cases and summarize the salient legal rules. Headnotes, however, are not authoritative. They have no precedential value. See *United States v. Detroit Timber & Lumber Company*, 200 U.S. 321 (1906).

[18] Batchelder, "Christopher C. Langdell," 440.

understood through the reading of a series of the leading cases.[19] Students adopted a judicial or juridical standpoint by engaging the very sources of the law, rather than accepting the word of textbook writers or professors. This was active learning.[20]

A LEGAL SCIENCE

The case method, however, was not simply a *method*, if by "method" we imagine a simple procedure – the reading of cases – for attaining an object: discovering the law. Rather, at least in its origins, the case method was truly a representation of, and the means to create and support, an intellectual discipline: an independent branch of study, a Langdellian *legal science*, which would both build upon, and significantly unsettle, the broadly natural-law foundations of earlier treatments of the legal system.

Langdell, in short, saw law as a science akin to physics, chemistry, or biology. In the preface to his first casebook, for instance, Langdell follows Blackstone and Story in describing law "as a science," consisting of "certain principles or doctrines."[21] "[T]he business of every earnest student of law," Langdell writes, is to "have such a mastery of these [principles or doctrines] as to be able to apply them with constant facility and certainty to the ever-tangled skein of human affairs."[22] If law was truly a science, however – or rather, if late-nineteenth-century Anglo-American law, as studied in a university context, were truly *to be* a science – then this legal science needed to consist of a finite number of principles or doctrines, akin to the finite chemical elements or laws of physics. While the content of the law seemed complex, even messy, Langdell maintained that the number of its core principles or doctrines was

[19] "The mere *ipse dixit* of the court is never accepted as final. In fact chief justices and chancellors are frequently overruled with surprisingly nonchalance." M, *Correspondence to the Editors*, 1 Columb. L. Times 4, 25 (October 1887).

[20] Years later, Langdell's great supporter President Eliot would dryly suggest, "Professor Langdell had, I think, no acquaintance with the educational theories or practices of Froebel, Pestalozzi, Seguin, and Montessori; yet his method of teaching was a direct application to intelligent and well-trained adults of some of their methods for children and defectives." Charles W. Eliot, *Langdell and the Law School*, 33 Harv. L. Rev. 518, 523 (1919).

[21] Langdell, *Selection of Cases*, vi. Few commentators note the affinities with Blackstone and Story. They suggest, instead, that Langdell marks a distinct break from previous traditions. Thomas Gray does note continuity, but suggests that we find a new rigor with "Langdell and his followers" who "took the view of law as science seriously and carried it out programmatically in a way that had no precedent in the common law world, erecting a vast discursive structure that came to dominate legal education and to greatly influence the practical work of lawyers and judges." Thomas Gray, *Langdell's Orthodoxy*, 45 U. Pitt. L. Rev. 1, 5 (1984).

[22] Langdell, *Selection of Cases*, vi.

"much less than is commonly supposed."[23] The varied guises under which the same legal principles or doctrines had appeared, he thought, concealed relative simplicity: a fog of confusion that the tools of modern science – not least classification and systematization – could dissipate.

A science, of course, has an object of study, and the material on which Langdellian legal science worked was not an abstract concept of justice, or, as for Story, a combination of history and reason. Rather, it was the written cases. The true specimens of legal science were the reported words of judges. Indeed, Langdell maintained that "*all* the available materials of that science are contained in printed books."[24] The research practices and attitudes of legal science rightly related, then, to the discovery and sifting of information from the law library, which he believed was:

> the proper workshop of professors and students alike; that it is to us all that the laboratories of the university are to the chemists and physicists, the museum of natural history to the zoologists, the botanical garden to the botanists.[25]

The law was to be discovered and extracted from its source, the written record of cases – particularly appellate opinions – by *induction*; the legal scientist was to infer principles and doctrines from the particular decisions of the courts. As knowledge of natural science was understood to rightly proceed from observation of particular organisms, or physical science from physical phenomena, so in legal science, the *stuff* of the common law – the written record of judicial opinions – was to be the sole source for the law. Accordingly, legal education was to teach the inductive derivation of principles and doctrines, never apart from the cases.[26]

To teach law in this way, thought Langdell, professors need not be experienced in the *practice* of the law. As *legal scientists*, professors' expertise was rightly "experience in learning law," not in its use.[27] They were to be

---

23   Ibid. Notice that Langdell's claim provides an answer to the problem of how to deal with the increasingly large numbers of reported law cases.
24   *The Harvard Law School*, 3 Law Q. Rev. 118, 124 (1887) (emphasis added).
25   Ibid. Langdell identified the library as the site of scientific inquiry on several occasions, including in his published reports to President Eliot. See, e.g., *Annual Reports of the President and Treasurer of Harvard College. 1872–73* (Cambridge: Welch, Bigelow, 1874), 63; and *Annual Reports of the President and Treasurer of Harvard College. 1873–74* (Cambridge, MA: John Wilson and Sons, 1875), 67.
26   Redlich, *Common Law and the Case Method*, 16.
27   The skills and purpose of the law professor for Langdell were "not the experience of the Roman advocate, or of the Roman prætor, still less of the Roman procurator, but the experience of the Roman jurisconsult." *The Harvard Law School*, 3 Law Q. Rev. 118, 124 (1887). A *jurisconsult* gave advice on questions of law as an aristocratic pursuit rather than as his career. He did not try cases or aid parties in their pleadings before courts, but rather gave

researchers in the laboratory of the law library. Langdell's student James Barr Ames (1846–1910), for example, was appointed an assistant professor immediately following his graduation from Harvard Law School, without any professional experience. In fact, Langdell was "inclined to believe that success at the Bar or on the Bench was, in all probability, a disqualification for the functions of a professor of law."[28]

Despite sharing some vocabulary, Langdell's understanding of law as science conflicted with the prevailing practitioners' view of law as a craft, and with the older collegiate vision of law as an art, rightly studied with philosophy and government as the means to form character. Proponents of legal science insisted instead that law was its own scholarly discipline with its own domain and method.[29] It was neither merely a preparation for practice nor one facet of a humanistic education.

Despite initial resistance to the introduction of the case method, the intellectual underpinnings of this new legal science were not unfamiliar to Langdell's contemporaries. "Science" was the emerging commonplace of a powerful new American vision for the research university. Inspired by Germany, not just the natural and physical sciences but even the humanities at Harvard, as elsewhere, were rebuilding on a scientific basis.[30] Congruence with observable phenomena, and not metaphysical or other categories, was to be the sole criterion for truth.

To establish the scientific character [*Wissenschaftlichkeit*] of legal study, Langdell's would-be legal scientists insisted both that law has a distinctive object of study (reported cases) and that its method (induction) was suitably objective. We might think that the very bareness of Langdell's casebook offered its own proof: What could speak more of the publicity and replicability

advice to a judge or a party to the case on the state of the law. See Cicero, *De Oratore. Loeb Classical Library.* (Cambridge, MA: Harvard University Press, 1942–48), 1:212, 148–49.

[28]   Eliot, "Langdell and the Law School," 520.

[29]   "Dean Langdell thought that English and American law should be studied by itself without admixture of other subjects, such as government, economics, international law, or Roman law." Ibid., 523.

[30]   Americans' enthusiasm for German universities nonetheless often confused German interest in *pure learning* – research pursued for its own merit, free from state and commercial demands – with *pure science*, the use of experimental methodologies in ever-increasing specialization. Americans generally ignored the contemplative aspects of *Wissenschaft*, and, especially in the *Humboldtsches Bildungsideal*, the integration of humanistic and scientific knowledge in the formation of students as (world) citizens. See Laurence Veysey, *The Emergence of the American University* (Chicago: University of Chicago Press, 1965), 121–79; and Chad Wellmon, *Organizing Enlightenment: Information Overload and the Invention of the Modern Research University* (Baltimore, MD: Johns Hopkins University Press, 2015), 210–233.

of law – necessary for law's scientific character – than the fact that, from its unadulterated materials of study, law students could inductively determine the law? "Under the influence of Germany," Oliver Wendell Holmes, Jr. told the assembled crowds at the 1886 celebration of Harvard's 250th anniversary, "science is gradually drawing legal history into its sphere."[31]

Langdell's vision of the law, then, places it alongside physics, chemistry, and biology. We might be tempted to link this vision to every facet of the nine-teenth-century enthusiasm for science and the scientific method. But yielding to this temptation obscures more than illumines. Beyond legal science's general scientific spirit, and its scientifically inflected building blocks – its content (legal principles and doctrines), its sources (law cases), its place of investigation (the law library), its method (induction), and its scientists (law professors not lawyers) – the connections between legal science and the natural and physical sciences are difficult to sketch with any exactitude.[32] What did it truly mean for case law to be "scientific"?

Recent commentators suggest case law's scientific influences and compara-tors. Robert Stevens, for instance, calls the case method "somewhat Darwinian," presumably as legal doctrine is refined through a series of cases with only the fittest parts surviving.[33] Bruce Kimball links Langdell with *Baconianism*, at least inasmuch as Bacon's thought was understood through popular mid-nineteenth-century philosophers of science, such as Samuel Tyler (1809–77).[34] Legal science, accordingly, is inductive and empiricist. Thomas Gray depicts the intellectual world of Langdell and his supporters as *idealist*: The legal scientist – the scholar, or a great judge or lawyer – discovers a previously unrecognized principle of the law, albeit immanent in

---

[31] Holmes continued: "The facts are being scrutinized by eyes microscopic in intensity and panoramic in scope. At the same time, under the influence of our revived interest in philosophical speculation, a thousand heads are analyzing and generalizing the rules of law and the grounds on which they stand. The law has got to be stated over again, and I venture to say that in fifty years we shall have it in a form of which no man could have dreamed fifty years ago." *The Harvard Law School*, 3 Law Q. Rev. 118, 120 (1887).

[32] But see Howard Schweber, *The "Science" of Legal Science: The Model of the Natural Sciences in Nineteenth-Century American Legal Education*, 17 Law & Hist. Rev. 421 (1999).

[33] Robert Stevens, *Law School: Legal Education in America from the 1850s to the 1980s* (Chapel Hill: University of North Carolina Press, 1983), 55.

[34] Bruce Kimball, "The Proliferation of Case Method Teaching in American Law Schools: Mr. Langdell's Emblematic 'Abomination,' 1890–1915," *History of Education Quarterly* 46, no. 2 (2006): 192–247, 198; Samuel Tyler, *A Discourse of the Baconian Philosophy*, rev. ed. (New York: Baker and Scribner, 1850); Samuel Tyler, "On Philosophical Induction," *American Journal of Science and Arts*, 2nd series, 5 (1848): 329–37. Francis Bacon had advocated science as the exhaustive survey of experience via induction involving multiple stages of abstraction and invention. Langdell took the induction, at least.

the cases, and articulates this principle with greater precision than hitherto, thereby furthering the science of the law.[35] Each depiction captures something of Langdell's approach, but risks overly neat interpretation.

Langdell's presentation of law-as-a-science – akin to the natural and physical sciences – was, in its time, a contribution to the still-unsettled question of whether law, and other professional disciplines, rightly belonged in the American university. The rhetoric of legal study as scientific investigation served to link university law schools with the prestige then enjoyed by the burgeoning experimental sciences. In his speech marking the 250th anniversary of Harvard, Langdell identified, and measured, the law school's success, past and future, by its ability to prove "that law is a science, and that all the available materials of that science are contained in printed books."[36] In Langdell's mind, the purpose of university education was exhausted by the scientific method, such that "[i]f law be not a science, it is a species of handicraft, and may best be learned by serving an apprenticeship to one who practises it." To be worthy of university study, then, the law had to be a science, with the library – not the lawyer's office or judge's chambers – its essential workshop.[37]

Natural-law understandings of the American legal system of Langdell's time (and earlier) had also understood law to be a science. The creation of Harvard Law School was advocated on the grounds, we should recall, that law is a "comprehensive system of human wisdom, derived from the nature of man in his social and civil state, and founded on the everlasting basis of natural justice and moral philosophy."[38] Determining the degree to which Langdell's legal science is in continuity with earlier natural-law treatments of the law, therefore, requires some care, particularly because later critics of Langdell rarely parsed the distinctions between competing nineteenth-century visions.

Josef Redlich (1889–1936) – an Austrian jurist who authored a 1914 Carnegie Endowment report on the case method – was unusual in attempting to clarify the relation of Langdell's "legal science" to other then-contemporary uses of

---

[35] Gray suggests that for Langdell and his supporters, this was understood to occur partly in judicial acknowledgment of the changing needs and conditions of society. While not mentioned by Gray, on this account, there is something of *Hegelian* idealism in Langdell's views: The truth is progressively realized through the working out of societal life.

[36] *The Harvard Law School*, 3 Law Q. Rev. 118, 124 (1887).

[37] Langdell suggests that if it is a science, as he contends, "it will scarcely be disputed that it is one of the greatest and most difficult of sciences, and that it needs all the light that the most enlightened seat of learning can throw upon it." Ibid.

[38] These words were spoken by Isaac Parker on April 17, 1816 in his inaugural address as the first Royall Professor of Law. His address can be found in Charles Warren, *History of the Harvard Law School and of Early Legal Conditions in America* (New York: Lewis, 1908), 302.

that term. "Legal science," said Redlich, can refer, as it did in Europe, to the study of law as a historical and social phenomenon. But this "sociological, legal-historical, and cultural investigation" is not Langdell's legal science.[39] *Langdellian* legal science, instead, is a science of the *positive* law: a study of those laws instituted or imposed by authority. (For Langdell, we have seen, this refers primarily to the authoritative opinions of English and American common-law judges, although statutes, too, are positive law.) Langdell's legal science, moreover, is a *positivist* account of positive law because it does not deal "with physical facts, but with the products of the human will."[40]

Redlich's distinctions are helpful. Again, however, they make precise what was ambiguous in Langdell's writings.[41] Redlich's typology separates Langdellian legal science from the natural and physical sciences – which "rest upon observation, experience, and investigation of natural phenomena" – despite the fact that Langdell's favored comparators were biology and physics.[42] And Redlich emphasizes the *source* of Langdell's law in authoritative legal judgments, while Langdell equally stressed the common law's internal conceptual coherence.[43] True, Langdell did seem to implicitly agree that in an important sense the normativity of the law comes from command (and thus its commander), but it seemed to him – as much as it is possible to tell, given his silence – that commands are not to be separated from the *principled* content of the common law. At the least, the very possibility of casebooks depends on the idea that the disciplined student of the law can *discover* the law's content in the cases. Case law reveals the *coherence* of common-law doctrine; to the trained eye, indeed, the pages of the leading cases display the development, even consecutive revelation, of legal principles.

---

[39] Redlich, *Common Law and the Case Method*, 55.

[40] Ibid., 56.

[41] Perhaps Redlich captures the logical consequences of Langdell's thought. But Redlich's account does not explain Langdell's own understanding of the law, or how Langdellian legal science was understood in its day.

[42] Redlich, *Common Law and the Case Method*, 56.

[43] This distinguishes Langdell's approach from many of his successors, even those employing the case method. The cases worthy of study, in Langdell's view, were those that confirmed doctrine. In today's lecture theaters, Langdell "has been turned on its head," says Martha Minow (dean of Harvard Law School, 2009–17). The cases worthy of study are precisely those that do *not* readily conform to doctrine. "We have conflicting principles and are committed to opposing values. Students have to develop some degree of comfort with ambiguity." Martha Minow, quoted in David Garvin, "Making the Case: Professional Education for the World of Practice," *Harvard Magazine* (September–October, 2003).

PRECEDENT AND THE PROBLEM OF JUSTIFICATION

In its avowal of both _command_ and _principle_ in common law, Langdellian science has been said to "straddle ... natural law and historical schools."[44] In one sense, Langdell's law is, indeed, historicist. He presents the law developmentally. To refer to a series of cases, after all, is to chart the growth and the refinement of legal doctrines and principles over time. In this aspect of his method, Langdell is meaningfully linked to the historical school of jurisprudence, best known in the work of Friedrich Carl von Savigny (1779–1861). For historicists, law is the product and reflection of the particular spirit of a nation's people [_Volksgeist_]. Langdell is a historicist inasmuch as he believes – with Joseph Story – that common law fundamentally develops as English and American society develops. But Langdell's law is also natural law-like. After all, for Langdell, as for natural-law thinkers, it is the _reasonability_ of legal rules that is discovered in the common law's development. The act of determining what is the law is an act of human will, yes, but the content identified is rightly coherent with the wider body of law, and thus in accord with reason (at least in its practical, commonsensical guise).

Principle, therefore, has prominence in Langdell's vision of the law, despite his recognition of the importance of precedent and custom. And of great practical significance, moreover, was Langdell's understanding – shared with Blackstone and the Litchfield school – that general principles of the common law transcend borders. Harvard Law School was a _national_ law school, for Langdell, not a preparatory school for the Massachusetts bar. It taught a legal system "unitary, self-contained, value-free and consistent," where its students were to identify principle and doctrine through the opinions of the English and American courts.[45] This denial of difference was a distinct challenge to those who understood each of the states to have a viable legal system and contributed to the scholarly downplaying of the importance of legislation, which was little taught at Harvard.

Unlike his peers, who remained more closely wedded to the language of natural law, however, Langdell has a justificatory problem.[46] _How does a judge's decision in a case relate to what is right or true?_ The veracity of theories and practices of the natural and physical sciences receives independent justificatory support from the direct evidences of our senses, which, on

---

44 Gray, "Langdell's Orthodoxy," 30.
45 Stevens, _Law School_, 53.
46 Gray, "Langdell's Orthodoxy," 22.

the whole, we trust.[47] The modern natural-law theories, known to earlier generations of American lawyers, likewise appealed to depictions of what it means to be human in society in order to ground the rightness of law. (Story spoke, for example, of human nature as motivated toward happiness, human beings as possessors of certain intellectual powers, and human life as consisting in various relations – individual, familial, communal – that are generative of duties.) This was not similarly true for Langdell. He does not appeal to human nature. Instead, the sole content of his legal science is the judicial decisions found in the reported cases. What independent support can be given to justify these judicial decisions?

The twentieth-century legal scholar Thomas Gray asserts that two arguments were available to Langdell to justify his proposed legal principles and doctrines. Langdell could have appealed to *intuition* or *precedent*.[48] On Gray's account, Langdell first could have suggested that intuition links a judge's decision with an independent justification. Gray sketches three forms this argument might take. Form One is an appeal to some sort of moral sense: the "supposed universal human faculty for the direct intuition of right and wrong in concrete situations."[49] Unlike his natural-law forebears, however, Langdell did not justify judicial decisions on the ground of moral sense.

---

[47] The truth of natural and physical science is determined by its correspondence with the realities we perceive. Adherence to the theory of evolution, for instance, first received initial justification through the examination of organism remains and fossil layers, the observation of similarities between living organisms, and the practices and outcomes of artificial selection. The likely veracity of the theory has increased, more recently, with the development of technologies that allow the observation of organisms' DNA similitude.

[48] Gray also notes that *today* we might simply admit the circularity of a practice like the law. We might think that "science" and its methods and epistemology are similarly circular, with no means to step outside our ways of perceiving and measuring the world. "Langdell's Orthodoxy," 20–22.

[49] Ibid., 22–28. College-educated or well-read judges – those, particularly of an earlier generation, who studied Hutcheson's *Short Introduction to Moral Philosophy* – would recognize the *moral sense* as that which receives approbation or condemnation independent of our will. In America, Hutcheson's thought was often combined – uneasily, in retrospect – with that of Thomas Reid (1710–96). See Sydney Ahlstrom, "The Scottish Philosophy and American Theology," *Church History* 24, no. 3 (1955): 257–72; S. A. Grave, *The Scottish Philosophy of Common Sense* (Oxford: Clarendon Press, 1960); Knud Haakonssen, "Scottish Common Sense Realism," in *A Companion to American Thought*, ed. Richard Wightman Fox and James Kloppenberg (Cambridge, MA: Blackwell, 1995), 618–20. For Reid, our initial intuitions concern matters as basic as our consciousness – without any external evidence, we accept, and rely upon, an intuition of our own consciousness. ("The operations of our minds are attended with consciousness; and this consciousness is the evidence, the only evidence which we have or can have of their existence." Thomas Reid, *Essays on the Intellectual Powers of Man*, ed. Derek Brooks and Knud Haakonssen (Edinburgh: Edinburgh University Press,

Form Two Gray calls *common sense*. This is the "generally shared tacit knowledge of the conventional morality of a particular society."[50] Historically, this has been an influential expression of the nature of the common law, and Gray underestimates the tacit support that this common sense – tried by times and experience – receives in Langdell's depiction of the common law.[51] Nonetheless, Langdell did not explicitly justify judicial decisions on the ground of common sense.

The final form of intuition that could have linked judicial decisions to an independent justification is *trained intuition*: "a specialized professional skill developed by lawyers in the course of their apprenticeship, and practice."[52] Here, Gray briefly references Roscoe Pound (1870–1964) as representative of a commonplace view to this effect. But its *locus classicus* is the argument of Edward Coke (1552–1634), who, in disputing Jacobean royal authority, appealed to the superiority of lawyers' "artificial reason" over the natural reason of the king or any other. In Coke's argument, the reason necessary for legal determinations is "an artificial perfection of reason, gotten by long study,

2002, 41.) And likewise the "first principles of morals," which are understood to ground our moral reasoning, do not generate a decision in particular cases, but concern that: certain actions merit praise and others blame; involuntariness and necessity remove moral blame; omissions may be blameworthy; we should inform ourselves of our duties; and we should cultivate our minds for right action. (Thomas Reid, *Essays on the Active Powers of Man*, ed. Knud Haakonssen and James Harris (Edinburgh: Edinburgh University Press, 2010), "Essay V. Of Morals. Chapter 1. Of the First Principles of Morals," 271. These first principles of morals govern but do not produce determinations in concrete cases. Even the more particular principles that Reid identifies remain at a sufficiently high level that they cannot reasonably be understood to produce a determination in a concrete case. For instance, Reid argues that we rightly prefer a greater, though more distant, good to a lesser good; comply with our constitutions as human beings (this being understood as the intention of nature); are born not simply for ourselves; should act toward another as we would judge right for another to act toward us; and see that "veneration and submission" to God are self-evident to those who believe in "the existence, the perfections, and the providence of GOD." (Ibid., 272–76, 276.) Now, Reid's self-evident moral principles may be less self-evident than he imagined, but they nonetheless do not straightforwardly suggest determinations on factual grounds. If the emphasis is on Reid rather than Hutcheson, then the thought that judicial decisions should at some basic level accord with *moral sense* is less obscure than Gray seems to suppose.

50 Gray, "Langdell's Orthodoxy," 23.

51 "In the common law country, the law appears in the national thought as a quality which to a certain extent comes of itself to men and to the relations which bind men together, as something that is always there and for that reason is known and understood by every one of the people themselves." Redlich, *Common Law and the Case Method*, 37. A classic expression of common law as custom is found in Thomas Hedley's parliamentary speech of June 28, 1610: "the Comon lawe tried by tyme, which is wiser then all the Judges in the land. By tyme out of mynde." *Parliamentary Debates 1610*, ed. Samuel Rawson Gardiner (London: Camden Society, 1862), 71–77, 73.

52 Gray, "Langdell's Orthodoxy," 23.

observation and experience."[53] Once again, however, Langdell did not justify his legal science on the basis of intuition.

Ultimately, neither moral sense, nor common sense, nor trained intuition, nor some combination of the three provided the justification for Langdell's claim that the law is known inductively through the case law. Instead, Langdell looked to *precedent*.[54] Judicial decisions receive justification by following the previous decisions of the courts. Precedent is distinguished from intuition by a particular understanding of authority. In England and America, this plays out in the legal doctrine that precedents should be followed because of the authority of the prior decider. Inferior court judges, for instance, must follow the binding opinions of superior courts.[55]

Gray ultimately argues, then, that it is this resort to precedent that saves Langdell's understanding of the law from a vicious circularity.[56] A decision in a particular case is justified because the decision is based on a rule previously expressed by the court, and this rule itself is understood as binding because the

---

[53] "[R]eason is the life of the law, nay the common law itself is nothing else but reason; which is to be understood of an artificial perfection of reason, gotten by long study, observation and experience, and not of every man's natural reason; for *Nemo nascitur artilex.* This legal reason *est summa ratio.* And therefore if all the reason that is dispersed into so many several heads, were united into one, yet could he not make such a law as the law in England is; because by many successions of ages it hath been fined and refined by an infinite number of grave and learned men, and by long experience grown to such a perfection, for the government of this realm, as the old rule may be justly verified of it, *Neminem oportet esse sapientiorem legibus:* No man out of his own private reason ought to be wiser than the law, which is the perfection of reason." Co. Litt. 97b.

[54] Gray too sharply divides intuition from precedent. Their distinction is not, as it might first seem, about time: intuition as immediate, precedent based on history. *Common sense* and *trained intuition* – that is, societal morality, and lawyers' artificial reason – are themselves creatures of history: formed over time and through deliberation. Apart from Gray's understanding of intuition as *moral sense* – a universal faculty for direct intuition of right and wrong – precedent, therefore, is not distinguished from intuition by its connection to history or the passage of time.

[55] In a legal system where precedent is important, even the top court in a given jurisdiction may feel bound to ordinarily follow its own precedents. This is the doctrine of *stare decisis* ("to stand by decided matters"). For instance, through much of the nineteenth and early twentieth centuries, the United Kingdom's top appellate court (the judicial committee of the House of Lords) treated its own previous decisions as binding. This convention was only abolished in 1966. *Practice Statement (Judicial Precedent)* [1966] 1 WLR 1234 (HL).

[56] It seems that neither Gray nor Langdell consider the option that precedent itself may be the fruit of natural-law reasoning. There are obvious goods in the finality offered by precedent. There is a legitimacy gained from settled law that does not change on the whim of judges or other decision-makers. And settled expectations allow people to organize their lives without the anxieties of regular change. For an argument for the "inner morality" of law based off of such considerations, see Lon Fuller, *The Morality of Law* (New Haven, CT: Yale University Press, 1963).

court that expressed the rule is itself recognized as having the authority to determine the law.[57] Gray helps us see the justificatory pressure on Langdell to embrace precedent.

But this appeal to precedent compromises the "universally formal conceptual order" that Langdellian science assumed and promised.[58] To exalt precedent, after all, means to accept that long-standing, widely followed though seemingly *un*principled doctrine must be followed, too. The "wrong" gets followed as much as the "right." The role of consideration in contract law is a classic example. This is the doctrine that each party must give something up if a promise is to be binding and enforceable. The doctrine of consideration, Langdell recognized, can sometimes cause hardship and seeming unfairness, and is unnecessary in principle. Yet, Langdell determined, consideration is simply too well established in common law practice to be abandoned.[59] Precedent seems to win over principle.

LEGAL SCIENCE AND NATURAL LAW

The twentieth-century triumph of the case method has mostly obscured the controversy and dissension that surrounded its nineteenth-century introduction. Older forms of teaching remained standard. A history of legal education written in 1904 declared that "[t]he method of instruction in vogue in most of our law schools at the present day, as it was in all until a comparatively recent date, is that of the lecture."[60] With the case method's 1870 introduction at Harvard, student numbers dropped, and "[h]ardly one of the Boston lawyers had any faith in it."[61] When Langdell retired in 1895, only six other schools had

---

[57]   Most contemporary legal philosophers – following H. L. A. Hart (1907–92) – understand this type of recognition of authority as some form of a *social rule*: a complex practice imposing a duty on officials to follow and apply the rule.

[58]   Gray, "Langdell's Orthodoxy," 26.

[59]   By Langdell's time, in common-law jurisdictions, a valid contract – in its simplest form – was formed where there was an offer and its acceptance, the parties intended to create a legal relationship, and there was valid consideration. In Langdell's chosen words, consideration is "the thing given or done by the promisee in exchange for the promise": in a contract, the recompense or equivalent for what one party does or undertakes for the other party. As a matter of principle, however, Langdell felt – as have many before and since – that consideration is unnecessary. In European civil law, promises are enforceable without consideration, as they are too in the common-law world where an agreement is undertaken while employing sufficient formalities as, for example, with a deed, where a legal disposition is written, sealed, and delivered. Langdell, *Selection of Cases*, §45, 58.

[60]   Edwin Dexter, *A History of Education in the United States* (New York: Macmillan, 1904), 326.

[61]   "The number of students declined more than either of us had expected, and the demonstration of success achieved in prominent law offices and in practice by graduates of the School,

adopted the case method, and, as we have seen, it remained sufficiently controversial in the ensuing decades that, in 1914, the Carnegie Endowment for the Advancement of Teaching commissioned Redlich's study of its utility. The method's widespread adoption came only as prominent students of Langdell came of age and praised the system in which they were trained, and as the case method's use slowly became an institutional mark of prestige. Even if its uptake was small, the case method was used, its supporters noted, "in nearly all the best schools."[62]

The case method's twentieth-century success, moreover, has obscured not only the cautious initial uptake of the method, but its connection to the wide range of nineteenth-century voices on the nature and purpose of law, explicit natural-law accounts included. Over the twentieth century, Langdell became a too-convenient symbol for his era and his methodological proclivities as definitive of the age's particular genius.[63]

If, by embracing precedent over reason, Langdell's science of the law – known and perpetuated in the case method – helped to displace natural-law forms of thinking about the law, however, this was not necessitated by Langdellian legal science. In ways strange to twentieth-century positivists, Langdell took for granted that precedent – the historical development of legal principles and doctrines – determined the right answers. He viewed the common law, in other words, as having both a precedential authority *and* a persuasive authority. Common law's authority comes from rightly guiding *and* commanding action.

The case method, we have seen, both relies upon the tracing of doctrinal development through the leading cases, and presumes – in Langdell's version – that there are, in fact, correct principles that the law student can identify by reading the cases.[64] So Langdell could believe in the superiority of precedent while also being "inexorable in his search for the truth."[65]

---

who had enjoyed Langdell's system and thoroughly utilized it, came more slowly than we had anticipated." Charles Eliot, *Langdell and the Law School*, 33 Harv. L. Rev. 518, 522–23 (1920). James Barr Ames, "Christopher Columbus Langdell," in *Lectures on Legal History and Miscellaneous Legal Essays* (Cambridge, MA: Harvard University Press, 1913), 467–84.

[62] Ames, "Christopher Columbus Langdell," 478.

[63] "If Langdell had not existed," wrote Grant Gilmore, "we should have had to invent him." *The Ages of American Law*, 2nd ed., with a final chapter by Philip Bobbitt (New Haven, CT: Yale University Press, 2014), 38.

[64] "Each of these doctrines has arrived at its present state by slow degrees; in other words, it is a growth, extending in many cases through centuries. This growth is to be traced in the main through a series of cases; and much the shortest and best, if not the only way of mastering the doctrine effectually is by studying the cases in which it is embodied." Ibid., vi.

[65] This was the recollection of his first students. Franklin Fessenden, *The Rebirth of the Harvard Law School*, 33 Harv. L. Rev. 493, 513 (1920).

Langdell's twentieth-century critics reject this combinative possibility. Indeed, it is Langdell's commitment to the pervasive reasonability of the law that has left many commentators convinced that his legal science is, in fact, a restatement of "the natural-law argument for judicial supremacy, albeit with a glossy 'law is a science' label."[66] Certainly, Langdell and his supporters notably offer little philosophical basis for principles and doctrines. They fail to answer the question, in other words, of how principles are uniform in the legal system if based solely on the decisions of individual judges. The case method is the process for *identifying* principles, not their explanation. Earlier natural lawyers might explain principles as according with shared human inclinations, but for Langdell, the historical determinations of judges provide the material of the law, and not human nature or philosophical reflection thereon.

Langdell's science, therefore, departed from the natural-law tradition in its clear affirmation of positive law – as promulgated by judges and, secondarily, legislators – as the sole source of the law, rather than morality or even custom. For this reason, Langdell is sometimes listed as a pioneer of legal positivism. John Witte, Jr. and Frank Alexander, indeed, treat Langdell as the American exemplar of legal positivism.[67]

Yet the commitment to principle and internal coherence in Langdell's science – which generates a normativity of persuasive authority even if

---

[66] In the eyes of those influenced by legal realism – who emphasize law as a matter of societal and political power, and not formal principle – the congruence of the *results* of Langdellian legal science with those of earlier natural-law approaches show them to be only trivially distinct. Langdellian legal science supports "political beliefs every bit as conservative as those of Joseph Story." Seligman, *High Citadel*, 36. Intriguingly, the victory of the case method in the early decades of the twentieth century has also led to the reverse: curious readings of evidently natural-law visions of American law *as* Langdellian legal science. For instance, Robert Stevens, usually a reliable guide to law schools, presents developments at Catholic University's law school in the 1890s as evidence of Langdell's influence. For William Robinson, the school's reforming dean, "law as a science is a body of fundamental principles and of deductions drawn therefore in reference to the right ordering of social conduct." Stevens, *Law School*, 122. Stevens connects this to Langdell. However, Robinson's attention to "logical deductions from immutable and universal principles" combined with his belief in law as "an ethical science [with its] origin in the reason, not in the will," shows greater correspondence with the neo-Thomism of the period than Langdellian legal science. William Robinson, *A Study on Legal Education: Its Purposes and Methods* (Washington, DC: Stormont & Jackson, 1895), 4, 5. Of course, expressions of neo-Thomism are, themselves, linked to the changes in thinking wrought by the scientific revolution.

[67] Witte and Alexander place Langdell beside England's John Austin. Langdell and Austin, they say, believed "[l]aw is simply the concrete rules and procedures posited by the sovereign and enforced by the courts." *The Teachings of Modern Christianity on Law, Politics, and Human Nature*, ed. John Witte, Jr. and Frank Alexander (New York: Columbia University Press, 2006), xxii.

precedent is the ultimate practical referent – places it apart from consequentialist visions of the law, whether nineteenth-century utilitarianism, or the twentieth-century models that would come to dominate: where law is justified by its results in good public policy or economic rationalization, and legal success understood as the match between courtroom outcomes and political desires.

* * *

The figure of Langdell serves as a helpful example of the uneasy relationship of natural law and positivism in late-nineteenth-century accounts of common law. Some commentators treat Langdell's turn to the natural sciences as continuous with Blackstone and Story's understanding of law as a science. Others herald or bemoan Langdell as a nascent legal positivist. Langdell, we have seen, affirms the positive law of judges and legislators as the sole source of law, not morality or even custom, and turns to precedent to ultimately explain the particular content and binding quality of American common law. Yet, Langdell also presumes law's internal coherence. When students engage in the case method, he says, they find principles at the heart of the common law.

In this, Langdell arguably offers an example of a natural-law account of common law that is inductionist. He offers, in other words, a vision of law where more general laws or principles are formed by inference from the decisions of particular legal cases. This approach is distinct from prominent forms of the natural-law tradition – especially in its modern guise – which work *deductively*: that is, by applying a priori principles (concerning human nature, say) to particulars. Of the modern natural lawyers, only Hugo Grotius allows for both induction and deduction. Thomas Hobbes, Samuel Pufendorf, and John Locke, instead, solely work by deduction.[68] Definitions begin their treatises. Mathematics is their model. In favoring induction, Langdell looked instead to cases not principles, and the natural sciences not mathematics.

But this inductionist account is haunted by questions of justification, as we have seen: Why should we expect to find case law reasonable? It is Langdell's silence on this question that allows his interpretation as either natural lawyer or positivist. He neither adopts the position of Story, who suggested that history – and thus the refinement of case law – works out reason, nor the legal realists who would follow, who looked to standards external of the law.

---

[68] For extracts of the relevant discussions by Grotius, Hobbes, Pufendorf, and Locke, see J. B. Schneewind, *Moral Philosophy from Montaigne to Kant* (Cambridge: Cambridge University Press, 2003), 88–200. The same ground is covered by Knud Haakonssen, "Natural Law in the Seventeenth Century," in *Natural Law and Moral Philosophy: From Grotius to the Scottish Enlightenment* (Cambridge: Cambridge University Press, 1996), 15–62.

Without an explicit answer to the question, Langdell turned to precedent. Yet he retained a belief – bolstered by his scientific method – that common law is, at its heart, reasonable. His was an age when the power of the scientific method promised progress in all aspects of life. Following in the mainstream of the natural-law tradition, Langdell assumed, too, that all reasonable people would see the truths of his legal science. In the next chapter, we will see what happened when such belief turned to disbelief: For Oliver Wendell Holmes, Jr. and the American legal realists, common law had no intrinsic rationality.

6

Breaking with Natural Law

Oliver Wendell Holmes and the Legal Realists

Christopher Columbus Langdell's vision of the law did not go unchallenged, even in his own day. Yes, leading universities adopted his case method, but it remained sufficiently controversial that reports gauging its utility were still being written thirty years after its classroom introduction. An older lecture-driven vision of legal education remained the norm in most university legal education into the early years of the twentieth century, and apprentices continued to glean professional competency from experienced practitioners and their copies of treatises by Blackstone, Story, and their successors.

Pedagogical conservativism aside, Langdell's legal science faced a striking further challenge. Oliver Wendell Holmes, Jr. (1841–1935) – a justice of the Massachusetts Supreme Judicial Court (1882–1902) and of the U.S. Supreme Court (1902–32) – dismissed Langdell's belief in the principled cohesion of the common law.[1] Holmes's skeptical and pragmatic jurisprudence – known best through his widely read *The Common Law* (1881) and "The Path of the Law" (1897), together with his famous dissents from the Supreme Court bench – rejected Langdell's "formalism" and articulated a thoroughgoing positivism

---

[1] Holmes's major works are included in Sheldon Novick, ed., *The Collected Works of Justice Holmes: Complete Public Writings and Selected Judicial Opinions*, 3 vol. (Chicago: University of Chicago Press, 1994). Holmes's diaries and letters were edited by Mark DeWolfe Howe: *Holmes-Pollock Letters, The Correspondence of Mr. Justice Holmes and Sir Frederick Pollock, 1872–1932* (Cambridge, MA: Harvard University Press, 1941); *Touched with Fire: Civil War Letters and Diary of Oliver Wendell Holmes, Jr.* (Cambridge, MA: Harvard University Press, 1946); and *Holmes-Laski Letters: The Correspondence of Mr. Justice Holmes and Harold J. Laski, 1916–1935* (Cambridge, MA: Harvard University Press, 1953). Recent biographies include: G. Edward White, *Oliver Wendell Holmes, Jr.* (New York: Oxford University Press, 2006); Albert Alschuler, *Law without Values: The Life, Work, and Legacy of Justice Holmes* (Chicago: University of Chicago Press, 2000); and Sheldon Novick, *Honorable Justice: The Life of Oliver Wendell Holmes* (Boston: Little, Brown, 1989).

that was embraced by a succeeding wave of legal thinkers.[2] If the effects of Holmes's thought on legal education were minimal at first, his influence was ultimately profound; refracted through the work of the twentieth-century legal realists, to whom we will shortly turn, Holmes's thought indisputably changed American conceptions of law.

HOLMES AND THE NATURE OF THE LAW

Holmes has been called the "hero of American law"; the "great oracle of American legal thought"; and the "most illustrious figure in the history of American law."[3] His renown today is as a judge and man of letters, a towering statesman and individual thinker, but he was also an influential conduit of a stream of pragmatist thought. Despite his overt rejection of philosophical pragmatism as a whole, Holmes's legal writings are inconceivable without C. S. Pierce (1839–1914), William James (1842–1910), and John Dewey (1859–1952), the pioneers of pragmaticism.[4] Holmes shared their distaste for the formal, the deduced, and the abstract, and, with them, argued for evolution and change over tradition and consistency.[5] He embraced James's commitment to "*look . . . away from first things, principles, 'categories,' supposed necessities*" and look instead "*towards last things, fruits, consequences, facts.*"[6] And in determining cases, Holmes sought to rely not on logic or deduction, but on what Dewey would call "inquiry, comparison of alternatives, weighing of facts."[7]

Holmes's attention to consequences undergirds his "prediction theory of law." Holmes claims that the *nature* of law – and thus the proper "object of study" for the law student and practitioner alike – is simply "the prediction of the incident of the public force through the instrumentality of the courts."[8] What law is, in other words, is just what the courts do. Law has no existence

[2] *The Common Law* (Boston: Little, Brown, 1881); *The Path of the Law*, 10 Harv. L. Rev. 457 (1897). Holmes's most famous dissent was in *Lochner v. New York* 198 U.S. 45, 74 (1905).
[3] See Alschuler, *Law Without Values*, 14–15.
[4] Against the pragmatists, Holmes believed in mind-independent reality. And Holmes dismissed William James's perceived support of religion and cosmic beneficence, calling James's ideas "an amusing humbug." "Holmes to Pollock. June 17, 1908," in Howe, ed., *Holmes-Pollock Correspondence*, 1:139.
[5] Wilfred Rumble, *American Legal Realism: Skepticism, Reform, and the Judicial Process* (Ithaca, NY: Cornell University Press, 1968), 6.
[6] *Pragmatism: A New Name for Some Old Ways of Thinking: Popular Lectures on Philosophy* (New York: Longmans, Green, 1907), 29 (italics in original).
[7] John Dewey, *Logical Method and Law*, 10 Cornell L. Rev. 17, 17 (1924).
[8] Holmes, "Path," 457.

apart from a judge's decision. The task of lawyering, therefore, is the prediction of the decision a court will make, not the determination of a right answer.

No one would dispute that, as a matter of strategy, lawyers offer predictions to their clients. Lawyers help their clients understand the strength of their case, and – particularly in civil litigation – help them weigh costs and risks against the potential for success. But Holmes's attention to the consequences of court decisions was not a matter of strategy but ontology. Rather than think that the law concerns duties, say, or "inner states" – intention, recklessness, negligence, and so forth – Holmes concentrates almost solely on consequences. Take, for instance, the agreement reached in a contract. Holmes suggests that "[t]he duty to keep a contract at common law means a prediction that you must pay damages if you do not keep it, – nothing else."[9] Gone in Holmes's account of contracts is any reference to promises or duties as ordinarily understood as obligations, which *ought* to be fulfilled. The "only universal consequence" of entering into a contract, he says, is that "the law makes the promisor pay damages if the promised event does not come to pass."[10]

If law is best understood as a matter of predictable consequences, then the viewpoint of "the bad man" best apprehends the law's scope and content. Dispelling "a confusion between morality and law," Holmes argues that "[a] man who cares nothing for an ethical rule which is believed and practised by his neighbors is likely nevertheless to care a good deal to avoid being made to pay money, and will want to keep out of jail if he can."[11] Hence, if the law student is to know the law, he "must look at it as a bad man, who cares only for the material consequences which such knowledge enables him to predict, not as a good one, who finds his reasons for conduct, whether inside the law or outside of it, in the vaguer sanctions of conscience."[12]

Holmes thinks that taking the viewpoint of the bad man clarifies the nature of the law. The law is not "a system of reason," then, or "deduction from principles of ethics or admitted axioms or what not," as, arguably, Blackstone or Story contend.[13] Instead, law for Holmes is simply "what is decided by the

---

[9] Ibid., 462.

[10] Holmes, *Common Law*, 301.

[11] A "confusion," he says, "which sometimes rises to the height of conscious theory, and more often and indeed constantly is making trouble in detail without reaching the point of consciousness." Holmes, "Path," 459.

[12] Ibid.

[13] Ibid., 460. As we have seen, however, Blackstone and Story do not neglect the role that courts play in specifying common law. On their accounts, common law does indeed relate to a system of reason and is partially deducible from principles (although not on indifferent matters). But from reason and principle, courts determine what the law is and put it into practice.

courts of Massachusetts or England."[14] The bad man – and, accordingly, the lawyer and the jurist – do not "care two straws for the axioms or deductions," but "want to know what the Massachusetts or English courts are likely to do in fact."[15] And thus "the prophecies of what the courts will do in fact, and nothing more pretentious" are what Holmes means by "law."[16] Holmes looks solely to the facts of a case and its likely outcome. Gone is the thought that reasoning on principles is the necessary intermediary.

For Holmes, then, to speak of "law" is to speak predictively of the actions of the courts of a particular legal jurisdiction. The common law is thus "the articulate voice of some sovereign or quasi sovereign," and not "a brooding omnipresence in the sky ... some mystic overlaw that [the U.S.] is bound to obey."[17] Echoing the philosophical pragmatists, Holmes believes that there is nothing "beyond" or "outside" of the bare practice of adjudication. Law has no independent existence. In one of his famous dissents, Holmes charges that his colleagues on the Supreme Court bench fallaciously used their "independent judgment" to determine the content of "a transcendental body of law outside of any particular state but obligatory within it" when, in fact, "there is no such body of law."[18] There is no *common* common law – no "common law in abstracto" accessible by judicial reason – but only the particular common law of Massachusetts, say, or of England.[19]

It remains possible, of course, to ask *why* particular courts make the decisions they do. But, so framed, this is now a descriptive rather than a normative question. As Holmes famously puts it at the beginning of *The Common Law*:

---

[14]   Holmes, "Path," 460.

[15]   Ibid., 461.

[16]   Ibid.

[17]   Letter of January 29, 1926, to Harold Laski. In Richard Posner, ed., *The Essential Holmes: Selections from the Letters, Speeches, Judicial Opinions, and Other Writings of Oliver Wendell Holmes, Jr.* (Chicago: Chicago University Press, 1992), 235. The more familiar use of his phrase "brooding omnipresence in the sky" is found in his dissent to *Southern Pacific Company v. Jensen*, 244 U.S. 205, 222 (1917): "[T]he common law is not a brooding omnipresence in the sky, but the articulate voice of some sovereign or quasi sovereign that can be identified; although some decisions with which I have disagreed seem to me to have forgotten the fact."

[18]   *Black & White Taxi Co. v. Brown & Yellow Taxi Co.*, 276 U.S. 518, 533 (1928) (Holmes, J., dissenting). The Supreme Court ruled that, when federal courts sit in *diversity jurisdiction* – most usually when the parties are from different states – they need not apply state common law. Ten years later, in *Erie Railroad Co. v. Tompkins*, 304 U.S. 64 (1938), the Court determined that, in fact, it did *not* have the power to create federal common law when hearing state law claims under diversity jurisdiction.

[19]   "The late [Justice John Marshall] Harlan, [Justice William R.] Day, and a majority of others have treated the question as if they were invited to speculate about *the* common law *in abstracto*." "To Harold Laski, January 29, 1926," in Posner, ed., *Essential Holmes*, 235.

"The life of the law has not been logic: it has been experience."[20] It is not enough, as for Langdell, to "show that the consistency of a system requires a particular result." Law is not a matter of "axioms and corollaries of a book of mathematics." To know the law in Holmes's world – that is, to predict how judges will determine cases – is to consider "[t]he felt necessities of the time, the prevalent moral and political theories, intuitions of public policy, avowed or unconscious, even the prejudices which judges share with their fellow-men." The "grown-up" legal mind, in Holmes's view, is not concerned with the aptness or otherwise of felt necessities, however, or the rightness or wrongness of moral and political theory, but simply how such prejudices might suggest how a judge will decide a case.

HOLMES AND MORALITY

Holmes was not new in distinguishing law and morality. And neither was he new in suggesting that law and morality are not necessarily connected; legal positivism has a long history.[21] (Indeed, the very idea of "positive law" itself is likely the creation of the medieval minds closely associated with the natural-law tradition.[22]) The more proximate genealogy of Holmes's thought, however, included Thomas Hobbes (1588–1679) and David Hume (1711–76), who stressed political arrangements as conventional; Jeremy Bentham (1748–1832), who suggested an alternative to Blackstone's natural-law vision of English law in utilitarian consequentialism; and John Austin (1790–1859), who, expanding on Bentham, presented law as the traceable command of a sovereign. Holmes used this particular positivistic inheritance to explain and critique American common law, and, thereafter, has himself served as a touchstone for an American tradition of legal positivism.

What are the consequences of embracing positivism? Holmes sometimes suggested that separating law and morality is simply for analytical advantage. In "The Path of the Law" he argues, "[w]hen I emphasize the difference between law and morals I do so with reference to a single end, that of learning and understanding the law."[23] Indeed, he stresses the unavoidability of morality in the practice of law, for, whether we like it or not, "[t]he law is the

---

[20] Holmes, *Common Law*, 1.
[21] For examples from antiquity of "non-realist" conceptions of law, even divine law, see Christine Hayes, *What's Divine about Divine Law?* (Princeton, NJ: Princeton University Press, 2015).
[22] See John Finnis, "The Truth in Legal Positivism," in *The Autonomy of Law*, ed. Robert P. George (Oxford: Clarendon Press, 1996), 195–214.
[23] Holmes, "Path," 459.

witness and external deposit of our moral life. It is history of the moral development of the race."[24]

From these statements alone, we might conclude that Holmes understands legislators, judges, and society at large to have moral and social views, which – consciously or otherwise – find shape in the law, but that students of law, notwithstanding this, should focus on law proper without backward reference to the moral and social views that brought it into being. But that conclusion is not quite right.

Holmes's other writings suggest a stronger rejection of morality. In his private letters, indeed, Holmes more often than not treats morality as an enemy to be defeated. True, by "morality" Holmes seems to have in mind a particular Kantian conception concerned with exceptionless rules. He dismisses, for instance, "ordinary Christian morality" and its "slapdash universal (Never tell a lie. Sell all thou hast and give to the poor etc.)."[25] And in *The Common Law* he is at pains to prove that a "true account of the law as it stands" shows that the law "treat[s] the individual as a means to an end," and therefore does not instantiate (Kantian) morality.[26]

But Holmes does not just reject one articulation of morality, Christian or Kantian. Instead he finds the concept itself at best useless. In this, he is a "naturalist" in morals. A moral statement, for Holmes, does not pick out an independent value in the world, or refer to a truth. A moral statement is rather "an imperfect social generalization expressed in terms of feeling."[27] This naturalistic understanding of moral statements, however, is not enough for Holmes. Even so recognized, moral statements and the system they instantiate remain unhelpfully tied to "feeling." It would be far better, in Holmes's view, to "omit the emotion," and, instead, "ask ourselves what those generalizations are and how far they are confirmed by fact accurately ascertained."[28] We look around and see what is happening. So-called morality is thus known through "the same science as other observations of fact."[29]

---

[24] Ibid.

[25] "To Lewis Einstein, July 31, 1906," in Posner, ed., *Essential Holmes*, 58.

[26] Holmes, *Common Law*, 46–47. Kant's formulation of humanity of his categorical imperative reads, "So act that you use humanity, whether in your own person or in the person of any other, always at the same time as an end, never merely as a means." Immanuel Kant, *Groundwork of the Metaphysics of Morals*, trans. and ed. Mary Gregor (Cambridge: Cambridge University Press, 1998), 34, Ak. 4:429.

[27] "To Lewis Einstein, May 21, 1914," in Posner, ed., *Essential Holmes*, 114.

[28] *Ideals and Doubts*, 10 Ill. L. Rev. 1 (1915). Morality, he suggested, is best treated "like a physical phenomenon . . . to be combated or got around so far as may be, if one does not like it, as soon as fully possible." "To Patrick Sheehan, October 18, 1912," in Posner, ed., *Essential Holmes*, 7.

[29] "To Harold Laski, June 24, 1929," in Posner, ed., *Essential Holmes*, 116.

Unlike a Bentham or a John Stuart Mill, Holmes does not suggest a standard by which to judge the imperfect social generalizations of conventional morality, except perhaps a social Darwinist's belief in "progress."[30] This reticence is ultimately because Homes treats not just morality but also truth itself as purely conventional. "Truth," as we know it at least, "is the unanimous consent of mankind to a system of propositions."[31] Or as he archly elaborates: "Do you like sugar in your coffee or don't you?"[32] And answers: "You admit the possibility of difference and yet are categorical in your own way, and even instinctively condemn those who do not agree. *So as to truth.*"[33]

If positivism severs law and morality, so severed they are equally social conventions, insists Holmes. And in morals, unlike law, there is "no superior tribunal to decide" between alternatives.[34] Thus he can write to his friend Harold Laski and suggest that "logically the Germans stood as well as we did" in using chemical weapons in the First World War, despite Allied protestations: "I often think of the way our side shrieked during the late war at various things done by the Germans such as the use of gas. We said gentlemen don't do such things – to which the Germans: 'Who the hell are you? We do them.'"[35] And, likewise, Holmes can say similarly of law that "the first requirement of a sound body of law is, that it should correspond with the actual feelings and demands of the community, whether right or wrong."[36]

But by what standard can he say that community feelings and demands are "right" or "wrong"? Critics of Holmes have long suggested that his judicial philosophy tends toward *might makes right*. His supporters cast aspects of this propensity as *judicial restraint*. Holmes, they say, acquiesces to the will of the people known through elected government. It would be fairer and more accurate, however, to think that, for Holmes, it is not so much that might makes right, but that might is all there is. There is only the sheer fact of power. Holmes does have his own "moral" convictions, however much he presents them as just a matter of efficiency – "every lawyer ought to seek an understanding of economics" – or of taste: "beliefs and wishes have a transcendental basis in the sense that their foundation is arbitrary," but "[y]ou can not help

---

[30] For a relatively sympathetic treatment, see J. W. Burrow, "Holmes in his Intellectual Milieu," in *The Legacy of Oliver Wendell Holmes, Jr.*, ed. Robert Gordon (Stanford, CA: Stanford University Press, 1992), 17–30. For an excoriating treatment, see Alschuler, *Law without Values*, particularly chapter 2, "A Power-Focused Philosophy."

[31] "To Harold Laski, April 6, 1920," in Posner, ed., *Essential Holmes*, 115.

[32] "To Lady Pollock, September 6, 1902," in Howe, ed., *Holmes-Pollock Letters*, 105.

[33] Ibid. (emphasis added).

[34] "To Harold Laski, April 18, 1930," in Posner, ed., *Essential Holmes*, 117.

[35] Ibid.

[36] Holmes, *Common Law*, 41.

entertaining and feeling them, and there is an end of it."[37] And the law, he notes, does have advantages. It provides convenience and consistency, and channels unruly passions for revenge into a stable public process.[38] Even so, for Holmes, power is all there is.

HOLMES AND THE CASE METHOD

Despite his distinctive understanding of the nature of the law, and of law and morality, Holmes did not wholly disagree with the 1870 reforms of Christopher Columbus Langdell. There were merits to Langdell's teaching methods. Speaking in 1885, Holmes agreed with Langdell that "the number of legal principles is small," and that "therefore they may be taught through the cases which have developed and established them."[39] There were good pedagogical reasons, too, thought Holmes, for Langdell's case-based instruction: "Why, look at it simply in the light of human nature. Does not a man remember a concrete instance more vividly than a general principle?"[40] And even Langdell's focus on precedent and tradition has some practical value – an inherited body of law has the advantage against other options, at least, "that we know what it is."[41] And in "our short life" it make sense "to take on faith at second hand most of the rules on which we base our action and our thought."[42]

But these are mere concessions to practicality. Holmes sets aside the idea that the common law progressively develops a body of reason. A long-standing rule, he says, continues in force neither because it captures reason nor on account of the sheer fact that "our fathers always have followed it," but rather because the rule helps bring about "a social end which the governing power of the community has made up its mind that it wants."[43]

While Holmes does not reject outright Langdell's commitment to the coherence of a body of law, the imagined form of coherence is significantly reframed. Holmes's favored *prediction* replaces Langdell's precedent and reason: "The number of our predictions" – not Langdell's "principles and

---

[37] Holmes, "Path," 474; Oliver Wendell Holmes, *Natural Law*, 32 Harv. L. Rev. 40, 41 (1918); and Holmes, *Common Law*, 41.

[38] Holmes, *Common Law*, 41–42.

[39] "The Law. Suffolk Bar Association Dinner, February 5, 1885," in Posner, ed., *Essential Holmes*, 223.

[40] Ibid.

[41] Oliver Wendell Holmes, "Twenty Years in Retrospect. Speech at a Banquet of the Middlesex Bar Association, December 3, 1902," in Posner, ed., *Essential Holmes*, 151.

[42] Holmes, "Path," 468.

[43] Holmes, *Law in Science and Science in Law*, 12 Harv. L. Rev. 443, 452 (1899).

doctrines" – "when generalized and reduced to a system is not unmanageably large. They present themselves as a finite body of dogma which may be mastered within a reasonable time."[44] Gone from Holmesian prediction is any "theological working out of dogma or ... [its] logical development as in mathematics."[45] The coherence of a body of laws, therefore, "consists in the establishment of its postulates from ... accurately measured social desires instead of a tradition."[46] A body of laws coheres if it reflects the will of the people or their rulers, not on account of its rationality.

Nonetheless, some commentators treat Langdell and Holmes as engaged in a similar enterprise, despite Langdell's "internal" focus on doctrine and Holmes's "external" concern for social convention. Both share a "modern," mostly positivistic project, they say, which broadly rejects a natural-law basis for decision-making, but still assumes some principled basis for decisions.[47] Langdell treats law as an internally coherent science, whereas Holmes looks for coherence in history, anthropology, and the politics of his day. Therefore, even if for Holmes morality is arbitrary and the law with it, at an intermediate level, at least, the law makes sense. Legal education, then, can still rightly proceed from the body of developed case law. The law of Massachusetts has its own rules, even if these are only responsive to the economic, social, and political powers of the day. If this is so, Holmes can even seek to "discover whether there is any common [nonmoral] ground at the bottom of all liability in tort," for instance, and thus "reveal the general principle of civil liability at common law."[48] Between Langdell and Holmes, the rational underpinnings of legal education may have faltered. But the case method persisted.

---

44 Holmes, "Path," 458; and C. C. Langdell, *A Selection of Cases on the Law of Contracts: With References and Citations: Prepared for Use as a Text-book in Harvard Law School* (Boston: Little, Brown, 1871), vi.
45 Holmes, "Law in Science and Science in Law," 452.
46 Ibid.
47 Stephen M. Feldman, for instance, conceptually divides the law into a "premodern" variant (concerned with universal, eternal principles); a "modern" variant (antitraditionalist, proto-individualist, believing in progress through human endeavor); and a "postmodern" variant (rejecting foundational knowledge, individual autonomy, and endless social progress). On this account, Langdell belongs to rationalist modernity – creating order from reason – while Holmes and the realists are empiricist moderns who look to the external world (not reason) for truth. *American Legal Thought from Premodernism to Postmodernism: An Intellectual Voyage* (New York: Oxford University Press, 2000).
48 Holmes, *Common Law*, 77. Holmes likewise speaks of a general principle of *criminal law*. Ibid., 74. Some contemporary supporters of Holmes see this search for common ground as a lack of discipline in Holmes's thought and chide the "backslidings to formalism ... evident in a number of Holmes's judicial opinions and other writings." Posner, ed., *Essential Holmes*, xi.

THE AMERICAN LEGAL REALISTS

The case method became more and more the standard medium of university legal instruction in the early decades of the twentieth century, but its connection to Langdellian legal science was increasingly unstuck.[49] A profound break came with the rise of the *legal realists*. Their skepticism about the objectivity of legal rules permeates legal teaching and scholarship to this day, even if the particularities of their position were soon ignored.[50] For followers of the legal realists, Langdell's confidence in a rationally coherent system of law seemed, at best, a quaint relic and, more likely, an obscurantist obstacle to social progress.[51]

An attitude more than a movement, legal realism was cultivated and explicated most particularly in the 1930s at Columbia and Yale law schools, and the short-lived Johns Hopkins Institute of Law.[52] Legal realists found precursors – even heroes – in Oliver Wendell Holmes, Jr., embracing his skepticism, and Roscoe Pound (1870–1964), dean of Harvard Law School from 1916 to 1936, embracing his belief in law as socially engineering a better society.[53] Legal realists' basic orientation was to study law as it "really"

---

[49] The leading realist Jerome Frank rejected Langdell's focus on written appellate judicial opinions and advocated instead for student engagement in actual legal practice. See the legal education chapter of his *Courts on Trial: Myth and Reality in American Justice* (Princeton, NJ: Princeton University Press, 1949), 225–46. This chapter collects the thought of his earlier work on the subject, including *Why Not a Clinical Lawyer-School?*, 81 U. Pa. L. Rev. 907 (1933); and *What Constitutes a Good Legal Education?* 19 ABA J. 723 (1933): 723.

[50] Despite the influence of legal realism, its contemporary supporters suggest that it is frequently mischaracterized. See Brian Leiter, *Rethinking Legal Realism: Toward a Naturalized Jurisprudence*, 76 Tex. L. Rev. 267 (1997): 267–315.

[51] Important secondary literature on the American legal realists includes Justin Zaremby, *Legal Realism and American Law* (New York: Bloomsbury Academic, 2014); William Twining, *Karl Llewellyn and the Realist Movement* (Cambridge: Cambridge University Press, 2012); Brian Leiter, "Legal Realism and Legal Positivism Reconsidered," *Ethics* 111, no. 2 (2001): 278–301; John Henry Schlegel, *American Legal Realism and Empirical Social Science* (Chapel Hill: University of North Carolina Press, 1995); Laura Kalman, *Legal Realism at Yale, 1927–1960* (Chapel Hill: University of Carolina Press, 1986); Edward Purcell, "American Jurisprudence between the Wars: Legal Realism and the Crisis of Democratic Theory," *American Historical Review* 75, no. 2 (1969): 424–46; Wilfred Rumble, *American Legal Realism: Skepticism, Reform, and the Judicial Process* (Ithaca, NY: Cornell University Press, 1968); and Julius Paul, *The Legal Realism of Jerome N. Frank: A Study of Fact-Skepticism and the Judicial Process* (The Hague: Nijhoff, 1959).

[52] For a helpful collection of primary documents from the leading figures of legal realism, see William Fisher, Morton Horwitz, and Thomas Reed, ed., *American Legal Realism* (New York: Oxford University Press, 1993). In his revisionist account of legal realism, John Henry Schlegel offers a brief preface that outlines the "standard story" of the realists. *American Legal Realism and Empirical Social Science*, 15–21.

[53] Holmes was widely praised by the realists although their interpretation of his thought differed significantly. Roscoe Pound had been Holmes's champion, but Jerome Frank treated Pound

functions: Holmes, we have seen, insisted that experience not logic undergirds and animates the law; and Pound distinguished "law in books" and "law in action."[54] The realists agreed that the law is "really" found in the actions of judges and other officials, and not in the pages of law reports or statute books.[55]

The legal realist attitude relies on a number of intellectual commitments rarely spelled out by its adherents. Believing there to be a distinction between "law in action" and "law in books" is not enough. This is commonsensical to the point of banality. Indeed, the purported priority of law in action over law in books in realist thought, far from an innovation, is common-law orthodoxy. If, in practice, adherents of Langdellian legal science mechanically judged law in action against principles recorded in "books," they were nonetheless committed to the priority of the authoritative speech-acts of judges and other officials, albeit recorded in case reports and, perhaps, explained, simplified, and probed in treatises. The realists' break with their predecessors, then, was not the recognition that law in action differs from its presentation, nor even the recognition that this law in action has priority over principle, but rather that this law in action is not necessarily tied to legal rules. Realists condemned as "formalists" those who thought law exhausted by the text of legislation or the argument of judicial opinions.[56]

The realist attitude is typified, then, by a skepticism toward rules, and a sharp attention to what judges and officials do, irrespective of what they

---

as a "right-wing traitor who distorted Holmes's legal teaching." Pound's crime, in Frank's view, was to include people's *ideas* about the law – and not just the empirical consequences of adjudication – in his presentation of the legal system as it *really* is. See Paul, *The Legal Realism of Jerome N. Frank*, 19; and Jerome Frank, *Are Judges Human?* 80 U. Pa. L. Rev. 17, 18 (1931).

54   Roscoe Pound, *Law in Books and Law in Action*, 44 Am. L. Rev. 12, 15 (1910).

55   William Rumble, Jr. – who tried to capture the genius of legal realism after its post-war fading – answers the question "what was legal realism to its adherents?" with "[t]he best answer is that 'realism' meant to them what it has meant in art and literature. It meant the attempt to represent things as they actually are." *American Legal Realism: Skepticism, Reform, and the Judicial Process* (Ithaca, NY: Cornell University Press, 1968), 44.

56   Richard Posner has offered typological definitions of "formalism" and "realism" that aim to describe rather than evaluate the positions. By "formalism," he means "the use of deductive logic to derive the outcome of a case from premises accepted as authoritative. Formalism enables a commentator to pronounce the outcome of the case as being correct or incorrect, in approximately the same way that the solution to a mathematical problem can be pronounced correct or incorrect." And by "realism," Posner means "deciding a case so that its outcome best promotes public welfare in nonlegalistic terms; it is policy analysis. A 'realist' decision is more likely to be judged sound or unsound than correct or incorrect – the latter pair suggests a more demonstrable, verifiable mode of analysis than will usually be possible in weighing considerations of policy. Such equity maxims as 'no person shall profit from his own wrongdoing,' which Professor Ronald Dworkin calls 'principles,' are in my analysis 'policy considerations.'" *Legal Formalism, Legal Realism, and the Interpretation of Statutes and the Constitution*, 37 Case W. Res. L. Rev. 179, 181 (1986).

say they do.[57] Karl Llewellyn (1893–1962) gives vigorous early expression to the realists' skepticism in *The Bramble Bush* (1930), his lectures to Columbia Law School's incoming students: "What these officials do about disputes is, to my mind, the law itself."[58] Rules, in this understanding, are only "important so far as they help you ... see or predict what judges will do ... That is all their importance, except as pretty playthings."[59] The challenge to natural lawyers – indeed, to almost all those who preceded – was radical. The legal system, they were told, is not a coherent, principled body of law, but merely the actions of officials.

Even more so than other intellectual movements, the boundaries of "legal realism" are difficult to define with any exactitude.[60] Three sets of ideas, however, can help us understand the change wrought by the realists, and the corresponding breaks with the natural-law and Langdellian past: *secularization, indeterminacy,* and *nonobjectivity.*

Many commentators adopted the language of *secularization* to explain the realist change. Writing in the late 1960s, Calvin Woodard suggested that over the last four hundred years three "interrelated propensities" have been increasingly influential in the West.[61] The first two – *rationalism* and the *scientific*

---

[57] Brian Leiter gives many examples in the first three chapters of his *Naturalizing Jurisprudence: Essays on American Legal Realism and Naturalism in Legal Philosophy* (Oxford: Oxford University Press, 2007). In the context of commercial law, for instance, realists suggest that judges reach the "right outcome" not by working through legal rules, but by considering – consciously or otherwise – the standard business culture and practices of their time and place.

[58] *The Bramble Bush: Some Lectures on Law and Its Study* (New York: Tentative Printing for the Use of Students at Columbia University School of Law, 1930), 3 (emphasis removed). In the second edition, Llewellyn retreats from this bald statement.

[59] Ibid., 5.

[60] We will consider key figures – those recognized by all as within the fold of "legal realism" – as illustrative of a broader shift in scholarship and thought. The question of others who might be included in the fold is left open. Some contemporary scholars, however, would reject even this approach. Morton Horowitz, for instance, counts all critics of "formalism" as "realists." He argues that there was not much difference between key so-called realist figures and Roscoe Pound, whose "sociological jurisprudence" is usually treated as anticipatory of, and distinctive from, realism. Indeed, Horowitz suggests that seeking precise delineations of the movement wrongly casts the realists in an "academic" light when, in fact, their work was practically directed to administrative reform. See his chapter "Defining Legal Realism," in *The Transformation of American Law 1870–1960: The Crisis of Legal Orthodoxy,* 169–92 (Oxford: Oxford University Press, 1992). Brian Tamanaha argues, however, that nineteenth-century judges had long held the realists' skeptical views, at least as to the practice of day-to-day adjudication. In other words, there was no revolt against formalism. *Beyond the Formalist-Realist Divide: The Role of Politics in Judging* (Princeton, NJ: Princeton University Press, 2010).

[61] Calvin Woodard, *The Limits of Legal Realism: An Historical Perspective,* 54 Va. L. Rev. 689, 691 (1968).

method – were evident in Langdell's era. But with the realists' age came something new: an understanding of law as *technology* or *applied science*. This was not Langdell's science. Langdell had emphasized law as an independent, pure branch of study, with its own internal purpose, domain, and method. Nor was this the science of Isaac Parker, who had presented the science of law as the studied derivation of principles and rules from human nature and life in society. No, as an *applied* science or technology, law for the realists was functional. It was a technique or set of techniques. Gone were appeals to truth or the transcendent. On this account, the relevant realist secularization of the law, therefore, was the desire "simply to make the law – the science of law – more useful."[62] The legal system is rightly pragmatic, the realists thought, and legal rules and their operation are accordingly judged on their consequences: the social progress they afford.[63] If what the realists meant by "social progress" receives surprisingly little treatment in their work, most presented the achievements of New Deal progressivism as its fruit. Irrespective of the extract referent, when judged by its social consequences, a definition in the law – said Felix Cohen (1907–53) – is *"useful* or *useless*. It is not *true* or *false*."[64]

A further valence in the realist secularization narrative is that realists were "hard-headed" or "tough-minded": terms used in approbation, denoting a practical orientation and lack of sentimentality.[65] The purported

---

[62] Ibid., 704.

[63] The realists therefore shared Holmes's commitment to the law as a means to "get things done." However, many did not share the Holmesian opposition of utility and morality: "I think 'Whatsoever thy hand findeth to do, do it with thy might,' infinitely more important than the vain attempt to 'love one's neighbor as one's self.'" "Speech at a dinner given for Chief Justice Holmes by the Bar Association of Boston, March 7, 1900," in Posner, *Essential Holmes*, 79. Holmes, of course, *did* have a set of values of sorts, albeit usually expressed in distinction to what he termed "morality": The man who is a "true jobbist," he says – who gets practical things done – "will find on the Day of Judgment that he has been a better altruist than those who thought more about it." "To Harold Laski, December 9, 1921," in Posner, ed., *Essential Holmes*, 115.

[64] *Transcendental Nonsense and the Functional Approach*, 35 Columb. L. Rev. 809, 835 (1935). In Cohen's account, the New York Court of Appeals treated a question of whether a corporation chartered in New York could be sued in Pennsylvania not – as he would have it – by reference to *useful* economic, sociological, political, or ethical considerations, but instead by reference to metaphysical, *truth*, questions: "Where is a corporation? Was this corporation really in Pennsylvania or in New York, or could it be in two places at once?" *Tauza v. Susquehanna Coal Company*, 220 N.Y. 259 (1917).

[65] The term is used with surprising frequency in scholarly work that considers the realists. For just one example in nonlegal writing, see Hindy Lauer Schachter, "A Gendered Legacy? The Progressive Reform Era Revisited," in *The Oxford Handbook of American Bureaucracy*, ed. Robert Durant (Oxford: Oxford University Press, 2010). Woodard also uses the term. "Limits of Legal Realism," 6.

secularization wrought by the realists, then, is that in rejecting the "transcendental nonsense" of their forebears, they saw the law for what it truly is.[66] The realists' secularity, in this view, is synonymous with seeing aright. Holmes pioneered this rhetoric. He criticized Langdell, for instance, by dubbing him "the greatest living legal theologian."[67] Supporters of the realists, indeed, frequently adopt an anticlerical timbre: as human beings mature, they throw off legal obscurities; "the ghost-world of super-natural legal entities ... vanishes; in its place we see legal concepts as patterns of judicial behavior."[68] To see aright, then, is to see patterns of behavior empirically through the tools of the social sciences.[69] To see aright is to reject "[*l*]*egal concepts* (for example, *corporations* or *property rights*) [as] supernatural entities which do not have a verifiable existence except to the eyes of faith."[70] If toughmindedness suggests a concern for epistemology, truly ontological results nonetheless follow: Realists, on the whole, rejected that legal doctrines and principles exist.

This is secularization as "killing the idea of 'the system' altogether."[71] This is radical indeed. If there is no system, the law's "secularization" is, in part, a rejection of the idea that the law possesses intrinsic purposes. The law has no obvious ends. Natural-law approaches to human positive law, we have seen, have suggested that law is capable of aiding the flourishing of community, or, at least – in its limited, modern natural-law guise – maintaining a world of peaceable neighbors. The realists thought, instead, that ends must always be specified from outside. By itself, the law is merely a set of actors, institutions,

---

66   Cohen, "Transcendental Nonsense."
67   Book Notices, 14 Am. L. Rev. 233, 234 (1880).
68   Cohen, "Transcendental Nonsense," 828.
69   We are all creatures of our times, of course, but there is some irony that Frank's "scientific" framework for attacking formalism is unprovable tenets of psychoanalysis. Frank famously railed against *the basic myth of law* (that legal rules are certain and exact), and explained it as childish clinging to a Father-Substitute: "To the child the father is the Infallible Judge, the Maker of definite rules of conduct. He knows precisely what is right and what is wrong and, as head of family, sits in judgment and punishes misdeeds. The Law – a body of rules apparently devised for infallibly determining what is right and what is wrong and for deciding who should be punished for misdeeds – inevitably becomes a partial substitute for the Father-as-Infallible-Judge. That is, the desire persists in grown men to recapture, through a rediscovery of a father, a childish, completely controllable universe, and that desire seeks satisfaction in a partial, unconscious anthropomorphizing of Law, in ascribing to the Law some of the characteristics of the child's Father-Judge." *Law and the Modern Mind* (New York: Brentano's, 1930), 19.
70   Cohen, "Transcendental Nonsense," 828. Holmes typically saw "rights" as an articulation of power. "I always have said that the rights of a given crowd are what they will fight for." "To Harold Laski, July 23, 1925," in Posner, ed., *Essential Holmes*, 141.
71   Robert Stevens, *Law School: Legal Education in America from the 1850s to the 1980s* (Chapel Hill: University of North Carolina Press, 1983), 156.

and procedures used by individuals to advance their interests. The realists readily embraced political and economic systems to specify ends for which the secularized law was now rightly the handmaiden.[72]

Other narratives of the realist change speak not of secularization but *indeterminacy*. In this telling, the break with the natural-law past is best understood through the realists' claim that legal rules do not determine legal judgments. What does this mean precisely? The realists' primary focus is *adjudication* – how judges decide cases – and their primary target of critique is *formalism*: the idea, as Jerome Frank (1889–1957) put it, that "the judge begins with some rule or principle as his premise, applies this premise to the facts, and thereby arrives at his decision."[73] In other words, "formalism" – a mostly pejorative term – holds there to be distinct *legal* rules, which a judge uses to come to a *particular*, correct decision. The realists contend that thinking in terms of this "mechanical jurisprudence" fails to capture what judges actually do, and obscures the reality that the *nonlegal* facts of a case (the economic, political, and social dimensions of a particular case, for instance) determine the decision.[74]

While individual realists differed in the details, two related claims about the indeterminacy of legal rules help explain the realists' position, and thus their rejection of the tradition of natural-law reflection on the common law.[75] Legal rules are, first, on the realists' account, *rationally* indeterminate for deciding a legal case. In other words, the reasons that legal rules provide a court to rule one way or another do not in themselves justify a decision. Applying rules to particular facts does not justify a unique decision. And legal rules for the realists are, second, *causally* or *explanatorily* indeterminate for deciding a legal case: We cannot follow a judge's reasoning process, they say, from

---

[72] Holmes's skepticism was thoroughgoing. He understood human reason as more or less the slave of the passions. See Robert George, "Holmes on Natural Law," in *Nature in Philosophy*, ed. Jean De Groot (Washington, DC: Catholic University Press, 2012), 129. Many of the realists, however, thought that the newly authoritative empirical social sciences offered clear means to judge and channel the law for societal improvement.

[73] Frank, *Law and the Modern Mind*, 101. Formalism continues to get a bad name. Karl Llewellyn's *The Common Law Tradition: Deciding Appeals* is the *locus classicus* for the thesis that the common-law courts in the United States changed their opinion-writing style from an early nineteenth-century "grand style," involving broadly stated policy rationales, to a formal style, involving an established rule or doctrine to be applied in mechanical fashion to the facts. (Boston: Little, Brown, 1960), 62–75.

[74] A much used charge, *Mechanical Jurisprudence*, is also the title of an influential article by Roscoe Pound: 8 Colum. L. Rev. 605 (1908).

[75] Brian Leiter, "American Legal Realism," in *A Companion to Philosophy of Law and Legal Theory*, ed. Dennis Patterson (Walden, MA: Wiley-Blackwell, 2010), 249–66. And for his more constructive proposals, see his "Rethinking Legal Realism."

a set of facts through the application of a legal rule to a specific decision; legal rules do not suffice to explain why a judge makes the decision she does.

The realists differed, however, on how deadly they thought indeterminacy. Some thought that problems stemmed from legal rules being written at too high a level of generality, and hoped that specifying a particular rule to a greater degree would reduce, or even remove, the threat. Others, however, agreed with Herman Oliphant (1884–1939) that courts "respond to the stimulus of the facts in concrete cases before them rather than to the stimulus of over-general and outworn abstracts in opinions and treatises," and that *no* level of specification could change this.[76] As was true for Oliver Wendell Holmes, some realists were interested in how to *predict* judicial decisions not how to determine the correct legal answer. But if the result of a difficult case cannot be predicted by looking at legal rules, say the realists, then the good legal student, practitioner, or academic must look elsewhere.

How, then, does one predict the result of a case? Or, to put it another way: Why do judges determine what they do? The majority of the realists – dubbed the "sociological wing" by Brian Leiter – thought that there were predictable social patterns to judicial decision-making. For Oliphant, Llewellyn, and Cohen, judges' decisions are determined by social forces, particularly the prevailing norms of commercial culture or, better, some form of utilitarian calculus as to the "best" overall results for society.[77] The "idiosyncratic wing" of the realists thought instead that the particularities of individual judges, not general social forces, determine results: "[T]he personality of the judge," wrote Frank, "is the pivotal factor in law administration."[78] In a much-quoted article, Joseph Hutcheson (1879–1973) – a federal district court judge – suggested that judges act upon a "hunch": an intuitive sense of right or wrong.[79]

If Langdell's legal science looked to the natural sciences for its methods and authority, the realists – in their desire for predictability, and interest in the societal forces that shape judicial decisions – embraced the *social* sciences. For some, the social sciences provided merely the tools to adequately describe judicial adjudication by looking at the prevailing social, economic, or political patterns, or the psychology of particular judges. For most, however, the social sciences also provided norms for assessing judicial decisions: Did a decision promote social progress, they asked. And in the disciplines of sociology and economics, they found tools to provide an answer.

---

[76] Herman Oliphant, *A Return to Stare Decisis*, 14 ABA J. 71, 71–76, 107, 159–62 (1928).

[77] Leiter, "American Legal Realism," 259.

[78] Frank, *Law and the Modern Mind*, 111.

[79] Joseph Hutcheson, Jr., *The Judgment Intuitive: The Function of the "Hunch" in Judicial Decision*, 14 Cornell L.Q. 274 (1929).

A final way to understand how the realists broke with American law's natural-law past is by noting their rejection of the *objectivity* of legal rules. Langdellian science was purportedly *value-free*. But if, as the realists held, legal rules are dually indeterminate, and thus judges determine cases in reference to factors beyond the law – whether on the basis of prevailing social norms or their own individual idiosyncrasies – then legal rules are not objective. The individual realists differed on whether this *nonobjectivity* means that legal rules have no independent "existence," or that – in the more colloquial sense – judges' subjective feelings or opinions make their use of legal rules inherently partial. They agreed, nonetheless, that legal rules do not, by themselves, result in particular decisions.

The American legal realists' concern for nonobjectivity, however, was mostly practical. While their contemporaries in Scandinavia pursued nonobjectivity as nonexistence, deploying philosophical criticism – in particular semantics and epistemology – to debunk, in their minds, the metaphysical rot, thus rejecting terms such as "rights" as having no content – as straightforwardly meaningless – the Americans remained lawyers at heart, lawyers concerned to respond to the political situation of their day.[80] They were "technicians" focused on the practical aspects of a political task.[81] Indeed, many of the most prominent were New Deal lawyers serving in the Roosevelt administration: Frank was Chairman of the Securities and Exchange Commission; Oliphant was Chief Counsel of the Treasury Department; and Cohen served in the Solicitor's Office of the Department of the Interior.[82]

In the realists' minds, if the law is nonobjective it is thoroughly political. It is a tool to be used for good or ill. What this means for adjudication, however, is potentially troubling. Accepting a positivism that rejected the necessary link between law and morality, the realists were left simply with the view that judges often decide cases on the basis of their politics. While this insight convinced some realists that the law "made no sense," except in "striking

---

[80] For Axel Hägerströn – a leading Scandinavian realist – rights were "mysterious, supernatural powers and bonds" derived from "archaic magical conceptions," operating as "exterior forces that can be transferred to others through magical means." Patricia Mindus, *A Real Mind: The Life and Work of Axel Hägerström* (Dordercht: Springer Netherlands, 2009), 186. See also Jes Bjarup, *The Philosophy of Scandinavian Legal Realism*, 18 Ratio Juris 1 (2005). For the similarities between the Scandinavian and American legal realisms, see Gregory Alexander, *Comparing the Two Legal Realisms – American and Scandinavian*, 50 Am. J. Comp. L. 131 (2002).

[81] Woodard, "Limits of Legal Realism," 704.

[82] The standard view is that lawyers trained by the realists "brought their realism" to Washington, D.C. But see Neil Duxbury, *Patterns of American Jurisprudence* (Oxford: Oxford University Press, 1995), 155ff.

resemblance to the more despairing novels of Franz Kafka," for many it presented opportunities for reform.[83] Some saw their primary scholarly task as showing the nonobjectivity of the legal system and offering instead an objective, social scientific depiction of the law *as it is*.[84] The majority, though, embraced the law's nonobjectivity and proposed politically progressive alternatives to the status quo. For the latter, if the law is baldly political, then it must be used to achieve the best societal outcomes, determined – as their skeptical peers maintained – social scientifically. The law is *instrumental* to the achievement of social causes: "a means to an end, and is to be appraised only in the light of the ends it achieves."[85]

AFTER THE REALISTS

In its narrower form, legal realism – as a specific conversation undertaken by major scholars who self-identified with its aims – barely survived the 1940s. And yet it is "often said – indeed *so* often said that it become a cliché to call it a cliché – that we are *all* realists now."[86] The "we" here is the legal academy, and its near-universal acceptance, since the realists, that adjudication is more than a matter of applying legal rules to circumstances. Law schools came to embrace the idea that there are nonrational "reasons" behind many legal decisions.

The realists, then, successfully brought a new skepticism to the practice and study of law. But they faltered in proposing next steps. New waves of scholarship combined their skeptical attitude with clearer programs for legal and political reform. As a program of action, realism was swept from its academic bastion by "policy science." Destructive legal realism was replaced by

---

[83] Grant Gilmore, *The Ages of American Law*, 2nd ed., with a final chapter by Philip Bobbitt (New Haven: Yale University Press, 2014), 73. Gilmore found at least some expressions of realist "nihilism" admirable. Describing Wesley Sturges (1893–1962), dean of Yale Law School from 1945–54, Gilmore suggests he had "the courage of his bleak convictions. *Ex nihilio nihil.* He wrote almost nothing during the remainder of his long career . . . he was a lonely, great, and tragic figure." Ibid. See also Grant Gilmore, *Legal Realism: Its Cause and Cure*, 70 Yale L.J. 1037 (1961).

[84] John Henry Schlegel claims that realism can be understood as the law's late embrace of empiricism. While "new" disciplines in the nineteenth century – anthropology, economics, history, psychology, sociology – had sought objectivity through "scientific" empiricism, law already understood itself to be a (nonempirical) science of rational ordering. This differing view of scientificity delayed the embrace of empiricism. *American Legal Realism and Empirical Social Science.*

[85] Myres McDougal, *Fuller v. The American Legal Realism: An Intervention*, 50 Yale L.J. 827, 834–35 (1941).

[86] Michael Green, *Legal Realism as a Theory of Law*, 46 Wm. & Mary L. Rev. 1915, 1917 (2005).

a positive, conscious effort to "apply the best existing scientific knowledge to solving the policy problems of all our communities."[87] Realism had failed to integrate the social sciences toward specific policy ends. Among subsequent shifts in scholarship, the "law and economics" movement embraced legal realism's understanding of law as a social tool, but evaluated legal proposals against bodies of defined social scientific thought, including behavioral economics, game theory, and public choice theory.[88]

Moreover, while the realists treated the beliefs and attitudes of legal officials as distractions to knowing the law, resurgent post-World War II jurisprudence and political philosophy treated beliefs and attitudes as central to their task. As a legal theory, if not a theory of adjudication, then, legal realism was swept away by the widespread acceptance of sophisticated works of legal positivism, such as H. L. A. Hart's *The Concept of Law*.[89] Hart argues that what we recognize as "law" necessarily includes officials' internal view of the nature and purpose of the law. The law is not simply the threat of sanctions – as for Holmes's "bad man" – but the imposition too of obligations.

One continuing legacy of legal realism has transformed the law school professoriate. Many professors now come with doctorates in economics, history, or other disciplines. If the law is not fully explained by recourse to legal rules found in the cases, then experts in human behavior are needed. A more radical inheritance emerged with several waves of scholars who accepted the realist portrayal of the law, but rejected trust in the social sciences. These scholars embraced the instrumentalization of the law heralded by the realists, but not the subsequent belief that the social sciences could determine ends for this instrumentalization. If the law is essentially political, it must be exposed as such, they say, and directed toward articulated, political ends. Movements such as critical legal studies, and its feminist, critical race theory, and postmodern successors challenge current legal rules and norms as benefiting and legitimizing the powerful, and offer alternatives intended to benefit the powerless.[90]

---

[87] Myres McDougal, *The Law School of the Future: From Legal Realism to Policy Science in the World Community*, 56 Yale L.J. 1345, 1349 (1947). See also Harold Lasswell and Myres McDougal, *Legal Education and Public Policy: Professional Training in the Public Interest*, 52 Yale L.J. 203 (1943).

[88] For a recent treatment by one of its founders, see Guido Calabresi, *The Future of Law and Economics: Essays in Reform and Recollection* (New Haven, CT: Yale University Press, 2016).

[89] H.L.A. Hart, The Concept of Law (New York: Oxford University Press, 1961).

[90] Robert Ungar, *The Critical Legal Studies Movement* 96 Harv. L. Rev. 561 (1983), offers something of a manifesto. The realists' emphasis on *facts in themselves* appears naïve to postmodernists, of whatever form – the relationship between fact and value is not the clear-cut distinction the realists imagined. For a critical treatment of the "use" of the law to pursue

One pedagogical failure of legal realism is the continued prominence of casebooks. Jerome Frank thought that in accepting the reforms of Christopher Columbus Langdell, American legal education had been "seduced by a brilliant neurotic," and argued that "the sole way for those law schools to get back on the main track is unequivocally to repudiate Langdell's morbid repudiation of actual legal practice, to bring the students into intimate contact with courts and lawyers."[91] While clinical legal education has been added to law schools' curriculums to allow for experiential learning, casebooks nonetheless remain texts in "core" common-law courses.[92]

But if law students still turn to casebooks – thereby frustrating Jerome Frank and others who sought to pull the study of law from the decisions of appellate courts to the bustle and fact-finding of trial courts – their casebooks are not Langdell's bare extracts, but books of *cases and materials*: where social scientific and other literature is included to explain the law.[93] Moreover, as Martha Minow (dean of Harvard Law School, 2009–17) notes, where the case method is used today, it is often to disrupt as much as confirm the law as it stands. Where Langdell expected to find coherence in case law, after the realists, law school classrooms make conflicting principles prominent.[94]

* * *

Oliver Wendell Holmes and the realists alike rejected Langdell's idea that law is principled and coherent. They broke with the natural-law tradition in American common law. Legal rules – however well wrought in reason, or even pedigreed by precedent – underdetermine the results of judicial cases. Instead, legislative might or social convention, said Holmes, or sociology or psychology, said the realists, are the deciding factors, whatever the details of legal rules might say. To speak of "law," then, is to speak solely of specific legal decisions, not a principled body of doctrine. Legal decisions may be predicted, they say, but through attention to societal mores and contemporary common sense, not the exercise of internal legal reasoning.

---

    particular political agendas, see Brian Tamanah, *Law as Means to an End: Threat to the Rule of Law* (Cambridge: Cambridge University Press, 2006).

[91] A *Plea for Lawyer-Schools*, 56 Yale L.J. 1303, 1313 (1947). He makes this argument too in the legal education chapter of his *Courts on Trial*.

[92] See the website of the Clinical Legal Education Association, http://cleaweb.org, accessed March 1, 2017.

[93] "They study, almost entirely, upper-court opinions. Any such opinion, however, is not a case, but a small fraction of a case, its tail end. The law students are like future horticulturists studying solely cut flowers; or like future architects studying merely pictures of buildings." Frank, *Courts on Trial*, 227.

[94] Martha Minow, quoted in David Garvin, "Making the Case: Professional Education for the World of Practice," *Harvard Magazine* (September–October, 2003).

Holmes and the realists, nonetheless, differed on the basic question of what the law is for. Holmes's skepticism, we have seen, was thoroughgoing: extending beyond the law to morality, even truth. Law, for Holmes, channels the will of the strong, albeit with the helpful benefits of monopolizing legitimate violence and organizing human affairs. Law, for the realists, is a principal tool of social engineering, a means to bring about a fairer more humane society.

One significant realist legacy, accordingly, is to teach law interwoven with social policy, even desired social progress. Whereas Langdell sought value-free science, following the realists, twentieth-century American law schools were increasingly values driven. Not understood in the manner of a Blackstone or a Story, however, these values, whatever their flavor, were no longer seen as co-constituted by the common law, but specified from *without*.

Epilogue

American legal thinkers, from the seventeenth century into the twentieth, believed natural law and common law to be intertwined. To speak of "common law" – of routine court cases and printed judicial decisions – was to speak too of "natural law," a universally accessible morality tied to the mind or will of God, nature, or human reason. The essential details of what natural law and common law meant in specific times to particular people differed, even as – consciously or otherwise – legal thinkers and practitioners maintained continuity with the legal traditions they inherited.

The legal realists broke with those traditions. Their early-twentieth-century skepticism splintered law and reason. But our narrative – of Puritans and Revolutionaries, of Blackstone, Story, Langdell, Holmes, and the realists – is not the narrative of natural law's demise. The realists end one thread, yes, but the twentieth century offers new conceptions of natural law and common law, from universal human rights discourse – so powerful after the Second World War – to the civil rights movement to "the new natural law" and, more arguably, the antipositivist critiques of Lon Fuller, Ronald Dworkin, and their peers.[1]

Indeed, the relationship of law and morality was arguably *the* jurisprudential question of the twentieth century. Interestingly, though, the twentieth century's natural lawyers did not advance their arguments by burnishing their

---

[1] For surveys, see, John Finnis, "Natural Law: The Classical Tradition," 1–60, and Brian H. Bix, "Natural Law: The Modern Tradition," 61–100, in *The Oxford Handbook of Jurisprudence and Philosophy of Law*, ed. Jules Coleman and Scott Shapiro (Oxford: Oxford University Press, 2002). See also United Nations, *Universal Declaration of Human Rights* (1948); Martin Luther King, Jr., "Letter from a Birmingham Jail" (April 16, 1963), in *Why We Can't Wait* (Boston: Beacon Press, 2011), 85–110; John Finnis, *Natural Law and Natural Rights* (Oxford: Clarendon Press, 1980); Lon L. Fuller, *The Morality of Law*, rev. ed. (New Haven, CT: Yale University Press, 1964); and Ronald Dworkin, *Law's Empire* (Cambridge, MA: Harvard University Press, 1986).

natural-law inheritance. Instead, they largely accepted the realists' critiques of earlier centuries of legal thought – shared by most positivists – and simply moved on. Dworkin in his debates with the positivists, for example, set aside as distracting "some ghostly form of natural law" in order to advance his own account of law's integrity.[2] The new natural lawyers likewise disregarded metaphysical claims about human nature – so integral to many earlier accounts of natural law – to focus instead on practical reflections on how, and for what, humans act.[3]

Other responses were possible. The realists wrongly equated Langdell's natural law with the whole tradition and thus failed to respond to other potential visions of natural law. The "natural law" of the Puritans, Revolutionaries, Blackstone, and Story, then, perhaps remain viable. They will not convince everyone today, of course. They have their advantages and pitfalls. Their starting points or psychologies or historiographies are controversial: God, the triumph of reason, the ever-greater convergence of history, people, and morals. But whatever the range of possible criticism, contemporary appeals to natural law are not sudden aberrations. They come out of the four-hundred-year history we have charted. They add to a tradition. To adopt a natural-law interpretation of common law today, therefore, is necessarily to continue in conversation with foundational figures in American law.

* * *

How should law, morality, and religion interact in America today? The varied strands of natural-law reflection on common law offer resources and warnings to natural-law proponents and critics alike.

In reflecting on the stories of the preceding chapters, it becomes clear that common law is not simply "judge-made law," regardless of today's prevailing definition, nor is natural law necessarily divorced from human lawmakers, judges included. Common law and natural law are co-constitutive and, in at least some ways, inseparable in American history. Blackstone formed the system of modern common law, after all, in reference to natural law's rights and principles. Story treated natural law not merely as a source of common law's authority but as its structuring spirit: justifying specific enactments, defenses, and punishments, and coordinating moral and civic obligations. And yet, common law and natural law are mutable: The Puritans' natural law was a lodestar in a fallen world. The Revolutionaries' celebrated human

---

[2] Ronald Dworkin, *Law's Ambitions For Itself*, 71 Va. L. Rev. 173, 183 (1985).
[3] See Germain Grisez, Joseph Boyle, and John Finnis, *Practical Principles, Moral Truth, and Ultimate Ends*, 32 Am. J. Juris. 99 (1987).

rationality. Story's common law was a narration of America's history. Langdell's a science. Not merely the accretion of quotidian past practice, then, nor truth existent beyond our interpretation, common law and natural law are enmeshed in and articulated through the presuppositions of a particular time and place, our own included.

Index

Adams, John, 27, 63, 67
Alexander, Frank, 122
Ames, James Barr, 112
Ames, William, 8n26, 10, 19
Antelope, The, 100, 103
Aquinas. *See* Thomas Aquinas
Aristotle, 4, 19n64, 19, 20, 77
Arkes, Hadley, 54
Augustine of Hippo, Saint, 4, 53
Austin, John, 11n35, 63n93, 122n67, 129

Bacon, Asa, 73
Bacon, Francis, 13n40, 29, 69n117, 113n34, 113
Ballow, Henry, 57
Barlow, Joel, 31, 41n77
Beattie, James, 33
Bentham, Jeremy, 58, 59n70, 59n72, 63n93,
    129, 131
Bible. *See* scripture
*Black & White Taxi Co. v. Brown & Yellow Taxi
    Co,* 128n18
Blackstone, William, xiii, xiv, 46–69, 80, 85, 88,
    89, 90, 103, 108n12, 110n21, 110, 116, 123, 125,
    127n13, 127, 129, 145, 146, 147
  biography of, 47n5, 48
  as champion or critic of common law,
    58–59, 59n70, 71, 72
  cosmopolitanism of, 72
  definitions of law for, 49n17, 49, 50, 53
  denied English liberties pertain for
    American colonies, 63n94, 63
  distinguished common law and natural law,
    60–62
  groups named for, 64n102
  as organizer of common law, xi, 47, 48, 57–58

reception in America of, 62–69,
    66n107
  will and reason, their relation, for, 50–51.
    *See also Commentaries on the Laws of
    England*
Boorstein, Daniel, 59n71
Bramble Bush, The (Llewellyn), 136
Bretherton, Luke, 81n46
Britain. *See* England
Burke, Edmond, 63n95, 63
Butler, Joseph, 33

Calvin, John, 4n8, 4, 5, 6n16, 6,
    9n27
Carnegie Endowment for the Advancement of
    Teaching, 114, 121
Cases in Equity Pleading (Langdell), 107
Chamberlain v. Agar, 106–7
Cicero, Marcus Tullius, 5, 8, 19n64, 25n3, 37,
    38n61, 88n77. *See also* Stoic philosophy
civil law (applicable to members of a political
    community). *See also* common law;
    municipal law
  in Blackstone's thought, 55–56, 61
  in Puritan thought, 10–14, 23
  in Republican and revolutionary thought,
    34–39
civil law (derived from Roman law), 20, 68n115,
    68, 76, 77, 80, 93n96, 97, 120n59.
    See also Grotius; Pufendorf
Clap, Thomas, 17, 20, 22, 27,
    34n46
Cohen, Felix, 137n64, 137, 140, 141. *See also*
    legal realism
Coke, Edward, 66–67, 118–19

colleges and universities. *See also* curriculum;
     legal education
  Brown (College of Rhode Island), 35, 39,
     40n70
  Cambridge, University of, 1, 4, 16–19,
     19n64, 21
  in colonial America, 1–2, 14–18, 17n56, 24, 33,
     39, 43, 44
  Columbia (King's College), 16n51, 34,
     35n47, 43, 74, 78n37
  Dartmouth, 34–35
  Harvard, 1n2, 15, 16, 18–19, 19n66, 20, 33, 39,
     40n70, 42n79, 74n21, 113
  Oxford, University of, 16–18, 19n64, 21, 46, 47
  Pennsylvania, University of (College of
     Philadelphia), 35, 39n70, 39
  as preparatory for professions, 15, 20, 21n75
  Princeton (College of New Jersey), 18, 31–32,
     35n48, 35, 39, 40n70, 71
  as schools of the reformation, 17, 22, 24, 31, 33
  as schools of the Republic, 24, 30–32, 34–35
  Scottish, 16–18, 38
  Virginia, University of, 30, 43, 74
  William and Mary, 18n58, 30n24, 30, 32, 33,
     41, 42n79, 42n81, 42, 43, 74
  Williams, 36
  Yale, 17, 18, 19n67, 19, 20, 34n46, 40, 41, 75
Commentaries on Equity Pleadings (Story), 106
Commentaries on the Conflict of Laws
     (Story), 94
Commentaries on the Laws of England
     (Blackstone), 46n2, 46, 47n6, 47–62, 72,
     73, 75n24, 75, 103, 108n12
  as guide to law in America, 47, 68–69
  cited today, 49–56, 69n117, 69
  sales in America, 63–64
  structure of, 57–58.
  See also Blackstone
common law
  coherence of, 115, 116, 121–23, 124, 132–33
  contract, 57n61, 57, 92n95, 92–94,
     120n59, 127
  crime and punishment, 53, 59, 60, 97–98
  definition of, xi–xii, 57n63
  distinguished from natural law, in
     Blackstone's thought, 60–62
  equity, 90–92
  historicist views of, 80–81, 116
  incorporates or subsumes natural law, 78
  marriage, 94–96

negligence, 57
no *common* common law for Holmes, 128
obiter dicta, 102n140
organized through natural-law principles,
     57–58, 67, 72, 77, 78
  and precedent, 68, 73–74, 79,
     119–20, 121
  property, 60–62, 97
ratio decidenti, 102n140
  relationship to custom, history, and
     reason, xii, 41, 80–83, 116, 118n51, 119n53,
     123, 132
  sovereign as source of, 128n17
  and *stare decisis*, 119n55
  and threats to its survival in America, 67,
     79–80
  treatises, 79, 90, 105, 125
  writs, 57n64, 57
  See also Blackstone; *Dr. Bonham's Case*;
     England; legal education; right or rights
     (legal, moral, or natural entitlement)
Common Law (Holmes), 125, 128, 130
Common Law Tradition – Deciding Appeals
     (Llewellyn), 139n73
common sense (philosophy), 33–34, 35n48, 36,
     117n49
common sense (sociology), 2, 7, 29, 65n106,
     65–66, 118, 119n54, 144
Concept of Law (Hart), 143
conscience. *See* epistemology: conscience
constitution, ancient or British or English, 37,
     48n10, 48, 58, 66–67, 73, 82
Constitution, U.S., 27n12, 46n4, 64, 80n42, 80,
     83, 99n125, 100. *See also* originalism
     (U.S. constitutional interpretation)
Constitutional Convention, 44, 63n98
Continental Congress, 81–82
contract. *See* common law: contract
Cosgrove, Richard, 60n77
Cotton, John, 5, 7, 8n23
crime. *See* common law: crime and
     punishment
curriculum:
  apologetics, 33
  classics, 4n9, 4–5, 5n14, 17, 25n3,
     37n61, 43
  colonial and Puritan, 5, 14–15, 15n47, 22–23,
     39n67, 42n79
  disputations, 38–39, 39n70
  elective system, 15n46, 17n57

ethics, politics, and law, 20–23, 34–35, 42,
43, 44
liberal arts, 17n57, 20, 31,
48, 75
logic, 19n64, 19–20, 33, 39
moral philosophy, 20, 32–38, 33n41, 35n47,
44, 77
Protestant humanist, 22
Republican or revolutionary, 24, 26,
34–39, 44
scholastic, 18–20, 21n74, 39n67
specialization, 36, 42n79, 42, 43,
112n30
vocational, 17–18, 31–32, 37n61, 41.
See also colleges and universities; legal
education

Dane, Nathan, 76n28
De jure belli ac pacis (Grotius), 37
De jure naturae et gentium (Pufendorf), 37
De officiis (Cicero), 37
De officio hominis et civis (Pufendorf), 37
Declaration of Independence, 27n12, 27, 40n71,
40, 63n98, 64
Dewey, John, 126
Dr. Bonham's Case, 66, *See also* Coke;
common law
Dunster, Henry, 19n66, 19–20
Dwight, Timothy, IV, 72
Dworkin, Ronald, 100n127, 100, 135n56,
146, 147

Edwards, Jonathan, 26n7, 28
Eliot, Charles, 106n4, 108,
110n20
Encyclopædia Britannica, 48
Encyclopedia Americana, 84, 85, 95
England
American hostility toward, 13, 27, 40, 66–68
Americans as political subjects of, 14,
17n54, 17
and Church of England, 1n1, 2, 7n21
and continued role for its common law in
America, 73–74, 79, 108
and rights of Englishmen or English liberty,
67, 81–82
laws and procedures, 13–14
opposition to English common law in
America, 66n107, 68n115.
See also colleges and universities; common

law; constitution, ancient, British or
English
epistemology:
conscience, 3, 9, 11–12, 53, 55, 86, 88,
91n88, 127
contemporary, 117n48
deduction, 2n3, 6, 12, 29, 36, 77n34, 84, 89,
100n129, 122n66, 123, 126, 127n13, 128,
135n56
empiricism, 113, 133n47, 138, 139n72, 142n84
God and humanity, changing priority,
25–28, 33
idealism, 113, 114n35
induction, 29, 36, 100n129, 111, 112–13, 113n34,
119, 123
intuition, 117–19, 119n54,
140
justificatory problems in Langdell's thought,
116–20, 117n47
light of nature, 6, 9, 12, 39
modern natural law's differences from
Puritan views, 30
nature refuted, 28–29
non-miraculous, 26
prediction, 126–29, 133,
140
Puritan suspicion of human access to
knowledge, 7n20, 7,
29–30
revelation, 6n19, 6–9, 9n29, 10n32, 23, 24, 26,
28, 30, 34, 35, 52, 84, 87–88, 103
scientific character (*Wissenschaftlichkeit*),
112n30, 112–14, 142
self-evidence, 2n3, 24, 34,
117–18n49
social science, 139n72, 140,
143
truth's unity, 22, 28–30, 33, 44n90,
44, 80
universal access to knowledge, 24.
See also legal education; natural law;
rationality
equity. *See* common law: equity
Erie Railroad Co. v. Tompkins, 128n18

fall, humanity's, from original perfection.
See sin
Federalist Papers, 40
Feldman, Stephen, 133n47
Ferguson, Adam, 33

Feuerbach, P.J.A., 98
Finnis, John, xiii, *See also* natural law
formalism, 125, 133n48, 135, 136n60,
  139n73, 139
  definition of, 135n56
Frank, Jerome, 134n49, 134n53, 138n69, 139,
  140, 141, 144. *See also* legal realism
Fuller, Lon, 146

Giddings v. Brown, 66
Gilmore, Grant, 121n63,
  142n83
God:
  human duties toward (piety), 16n51, 36,
    84, 86
  known in nature, 6n19, 26, 27n12,
    34, 40
  known in two books of revelation and nature
    or reason, 29
  nature and attributes, 8n23, 88, 147
  will and reason, as natural law, xii, 50–51,
    88
Gorsuch, Neil, 69n117
Gray, Thomas, 110n21, 113, 117–20
Grotius, Hugo, xiv, 25, 37, 49–50, 51, 58, 61, 65,
  93n98, 123
Gustafson, James, 9n27

Hadot, Pierre, 5n13
Hägerströn, Axel, 141n80
Hale, Matthew, 69n117
Hamburger, Philip, 65n105
Hare, Charles, 43
Hart, H.L.A., 59, 120n57, 143
Hedley, Thomas, 118n51
Helmholz, R.H., 40n72, 65n104,
  89
Herdt, Jennifer, 36n52
Hobbes, Thomas, 55, 65, 88n77, 123, 129
Holmes, Oliver Wendell, Jr., xiii, 105, 108n12,
  113n31, 113, 124, 125–33, 134n53, 134,
  137n63, 138n70, 139n72, 140, 144, 145, 146
  bad man's view of law, 127–28
  judicial philosophy, 131–32
  morality, 129–32
  prediction theory of law, 126–29, 132
  view of the case method, 132–33
Hooker, Thomas, 8
Hopkins, Mark, 36
Horowitz, Morton, 136n60
Hume, David, 34n42, 129

Hutcheson, Francis, 28, 33, 35n51, 35, 117n49
Hutcheson, Joseph, 140

Ibbetson, David, 57
imago Dei, 4, 5, 8n25, 8, *See also* rationality
Institutes of Justinian, 51, 54, 84
international law, 77, 96n116, 100n129, 100–1,
  112n29
  customary, 100–2
  in Story's *Jeune Eugenie* decision, 99–103
  state practice, 100–3.
  See also Jeune Eugenie; law of nations;
    municipal law

James, William, 126n4, 126
Jay, John, 63
Jefferson, Thomas, 30n24, 31, 42n81, 43n87, 43,
  67n114, 87n73
Jeune Eugenie, La, 99–103, *See also* Story

Kames, Lord (Henry Home), 91n88
Kantian morality, 130n26, 130, *See also* right
  and wrong
Kaveny, Cathleen, 27n9,
  69n119
Kennedy, Duncan, 59
Kent, James, 38n61, 43, 68,
  78–79, 84
  biography of, 78n37
Kimball, Bruce, 113
King, Martin Luther, Jr., xiii, 53

Langbein, John, 72
Langdell, Christopher Columbus, xiii, 105–24,
  125, 133, 134, 137, 138, 144, 146
  case method, 108–10, 132–33
  justificatory problems, 116–20
  legal science, 110–15
  relationship to natural law, 120–23
  See also legal education
Langdon, Samuel, 27
law. *See* civil law; common law; international
  law; municipal law; natural law
law of nations, 39, 42, 54n45, 54, 76, 77n31, 77,
  100–2. *See also* international law;
    municipal law
Lawes and Libertyes of Massachusetts, 11–13
Lechford, Thomas, 13
legal education
  as apprenticeship, 21n75, 21, 70–71, 71n6, 72,
    76, 105, 114, 118, 125

as bachelor's degree in law, 42, 74
through case method, 105n3, 106n4, 106–10,
    113–14, 115n43, 120–22, 122n66, 125, 132–33,
    134, 144
as clinical, 144
collegiate professors in, 40–43, 74n21, 78
at Columbia Law School, 77n34, 77, 106n6,
    134, 136
through Dwight method, 106n6
English common law as university discipline
    in, 47–48
at Harvard Law School, 74–79, 76n28, 103,
    105–6, 108n12, 108, 109, 112, 114, 116,
    120, 134
independent study as, 71
influence of legal realists in, 142–44
at Inns of Court, 13, 21n74, 70n2
at Johns Hopkins Institute of Law, 134
law and economics in, 92n95, 143
lectures as form of instruction in, 21n76, 36,
    40n73, 41, 42n82, 42–43, 46, 73, 76, 78n37,
    109, 125, 136
as legal science, 110–15, 135, 137,
    140, 141
at Litchfield Law School, 72–74, 75, 116
at Lumpkin School of Law, 78
not for legal practice, 13, 14, 21, 22, 37, 41, 76,
    111, 112
as policy science, 142
at proprietary schools, 71–74, 103
in Republican and revolutionary colleges,
    32, 34–39, 71
through Socratic method, 109
at university law schools, in general, 74–78
at Yale Law School, 134
See also colleges and universities; curricu-
    lum; epistemology
legal positivism. *See* positivism
legal realism, xiii, 122n66, 124, 134–44, 146
as American movement, compared to
    Scandinavian, 141
and concern for social progress, 137
definition of, 135n56,
    136n60
law's ends specified from without,
    138–39, 142
and New Deal, 137, 141
reckons law indeterminate, 139–40
rejection of objectivity, 141–42
as secularization, 136–39
skepticism of legal rules, 135–36, 139–40

sociological and idiosyncratic wings of, 140
use of social science, 139n72, 140
See also Cohen; Holmes; Frank; legal
    education; Llewellyn; natural law;
    Oliphant; Pound
Leiter, Brian, 136n57, 140
Lincoln, Abraham, 46
Llewellyn, Karl, 136, 139n73, 140. *See also* legal
    realism
Lochner v. New York, 126n2
Locke, John, 2, 9n32, 9, 37n61, 37, 51–52, 61, 64,
    65, 85, 88n77, 123

Madison, James, 31, 32n33, 32, 71
Mansfield (William Murray, 1st Earl of),
    67n114
marriage. *See* common law: marriage
Marshall, John, 64, 100
Mason, George, 67
Mather, Cotton, 8n26, 16
Mather, Increase, 12
McClellan, James, 80n43, 88
McCosh, James, 33n40, 35n48
Milk for Babes (Cotton), 7
Mill, John Stuart, 131
Miller, Perry, 7n20, 9n29,
    22, 30
Minnow, Martha, 115n43, 144
Monroe, James, 31
Montesquieu (Charles-Louis de Secondat,
    Baron de), 64
moral philosophy. *See* curriculum
municipal law (law of a particular state), 13n40,
    54, 74. *See also* international law; law of
    nations

national jurisprudence
    in Langdell's thought, 116
    in Story's thought, 84
natural law
    allows civilization apart from knowledge of
        God's revealed will, 5–6
    in American popular thought, 65n105,
        65–66
    biblical basis for, 3
    Blackstone's, 48–62
    contemporary proponents and critics of, xi,
        xiii, xiv
    and content of revealed law, 8–9
    deductive approach to, 123
    definition of, xii–xiii, 2n3, 2, 84

natural law (cont.)
  distinguished from common law, in
    Blackstone's thought, 60–62
  first principles of, 51–52
  as God's mind or will, xii, 50–51, 64n102,
    88, 146
  happiness's role in, 52, 85
  inductive approach to, 123
  as justifying civil laws, 58–59
  and Langdell's legal science, 114, 116, 122,
    144
  limits of, 88–90
  and matters indifferent, 53, 56, 60, 89, 97,
    101, 127n13
  modern-natural-law forms of, 3, 24n1, 28, 48,
    52, 65, 123, 138
  new-natural-law forms of, xiii, 2n3, 23, 147
  operative in common law in Story's thought,
    90–104
  as philosophy of morals, 83–84
  and positive law, 50, 52n33, 52–54, 55, 60, 61,
    81, 83, 90, 93–96, 100, 101–2, 103n142, 104,
    122–23, 129, 138
  provides no saving knowledge of God, 5
  Puritan forms of, 2–7, 24
  realists' break from, 144
  scholastic forms of, 7n21, 19, 23,
    80n43
  and sociability, 5, 53, 85, 86, 87, 88, 92
  Story's account of, 83–103
  twentieth-century conceptions of, 146–47.
    See also common law; curriculum; episte-
    mology; God; legal realism; right or rights
    (legal, moral, or natural entitlement)
New Englands First Fruits, 1n2, 18
Newmeyer, Kent, 80n43, 83, 100, 102
Nolan, Dennis, 64n101
Nussbaum, Martha, 95n110

Oliphant, Herman, 140, 141, *See also* legal
  realism
originalism (U.S. constitutional
  interpretation), 46n4, 46,
  68–69

Paley, William, 33, 34n41, 84
Parker, Isaac, 75, 114n38, 137
Path of the Law (Holmes), 125, 129
Pierce, C.S., 126
Plato, 8
Porter, Noah, 44n90

positivism, 21, 59n71, 63n93, 115, 125, 128n17,
    128, 129–32, 133, 143
  and Blackstone, 55, 56, 60n77
  and Langdell, 122n67, 122
  definition of, xii, 11n35
  twentieth-century critiques of, 147
Pound, Roscoe, 79, 118, 134n53,
    134
pragmatism, 126, 128
property. *See* common law: property
Protestantism, 2, 4, 7n21, 7, 22, 23. *See also*
    Puritans
Pufendorf, Samuel, xiv, 25, 37, 49–50, 51–52, 53,
    57, 58, 60–61, 62, 65, 93n98, 93, 123
Puritans, xi, xii, xiii, xiv, 1–23,
    146, 147
  and civil law, 10–14, 23
  definition of, 1n1, 7n21
  relationship of human law and God's law,
    11–12
  suspicious of legal practice, 13
  See also civil law; colleges and universities;
    curriculum; epistemology; natural law;
    rationality

Quincy, Josiah, 19n66

Ramus, Petrus, 19, 22, 33
rationality
  and assumed connection with morality,
    10n32, 16, 20, 27, 28–30
  and Bacon's general dictates of reason, 13n40
  and invalidating laws, 66–67
  law lacking in, for Holmes, 127–28
  and legal indeterminacy, 139
  Puritan conceptions of, xiv, 4, 7–9, 8n23,
    29–30
  sufficient without revelation in modern
    natural law, 25, 44
  and will in Blackstone's thought, 50–51,
    56n59
  and will in Story's thought, 85, 86–87
  See also common law; epistemology;
    imago Dei
realism. *See* legal realism
Redlich, Josef, 114–15, 115n41, 121
Reeve, Tapping, 72–74, 75, 80
Reformed. *See* Calvin; Protestantism
Reid, Thomas, 33, 117n49
revelation. *See* epistemology: revelation;
    scripture

Revolution, American, xi, xii, xiii, 2–3, 17n54,
  24, 25n3, 40, 66, 81, 82, 146, 147
  and modern natural law, 2–3
  See also colleges and universities;
    curriculum
right and wrong
  cannot be obliterated by law, 101
  determined by law, 53, 54–55, 56,
    129, 131
  and laws *mala in se* (bad in themselves), 55,
    59n73, 59, 97
  and might makes right, 131, 138n70
  and precedent, 120
  should be students' concern, not law, for
    Locke, 37
right or rights (legal, moral, or natural
    entitlement)
  bestowed, 65, 90
  of conquest, 63n94
  contract confers, 79n41, 92, 94, 146
  differ in type and form for Story, 86n70, 89
  of discovery (claim to land), 97
  of discovery (compelled disclosure), 107
  and English liberty, 67, 81–82
  equity founded in, 90
  God's, 88
  human, xiii, 8n25, 58, 81
  in international law, 101
  law formed from, 83
  legal, 55–56
  in marriage, 95
  as meaningless, 141
  in modern natural law, 2, 27, 30, 37
  natural, 10, 49, 65, 86–87, 90
  to participate in government, 82, 89
  of property, 60–62, 61n87
  to punish, 58, 59n73, 59,
    98n124, 98
  of rebellion, 36, 39, 40
  to slavery, 100, 103
  as trump, 100n127
  unalienable, granted by God, 40
  See also common law; England;
    epistemology; international law;
    natural law
Roman Catholicism, 2–3, 7n21, 23, 122n66
Roman law, 4, 6, 21, 25, 41, 74, 80, 111n27, 112n29
Rumble, William, Jr., 135n55

sabbath, 6n19, 6, 7, 23
Savigny, Friedrich Carl von, 116

Schlegel, John Henry, 142n84
scripture, 3n6,3n7, 3, 4, 9, 12, 23,
    29, 39, 52
  First Corinthians, 3n7
  Genesis, 3n7, 3
  Hebrews, 3n7
  James, 3n7
  Romans, 3, 9, 11
  Second Corinthians, 3n7
  Ten Commandments, 5, 6n15, 6, 7.
  See also epistemology: revelation
Selden, John, 91n88
Selection of Cases on the Law of Contracts
    (Langdell), 109
Seneca, Lucius Annaeus, 5, 8, *See also* Stoic
    philosophy
Shaftesbury (Anthony Cooper, Third Earl
    of), 28
Shaw, Lemuel, 70
Shepard, Thomas, 6n19
sin, xiv, 4, 7n20, 7, 8, 9,
    29, 62
slavery, 89, 99n125, 99–103
Smith, William, 18n58
Socrates, 8
Stearns, Asahel, 74, 75n24,
    76n26, 76
Stevens, Robert, 21n75, 113,
    122n66
Stewart, Dugald, 33, 34n41
Stiles, Ezra, 19, 40n73, 40–41, 75
Stoic philosophy, 4–5, 25. *See also* Cicero;
    Seneca
Story, Joseph, xi, xiii, 64, 68, 76–77, 78–103,
    88n77, 105, 110n21, 110, 111, 116, 117, 123, 125,
    127n13, 127, 145, 146, 147
  and *Jeune Eugenie* case, 99–103
  biography of, 76n28, 78–79, 79n41,
    122n66
  scholarly approach of, 106–8
Sturges, Wesley, 142n83
Suárez, Francisco, 49–50, 88
System of the Laws of the State of Connecticut
    (Swift), 73

Tauza v. Susquehanna Coal Company, 137n64
Thirty Years War, 25n2
Thomas Aquinas, Saint, xiv, 2, 6n16, 53, 88n77,
    88, 122n66
Tucker, St. George, 68
Tyler, Samuel, 113

Ungar, Robert, 143n90
universities. *See* colleges and universities

Wales, Samuel, 8
Wightman v. Wightman, 84
Willard, Samuel, 6n19, 6
William, Ames, 8–9
Wilson, James, 42

Winterer, Caroline, 5n14
Witherspoon, John, 18n58, 32, 34n43,
   35n48, 35–36, 36n52, 45, 71
Witte, John, Jr., 122
Woodard, Calvin, 136
Woolsey, Theodore Dwight, 78
Writs of Assistance, 67
Wythe, George, 41–42